HIL

D0811657

STRATEGY AS ACTION

STRATEGIC MANAGEMENT SERIES

Editors
Michael A. Hitt, R. Duane Ireland, and Robert E. Hoskisson

Strategy as Action: Competitive Dynamics and Competitive Advantage
Curtis M. Grimm, Hun Lee, and Ken G. Smith

Strategy as Action

Competitive Dynamics and
Competitive Advantage

Edited by
Curtis M. Grimm
Hun Lee
Ken G. Smith

OXFORD
UNIVERSITY PRESS

2006

UNIVERSITY
OF NEW BRUNSWICK

AUG 2 1 2006

LIBRARIES

OXFORD

UNIVERSITY PRESS

Oxford University Press, Inc., publishes works that further
Oxford University's objective of excellence
in research, scholarship, and education.

Oxford   New York
Auckland   Cape Town   Dar es Salaam   Hong Kong   Karachi
Kuala Lumpur   Madrid   Melbourne   Mexico City   Nairobi
New Delhi   Shanghai   Taipei   Toronto

With offices in
Argentina   Austria   Brazil   Chile   Czech Republic   France   Greece
Guatemala   Hungary   Italy   Japan   Poland   Portugal   Singapore
South Korea   Switzerland   Thailand   Turkey   Ukraine   Vietnam

Copyright © 2006 by Oxford University Press, Inc.

Published by Oxford University Press, Inc.
198 Madison Avenue, New York, New York 10016
www.oup.com

Oxford is a registered trademark of Oxford University Press

All rights reserved. No part of this publication may be reproduced,
stored in a retrieval system, or transmitted, in any form or by any means,
electronic, mechanical, photocopying, recording, or otherwise,
without the prior permission of Oxford University Press.

Library of Congress Cataloging-in-Publication Data
Grimm, Curtis M.
Strategy as action : competitive dynamics and competitive
advantage / Curtis M. Grimm, Hun Lee, and Ken G. Smith.
p.   cm.—(Strategic management series)
Includes bibliographical references and index.
ISBN-13:978-0-19-516144-1
ISBN 0-19-516144-0
1. Competition.   2. Strategic planning.   I. Lee, Hun, 1962–   II. Smith, Ken G.
III. Title.   IV. Strategic management series (Oxford University Press)

HD41.G695 2005
658.4'012—dc22   2004010879

9 8 7 6 5 4 3 2 1

Printed in the United States of America
on acid-free paper

PREFACE

Curtis Grimm and Ken Smith arrived at the Robert H. Smith School of Business at the University of Maryland in August 1983, fresh Ph.D. degrees in hand. Although from different disciplinary backgrounds—Grimm from industrial organization economics and Smith from strategic management—we shared a keen interest in challenging current ways of thinking about strategy and competitive interaction. We were especially concerned with scholars' conception of strategy as inactive. To us, strategy was action! It was a high-stakes race of action and reaction, where timing of action is crucial to success. We subsequently developed a body of research on the actual competitive actions and reactions of real firms across a broad range of industries. The ideas presented in this book are drawn from that research, which has been reported in a wide variety of academic journals.

When should a firm be innovative or entrepreneurial, when should it aggressively take on rivals from a position of strength, and when should it cooperate? What is the right way to attack a rival, or the best way to defend an established position? When is it important to act quickly?

We have explored those questions over our 20-year collaboration, including the last several years with a former Ph.D. student, Hun Lee, Associate Professor of Strategic Management at George Mason University. The three of us have synthesized and advanced these ideas in a format designed to serve as a supplement to a basic strategy text for an MBA course or the undergraduate capstone course. The book would also be appropriate in an elective course on industry and competitor analysis. The ideas are of great relevance to current and future managers in today's competitive and fast-paced business environment. Researchers in strategy will also find value in reading the text.

More specifically, in chapter 1 we highlight the intensity of competition today, and stress the urgency of using an action perspective to gain competitive advantage. Chapter 2 reviews the different economic perspectives of competition and introduces game theory as an approach for investigating competitive advantage. Chapters 3 and 4 present frameworks that facilitate the analysis of a firm's relative market and resource position. Chapter 5 introduces the action model of advantage and shows how actions both consume and develop firm resources while influencing a firm's market position and performance. The chapter points out that actions provoke reactions, and that it is in the context of action and reaction that advantages are developed and eroded.

Chapters 6 through 8 all focus on engaging competitors to "win the battle" and improve the firm's resource and market position. In particular, chapter 6 examines the case of the firm with limited resources and a poor market position and argues that such firms must undertake entrepreneurial actions that delay reaction by exploiting competitive uncertainty and blind spots. Chapter 7 considers the case of the firm with a relative internal resource advantage over rivals and shows how it can exploit such a resource advantage through Ricardian actions. Ricardian actions based on resource advantages delay reaction because of resource scarcity. Chapter 8 presents the case of the market leader and explains how such a firm can use market power and intimidation to defend its markets through actions that deter competitors and delay reaction. In contrast to chapters 6 through 8, chapter 9 examines how firms can engage in cooperative actions when "winning the battle" is precluded by resource and market parity among firms. Competitive reaction is not as likely with cooperative actions. Chapter 10 demonstrates more specifically how managers can use the model and discusses the types and sources of information needed to do so. The final chapter summarizes the book's arguments and considers linkages across the resource positions presented in chapters 6 through 9. Attention is focused on firm evolution. A stage model of organizational development is offered as an integrative device to summarize and explain how firms build advantage over time.

We have used earlier versions of this material very effectively in the classroom and recommend that instructors of strategy consider its adoption. Importantly, the book is integrative, presenting a fresh perspective on strategy but one that fully incorporates and can be used with more traditional views. Porter's value chain, industry and SWOT analysis, and the resource-based view are all discussed within our framework. Our approach helps those ideas to come alive in an up-to-date and dynamic action context that has great practical relevance.

The book also integrates material on the legal, regulatory, and ethical environment of business. An instructor using the text can address those important issues completely within a strategy context rather than presenting them separately after fundamental strategy ideas have been covered. For example, the opening chapter discusses the evolving competitive environment, including the phenomena of deregulation and privatization, globalization, and technological change that motivate and necessitate the action-oriented approach we present. The chapters on co-opting actions and deterrent actions incorporate the antitrust laws and ethical standards with which managers must grapple. Rather than avoiding those issues, we face head-on the difficult tradeoffs managers often must make when an action that will improve firm profitability, and the manager's salary and status, is in a gray area of legality and ethics.

Many people contributed in important ways to this book. Duane Ireland, Mike Hitt, and Bob Hoskisson asked us to write a book on competitive dynamics for the Oxford University Press Series on Strategic Management and provided excellent assistance throughout, including detailed comments on a preliminary version of the manuscript. We thank John Rauschenberg and Keith Faivre, our editors at Oxford University Press, for their assistance and patience during the course of the project.

We gained much from our earlier collaboration with Martin Gannon in developing the ideas presented here. Several former doctoral students worked with us and sharpened our thinking, including Ming-Jer Chen, August Schomberg, Greg Young, Tom Quasney, Pam Derfus, and Wally Ferrier. We also thank MBA students Anthony Airoso, Sarah Bartholomen, James Parker, Kristi Vigil, and Elizabeth Welch and graduate research assistant Dharmesh Trivedi for their research, some of which is presented in chapter 10.

We owe a particular debt of gratitude to Pamela Derfus, a former doctoral student, who served as our research assistant and in-house editor. Pam contributed substantially to the clarity of our prose as well as to the substance of the material.

We have all received strong institutional backing in writing this book. The Robert H. Smith School of Business offered a uniquely supportive environment for writing this book. Dean Howard Frank has taught us much about leadership and the importance of taking action. Former Associate Dean Judy Olian provided consistent support and encouragement. George Mason University and Dean Rich Klimoski provided support by funding summer research and a study leave.

Many colleagues contributed comments, ideas, and inspiration, including Steve Carroll, Tom Corsi, Ed Locke, Lee Preston, Rhonda Reger, Brian Shaffer, Hank Sims, and Susan Taylor. Numerous doctoral students at Maryland, including Dax Basdeo, Kevin Clark, Yan Dong, Don Knight, Patrick Maggitti, Ayesha Malhotra, Cormac Mac Fhionnlaoich, Chris Lin, Daniel Simon, and Kefeng Xu, provided research assistance and helpful comments.

Last but not least, we extend special thanks to our families, who inspire, support, and motivate our efforts.

CONTENTS

Part I. The New Competitive Advantage

1: Disruptive Competition: Intensifying Actions
and Reactions in the Twenty-First Century 5

Part II. Strategic Paradigms of Competitive Advantage

2: Economic Theories of Competition and Competitive
Advantage: Neoclassical, Industrial Organization,
Game Theory, Schumpeterian, and Evolutionary
Economics 31

3: Knowing Your Relative Market Position 48

4: Knowing Your Relative Resource Position 68

**Part III. Action-Based Dynamic Model of Competitive
Advantage**

5: An Action-Reaction Framework for Building
Competitive Advantage 83

6: Avoiding Rivals with Entrepreneurial Actions:
Exploiting Competitive Uncertainty and Blind Spots   101

7: Engaging Rivals with Ricardian Actions:
Exploiting Ownership of Superior Resources   129

8: Defending against Rivals as a Dominant Firm:
The Role of Deterrent Actions   156

9: Winning the Peace: Taking "Co-optive" Actions
in the Absence of Resource Advantage   180

10: Using the Action Model: Predicting the Behavior
of Rivals   202

11: Strategy as Action: Integration and Evolution
of Resource Positions   223

Notes   239

Index   269

STRATEGY AS ACTION

Part I

The New Competitive Advantage

Chapter 1

DISRUPTIVE COMPETITION

*Intensifying Actions and Reactions
in the Twenty-First Century*

In the last two decades, a significant restructuring of business and industry has occurred through globalization, a worldwide renaissance of capitalism, and a resultant movement toward government deregulation and privatization, as well as an immense wave of technological innovation. The restructuring has already had an enormous impact and is likely to continue to affect the way business is conducted well into the twenty-first century. Many observers have argued that a new age of fast-paced competition or hypercompetition is emerging as a result of those significant changes.[1] The new age of competition is distinct because of the dramatic increase in competitive actions and reactions between firms. As a consequence of the accelerating rate of actions and reactions, the time firms have to make decisions has decreased, and the speed with which new ideas are created and brought to market has increased. Above all, the speed at which data, information, and knowledge pulse between competitors has skyrocketed. In this new age of competition, fast companies generate advantages and market power while faster ones generate more advantages and greater market power, and no one's advantages are guaranteed to last long.[2]

Let us consider the following examples. Competition among the wireless service providers reflects the new age of fast-paced competition. In mid-1998, AT&T Wireless introduced its Digital One Rate service, which combined local, long-distance, and roaming service into its pricing plans. Since then, nearly all major rivals have quickly and successfully imitated AT&T Wireless and offered their own similar services and pricing plans. AT&T Wireless's first-mover advantage was quickly eroded by rivals, but its competitive action ushered a dramatic growth in subscribers and transformed the wireless phone from a luxury into an affordable consumer necessity. The industry experienced a significant increase in number of subscribers from 34 million to 69 million over a four-year period from 1995 to 1998, but once the new services and pricing plans were initiated by most rivals, the number jumped to approximately 100 million subscribers in just over a two-year period by the end of 2000. The strong competition in this industry continues as other services, such as e-mail, Internet access, and instant messaging, introduced by first-movers have been quickly imitated by nearly all major rivals and as the Federal Communication Commission has eliminated restrictions on spectrum or wireless channel licenses that any wireless service provider can own in any given market.[3]

Let us consider an example of intense competition driven by technological change. Broadcasters in television and radio face an ever-increasing number of rivals from conventional and innovative entrants. Over the past decade, more than 600 new television stations and 3,000 new radio stations have entered the broadcasting industry. Furthermore, advancements in cable, satellite, and computer technologies have created numerous innovative entrants. Consumers can now choose from a variety of channels available and video-on-demand services from cable and satellite television companies (e.g., Dish Network and Direct TV). Consumers can also choose from thousands of radio-style music programs or numerous web sites to distribute or download music over the Internet and from a hundred channels offered by the emerging satellite radio companies (e.g., XM and Sirius). In fact, with evolving technologies, consumers are expected to have more viewing and listening alternatives even on the move through their cell phones and personal digital assistants.[4]

Let us consider an example of intense competition driven by globalization. The wireless handset industry is dominated by few global players such as Nokia and Motorola, which are first and second and together own 55 percent of the world market in 2002. However, a crowd of foreign competitors, especially from Asia, is persistently threatening the industry leaders. At the end of 2002, Samsung of Korea jumped from sixth to third, surpassing Siemens and Sony-Ericcson within just two years, while LG of Korea jumped to sixth from tenth in sales within a year. At the end of 2002, more than 20 Chinese companies had entered the wireless handset manufacturing market and captured approximately 20 percent of China's domestic market share, which is the world's largest, from nearly nothing within just three years. These Chinese competitors are expected to soon enter global markets outside of China and further threaten industry leaders with their cost advantages.[5]

Let us now consider another example drawn from the pet food industry. Ralston Purina is a market leader in this industry, especially in the dry food segment.[6] Quaker Oats's acquisition of Gaines Pet Foods and its principal product, Gravy Train, represented a major threat to Ralston because it made Quaker Oats the number two player in the dry food segment of the pet food industry.[7] Ralston's response was swift and aggressive. Within weeks of the acquisition, Ralston announced it would double its new product introductions. Ralston also quickly moved into the declining semimoist dog food segment, where Quaker Oats had the leading product, Gainesburgers. Ralston then acquired Benco Pet Foods, a single-plant operation that made Moist & Meaty, and immediately marketed that product nationally while also reducing its price, thus posing a direct threat to Quaker. Responding to Ralston's acquisition of Benco, Quaker Oats quickly introduced a semimoist imitative product named Moist 'n Beefy. Ralston retaliated by introducing a new dry dog food called Grravy, an unabashed mimicry of Quaker's Gravy Train brand. Amazingly, Ralston priced its 40-pound bag of Grravy at $10, significantly less than Quaker's $16 price for a bag of Gravy Train. Further, Ralston promoted its new brand with a $1.50 coupon, thereby beating Gravy Train's price by nearly 50 percent. Ralston apparently got the best of Quaker in this competitive skirmish; Quaker Oats recently sold its pet food line after losing a significant market share.

Finally, consider the following examples of intense competition driving firms to corporate spying. Oracle Corporation hired a detective agency to spy on its rival, Microsoft. The detective agency allegedly stole two laptops and offered $1,200 to janitors to obtain the trash of a trade group. Oracle believed that the trade group was misrepresenting itself as an independent advocacy group and was actually funded by Microsoft to influence public opinion during its federal antitrust trial. Procter & Gamble hired a competitive intelligence consulting firm to spy on a key rival in its hair care business. The consulting firm engaged in dumpster inspections on Unilever, attempting to gain information on its hair care business. A luxury-goods retailer hired Deloitte & Touche, which provides consulting in computer forensics. This engagement involved two of its consultants dressed as repairmen entering the closed offices of the client to copy the hard drives belonging to three employees. The retailer suspected that the three employees were stealing corporate secrets and customer information and providing them to a departed executive.[8]

These examples highlight both the innovativeness and the urgency of competition in this new age. The first example from the wireless service industry illustrates how quickly and easily rivals can imitate a first-mover's competitive action and how technological advantages may be short-lived and diffused throughout industry rivals. It also illustrates the role of government deregulation in intensifying competition. The second example from the broadcasting industry illustrates intensifying competition not only from traditional new entrants but also a new set of rivals created by technological innovations. The third example from the wireless handset industry illustrates the impact of globalization and foreign competitors in undermining the position of industry leaders. The fourth example portrays how warlike competition can become in industry segments as mundane as dry dog food. The final episodes of corporate espionage underscore the high-stakes nature of competition today. As Brian Holistein of the American Society for Industrial Security has noted, firms are reluctant to discuss their growing security problem: "Being a victim of industrial espionage is a lot like getting venereal disease. Many may have it, but nobody wants to talk about it."[9]

Key Insights about Competition

Many years ago, Joseph Schumpeter described competition as a perennial gale. "Every piece of business strategy acquires its true significance only against the background of that process and within the situation created by it. It must be seen in its role in the perennial gale of creative destruction."[10] The essence of Schumpeter's argument is that firms act and rivals react, and it is in the context of action and reaction that advantage is created and destroyed. Indeed, if competition is a perennial gale, every business advantage will eventually be eroded through competition. Schumpeter referred to that process as creative destruction. A successful new action, such as the introduction of Digital One Rate or Moist & Meaty, leads to creative reactions by rivals. When the stakes are high enough, firms may go to extremes to respond; for example, they might engage in multimarket competition or even industrial espionage. Initial advantages are quickly eroded through the creative destruction process.

The thesis of our book is that today's global business environment is becoming increasingly competitive and hostile, that every firm advantage will be quickly eroded and overcome by fast-paced competition in the perennial gale. Moreover, we expect the business environment to be even more warlike in the future. Figure 1.1 portrays the basic model of action and reaction—the disruptive competition. Our description of competition is analogous to Clayton Christensen's notion of "disruptive innovations" in describing the organizational challenges arising from continuous change and innovations.[11] We now consider the current business environment and the notion of disruption in competition in more detail.

The Increasingly Competitive
Business Environment

We have been studying competition and rivalry—action and reactions— in diverse industries for the past 15 years. In the context of action and

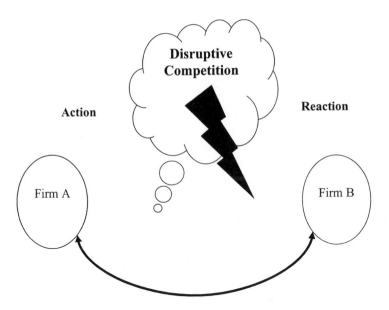

Figure 1.1 Disruptive Competition.

reaction, one important measure of fast-paced competition is the speed with which firms respond to one another's actions. As the average speed of firms' responses increases, so does the erosion of any single firm's advantage. Note that as the speed of response increases, the actual response time in days or months decreases. We have observed that in the U.S. airline industry, the average competitive response time, across a variety of different types of moves, dropped from 65 calendar days in 1984 to 34 days in 1986.[12] Today, airlines respond to one another's price cuts within minutes. We have observed that in the software industry, the average competitive response time dropped from 34 days in 1979 to just 1 day in 1991.[13] In other words, in 1991, rivals were responding virtually overnight to one another's actions. A study of competition between industry leaders and challengers in 41 different industries revealed that the average response time decreased from 90 days in 1988 to 54 days in 1992.[14] A study of new product rivalry in the brewing, telecommunications, and personal computer (PC) industries showed that the average time of response to new product introductions decreased dramatically in all of those industries between 1975 and 1989: from 2,381 to 181 days in the brewing industry, from 2,113 to 48 days in the telecommunications industry, and from 752 to 272 days in the PC industry.[15] These numbers highlight the imperative of speed in this new age of competition. As response time decreases, managers' decision-making time is compressed, and understanding competitors and their actions and reactions becomes more difficult. In addition, as response speed increases, the time window for earning first-mover advantages is narrowed. Studies have found that the returns of first movers who introduced new products significantly eroded as rivals respond with imitations[16] and the monopoly of first movers who introduced new products declined on average to 3.4 years (1967–86 period) from 33 years (1887–1906 period), contracting at rate of 2.93 percent per year.[17]

Consistent with the dramatic change in response times is the increase in the frequency with which firms act and react to one another. For example, in the airline industry the average number of firm moves, both actions and reactions, per year grew from 3.25 in 1978 to eight in 1986. In the software industry, the average number of moves per firm increased from just over one in 1980 to nearly nine in 1990. Among leaders and challengers across industries, the average number of moves increased from 15 in 1987 to 26 in 1992.

Figure 1.2 shows that the number of patents issued per year nearly doubled from 1990 to 2000, increasing from approximately 97,000 to over 180,000. Because many firms skip the patent process to avoid signaling competitors or making company secrets public, that increase may represent only a fraction of the new products actually invented. Moreover, the number of new products coming to market has increased. As detailed in figure 1.3, Marketing Intelligence Service reports that the number of new products introduced in consumer packaged goods, for example, have steadily increased from 1987 to 1997, growing from fewer than 6,000 to more than 9,000.

In many markets, the frequency in which new products are introduced has also accelerated. In the computer and wireless phone industry, where new models once had life cycles of nearly two years, product cycles have shrunk to as short as six months.[18] In the automobile industry, new car

Number of Patents Issued

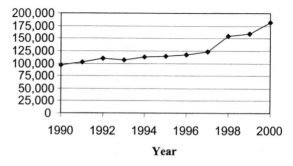

Figure 1.2   Patents Issued Per Year, 1990–2000. Source: Historical data from the U.S. Patent and Trademark Office, Commissioner of Patents and Trademarks Annual Reports.

Number of New Products

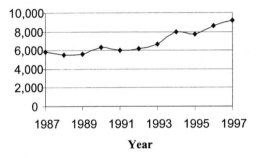

Figure 1.3   New Product Introductions of Consumer Packaged Goods, 1987–1997. Source: Historical data from Marketing Intelligence Service.

models used to be introduced every three to five years. Now, General Motors can introduce a new car in 20 months, and Toyota regularly develops a new car in 18 months or less. Toyota introduced the Corolla Spacio in 14.5 months and is attempting to cut its product cycle to one year on future cars,[19] while BMW intends to introduce a new or updated model nearly every three months.[20] In the telecommunication equipment industry, the sales cycles are sometimes longer than the new product development cycles. Before one competitor sells one generation of products, another competitor introduces its next generation of products, offering a faster capacity at a lower price.[21] In the electronics industry, Samsung planned to launch 95 new products, including 42 new television models, in 2003 and, at the same time, has reduced the time from new product concept to rollout from 14 months to 5 months over a recent six-year period.[22] These examples illustrate that the overall trend has been to increase the frequency of and reduce the time between new product introductions.

The increase in competitive activity and speed of response has largely resulted in increased price discounting for many products and services, although some highly and successfully differentiated products and services have not fallen prey to price discounting (e.g., luxury Mercedes-Benz automobiles and Rolex watches). One study found that prices have been dropping for products such as electric lamps, gasoline engines, refrigerators, and paper goods at annual rates between 1 and 3 percent and for integrated circuits and computers at an annual rate of almost 30 percent.[23] Airline ticket prices have declined 40 percent over the last 25 years, while the price of a two-liter bottle of Diet Coke has remained the same since 1985.[24] The average prices of a television and DVD player have declined 30 percent and 75 percent, respectively over the 1998–2002 period.[25] Even powerful brands such as Kraft, Frito-Lay, and Procter & Gamble have cut prices in response to increased competition from private labels.[26]

There seems to be no end to the price wars across many markets. Although price wars tend to harm the entire industry no matter who wins, they are increasingly becoming more common because of their ease and quickness in battles with rivals.[27] Let us examine the competition in the long-distance industry. Sprint introduced its nighttime long-distance rate of 5 cents per minute in mid-1999. Within two months, a price war had erupted as both MCI and A T & T matched or cut their long-distance rates to counter falling market share. On the day of the announcement of the price cuts, however, the stock prices of all three firms dropped.[28] In the video game industry, the top three competitors—Sony, Microsoft, and Nintendo—have been slashing prices to capture market share. In mid-2002, Sony initiated the price war by cutting its Playstation2 from $299 to $199. Two days after Sony's announcement, Microsoft followed by cutting its Xbox by the same amount. Nintendo, which initially announced no plans to lower prices, reduced its price from $199 to $149 several days later.[29] Further price cuts were expected in the following year, bringing the price of the Playstation2 and Xbox to $99 and Game Cube to $50.[30] In the computer server industry, Dell's entry strategy has been to undercut its rivals, such as IBM and Hewlett-Packard, by several hundred dollars. An industry executive noted that Dell's entry into the server market will increase price and overall competition.[31] Even in a relatively new industry such as laser eye surgery, price wars have erupted. When first available, laser eye surgery cost approximately $2,500 to $4,000 per eye. With increased competition from many doctors and laser surgery discounters, prices came down drastically to as low as $499 per eye.[32] Contributing to the price wars among doctors is the intensifying competition among the laser eye surgery equipment makers. Visx lowered the royalty fee it charges doctors for each use. Rivals Summit Technology and LaserSight matched the price cut by lowering the royalty fees from $250 to as low as $100.[33]

As we move farther into the twenty-first century, we will see firms linked in increasingly complex ways. Perhaps the most troubling result of the intense rivalry for managers is that success at one moment does not necessarily guarantee success in the next. Indeed, industry giants such as Boeing, General Motors, and Sears have faced significant challengers. Executives across the board generally agree that their focus on competitor analysis and overall competition among rivals is on the rise. Kunitake Ando, President of Sony, commented that he asks "for a report on what Samsung is doing every week."[34] Helmut Panke, chief executive of BMW, stated that one of his primary goals is to "beat out Mercedes-Benz as the number one maker of premium cars in the world" and that he "won't accept the position of number two."[35] Upon becoming president of

Table 1.1   Characteristics of Disruptive Competition

Response time	Short and getting shorter. Only one day in some industries.
Frequency of action	Increasing, even with more moves such as new product introductions that are difficult to implement.
Type of action	Price cuts, new products, and patents are on the rise.
Characteristics of business environment	More competitors, more failures, and generally more hostile rivalry.

Eastman Kodak, Patricia Russo described competition in the following way: "We have more competitors, and more formidable, aggressive competitors, than ever before... we are going through disruptive times."[36] Bill Gates of Microsoft reported that in the software industry, "[s]uccess depends not so much on how large the company is but rather on moving aggressively to the next advantage."[37] Table 1.1 summarizes the characteristics of today's competitive environment.

"Competitiveness" is the current buzzword of managers, economists, and policy analysts alike, and restoration of competitive vitality is an important goal for firms throughout the world. For many, a Japanese competitive achievement of the 1980s epitomized "beating the competition," and the frantic pace of Internet time of the 1990s represented the "new economy competition." Like superior athletes, firms that can run faster, jump higher, and outmaneuver their opponents are often simply those that are better trained and in better shape for the competition.

In an attempt to regain competitive vitality, firms are trying to "get fit." If surprise and first-mover activity are what wins, a firm must be prepared to use stealth and move fast. If winning takes world-class manufacturing, the firm must beat its competitors in the workshops. If it takes short development time, the firm must learn to be swift. If intimidation and market power are necessary to persuade the competitors to back down, the firm must be prepared to use its power. If a company cannot beat its competitors outright, it must find ways to join forces or work with other firms to improve its competitive position. Such are the realities of competition in today's disruptive competition.

Why a New Age of Competition?

There are several complex reasons for the increase in rivalry between firms. Here, we examine three important and interrelated trends: globalization, privatization and deregulation, and technological change. Figure 1.4 shows how they relate to each other and to action and reaction by firms.

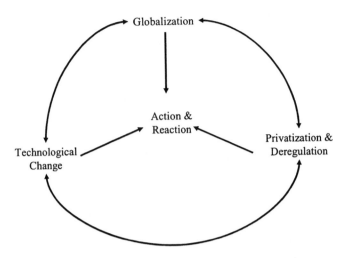

Figure 1.4   Competition in the Twenty-First Century.

Globalization.   In the last 20 years, national economies have become increasingly integrated into a complex web called the global economy.[38] A significant shift in the organization of business is behind this integration. Technological advances in telecommunications, information processing, and transportation have made possible the coordination of extremely complex organizational functions—from product design to manufacturing and marketing—in several countries simultaneously. Striving for efficiencies, firms have rationalized their operations across national boundaries on the basis of a variety of design, production, cost, and opportunity factors. Through technological networks and decreased costs of transportation, firms can effectively serve multiple markets with a diverse set of products and services.

In the past, a firm could separate markets into local, regional, and national. Now that trade barriers have been significantly reduced in regional trading blocks such as the European Union (EU) and North American Free Trade Agreement (NAFTA), and worldwide through the World Trade Organization (WTO), there is increasingly a focus on one market: the global market. As a consequence, American products and services compete in the global marketplace with those from many other countries. Another consequence is that new products and services from foreign competitors enter the American marketplace every day. New competitors are looking for market share in every market, and new brand names are striving to reach new customers. Firms are simultaneously marketing products in such diverse locations as Pawtucket, Rhode Island, and Pretoria, South Africa. Figure 1.5 shows that foreign imports almost tripled between 1960 and 2000 in the United States, and are expected to grow further into the

Percent

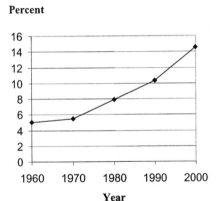

Figure 1.5 Foreign Imports as a Share of U.S. GDP. Source: Historical data from U.S. Department of Commerce, Bureau of Economic Analysis, National Income, 2002.

2000s. Figure 1.6 portrays the growing impact of imports in seven industrial sectors and in all manufacturing sectors combined. Imports have risen to nearly 35 percent in airplanes and 75 percent in vehicles.

Globalization has also brought diverse sets of competitors together in new and difficult-to-define markets that lack established rules of conduct. Asian, European, and American firms have different expectations and different norms and beliefs about how to compete.[39] When diverse sets of competitors come together, each with different goals and expectations,

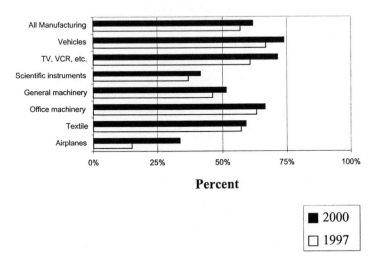

Percent

■ 2000
□ 1997

Figure 1.6 Percentage of Imports in Several U.S. Markets. Source: U.S. Census Bureau, U.S. International Trade in Goods and Services, series FT-900, Final Reports.

there is no basis for coordination, and rivalry is generally high. Trust between firms is minimal, and the social structure emphasizes competition, not cooperation.

Privatization and Deregulation. Another factor increasing the intensity of competition is worldwide microeconomic reform and economic deregulation.[40] During the 1970s and 1980s, steps were taken to lower regulatory boundaries throughout the world.[41] They included experiments with transportation and public utility deregulation, privatization, and liberalization. The range of such experiments is noteworthy: liberalization of transport regulation within the European community; extensive deregulation and privatization of telecommunications in many countries, including the United States, England, Japan, and the Netherlands; aviation deregulation in countries such as the United States, Canada, and Australia; and ambitious plans to transfer several state-owned enterprises to the private sector in New Zealand and Ireland. Privatization has also been pursued in less developed countries such as Nigeria, the Philippines, Bolivia, and Chile. Indeed, the nascent privatization of state enterprises in the former Soviet Union and throughout eastern Europe can be seen as part of the same worldwide phenomenon. A common theme in all of these undertakings is a disillusionment with state-owned and economically regulated enterprises and the belief that introducing market forces will enhance competition and economic efficiency.[42]

Many government regulations in the United States were initially developed during the Great Depression and appeared immediately after World War II in Europe and Japan. During that time, governments were interceding to protect businesses that created or provided jobs. Competition that forced firms to close in the economically depressed market was considered destructive for businesses, employees, and consumers. During World War II, when labor and resources were in short supply, any business that created new demand was also regulated. The most restrictive controls were lifted from the American market after the war, but many regulations remained. The government limited hours of work and operation, promoted fair pricing in general, and restricted entry and regulated monopolies in specific industries. As time went by, other restrictions were added during national emergencies, such as the wars in Korea and Vietnam.

In the U.S. banking industry, regulation persisted until the late 1970s, constraining consumer choice and capping rates. Competition was limited to banks in local markets; within the local markets, other financial institutions and out-of-state banks were not allowed to offer banking services. In retailing, hours of operation were often restricted by local governments, and many professionals, such as doctors and lawyers, could not advertise their services. In the transportation and communication industries, railroad, pipeline, and telecommunications firms were given local or national monopolies to prevent the development of costly duplicative infrastructures. In the airline, trucking, and other industries, regulations to combat excessive, destructive competition were adopted during the Great Depression. Patterns of regulation were similar in other developed countries in Europe and Asia.

Deregulation efforts have centered on a select group of industries that were protected from competition because of natural monopoly or concerns about excessive competition. Many of those industries, such as telecommunications, trucking, airlines, energy, and financial services, provided essential products and services to businesses and households. Table 1.2 highlights a set of industries recently deregulated in the United States. A similar deregulation pattern is evident in many other countries.

As a result of deregulation, many individual businesses are facing a major increase in the level of competition.[43] For example, because of new open access to natural gas pipelines, about 80 percent of the gas transported through the pipes is not owned by pipeline companies; before deregulation, that figure was only 3 percent. During the 1980s, nearly 15,000 megawatts of electric power were added to the national power supply by new electricity producers—50 percent more new power than was developed by existing utilities over the same period. Since the A T & T breakup, the company's long-distance market share has fallen from nearly 84 percent to 60 percent. More than 90 percent of consumers can now choose among several long-distance telephone carriers. Deregulation has also contributed to the emergence of interstate banking, the proliferation of cellular telephones and fax machines, and the development of the Fox and CNN television networks. Deregulation has thus increased the level of complexity and rivalry between firms. As noted in table 1.2, deregulation continues apace, most recently in the form of the landmark Telecommunications Act of 1996.

Technological Change. Technology also has changed rapidly in the last two decades, perhaps more so than at any other time in human history.[44] In fact, the pace and scope of technological change are so great that their consequences are difficult to predict. In the world of business, basic tenets of operation are under attack. Change is affecting the definitions of products and markets as well as the assumptions and processes of daily business. Managers face increasing ambiguity about business and industry definitions, decreasing ability to forecast industry trends and events, and subsequently growing uncertainty and risk.[45]

Knowledge is becoming an increasingly important parameter in the definition of businesses and in their ultimate success. In the past, the emphasis was on ownership of physical assets and resources, and the law

Table 1.2 U.S. Industries Recently Deregulated

Date	Industry	Change in Regulation
1978	Airlines	Airline Deregulation Act allowed entry and free competition through the system
	Natural gas	Natural Gas Policy Act decontrolled natural gas
	Energy generation	Public Utilities Regulatory Act encouraged nonutilities to provide power
1980	Railroads	Staggers Act provided substantial industry deregulation
1980	Trucking	Motor Carrier Act allowed substantial entry and market determination of rates
Early 1980s	Telephone	AT&T was broken up into the regional Bell systems and competitors were allowed to enter previously protected long-distance and equipment markets
1984	Cable to the home	The Cable Communications Policy Act barred restrictions on entry to new cable competitors
1986	Financial institutions	After a transition period, interest rate ceiling on interest payments by deposit institutions ended
1989	Natural gas	Natural Gas Wellhead Act decontrolled wellhead prices
1990–1991	Banking	All states permitted at least some freedom to out-of-state banks competing with in-state banks; the Federal Deposit Improvement Act introduced risk-based deposit insurance premiums to provide a more level competitive field
1991	International telecommunications	Competing with Intelsat permitted for international satellite communications
1992	Electricity	National Energy Policy Act increased competition
1995	Surface freight	Interstate Commerce Commission Termination Act eliminated oldest federal regulatory agency
1996	Telecommunications	Telecommunications Act of 1996 created process for entry across local and long-distance markets

of diminishing economic returns governed growth and profitability. Capital and labor are still critical to success, but rapid technological change has increased the value of knowledge and reduced the likelihood of diminishing returns. Growing numbers of industries are knowledge and technology intensive (electronics, pharmaceuticals, telecommunications, and computers), or they intensively use knowledge and technology (airlines, brokerage houses, banks, and electric utilities).[46]

Technological advances and the resultant cost advantages from their application are leading to significant structural changes in national economies and in the pattern of movement of goods, services, and capital throughout the world. To categorize all the major technological thrusts that are now underway is impossible, but at least four areas have been clearly transformed by technological revolutions: information, new materials, manufacturing, and transportation.

Integrated circuit technology is the key element of the information revolution. The accelerated pace of technological progress in integrated circuits is widely understood. As the cost per function has decreased by a factor of two, the complexity has doubled every year. In fact, technology of compression and miniaturization appears to have no limits. Work in photonics and the fiber-optic transmission of information has vastly expanded the transmission capacity of all information systems. Moreover, rapid improvements in semiconductor technology and digital electronics are affording similar advances in computer technology. The convergence of integrated circuit, fiber-optic, and semiconductor technology has provided significant economies of scale in both the accumulation and dissemination of information. The more powerful memories and the declining costs of information have made possible global forms of communication and control. Both basic and applied research have accelerated as past knowledge has become more readily available and experimentation has become easier with computers.

J. P. Clark and M. C. Flemmings noted in *Scientific American*[47] that advances in materials science and engineering now make it possible to start with a need and then develop a material to fit the need. That approach to materials technology is quite new. In the past, satisfying individual needs was limited by the raw materials available. The new approach has resulted in a swing from processing resources to creating new materials, such as optical fibers, superpolymers, and superconductors. An important aspect of these new materials is that they are often a superior substitute for traditional materials. For example, optical fibers are substitutes for copper in telecommunications, and ceramics, composites, and superpolymers are substitutes for ferrous and nonferrous metals. In the next decade, with increasing volume and decreasing costs, new materials will be a major force in competition and bring into question the viability of many traditional or older materials and their production facilities.

Industrial manufacturing processes are also undergoing significant technological change with the advent of computer-assisted design, computer-assisted manufacturing, and computer-integrated manufacturing. The emerging technology-intensive manufacturing paradigm, which is much more complex than machines replacing people, is challenging the dominant notion of mass production. The reorientation of manufacturing is based on multipurpose, programmable equipment and systems that make possible mass customization as opposed to standardization.[48]

New manufacturing systems provide much greater flexibility in that they can produce small or large production runs, quickly customize or standardize products, and speed responses to changing demands—all while reducing inventory requirements. As a result, the long-established emphasis on standardized products and services may be coming to an end. The ability to tailor a product or service to each customer's requirements will create a new form of competition. In the new age of competition, a single flexible business can respond to multiple customers in diverse markets. The transformation of manufacturing systems is shortening product life cycles, giving the edge to competitors with the shortest response or development times. Increased flexibility in manufacturing leads to increased strategic flexibility. Flexible firms are more able to compete in that they are better prepared to respond to technology and market opportunities, to diversify on the basis of their capabilities, to deploy resources effectively, and to be flexible in strategic decision-making.[49]

Changes in transportation technology, especially in aerospace technology, are bringing production centers and markets much closer together in terms of time and relative costs. Advances in transportation are related to the three previously discussed areas of technological change: information, materials, and manufacturing. Changes in those areas are driving the revolution in transportation, which in turn is enabling firms to speed their responses even further and compete more aggressively across a broader span of markets.

In sum, dramatic changes due to globalization, deregulation, and technology have redefined the nature of business by increasing competition. Significant increases in the speed of competitive response and the number of competitive actions and price cuts have also resulted. Those indicators highlight the intensity of competition. We believe those trends will continue unabated in the foreseeable future. Firms that have focused on developing effective response skills, as opposed to planning and forecasting skills, are best prepared to meet the uncertain challenges that lie ahead.[50]

Consequences of Increased Competition

Today's environment of disruptive competition has several important consequences. The most important implication for this book, however, is that the rules about how a firm should behave to build advantage must be reexamined and redefined. Traditional models of how firms build an advantage have emphasized the concept of sustainability or advantages that rivals cannot overcome. Yet our research suggests that in the current business environment, most advantages will eventually be eroded in an environment of disruptive competition. Other writers agree. Richard D'Aveni, for example, effectively argues that attempting to build a sustainable advantage under conditions of high competition is a distraction requiring misappropriation of resources that are sorely needed in intensely competitive environments.[51] He notes that in an environment where every advantage is rapidly eroded, attempting to increase or maintain an existing advantage hampers the development of new ones. Sustaining an existing advantage is a harvest strategy rather than a growth strategy. Even when attempting to sustain an advantage while presumably developing new ones, a firm must take action to be successful.

The problem is that many traditional models of strategy and advantage do not address the dynamics of competition, the constant amid increasing ebb and flow of rivals. The theories commonly assume that organizations and environments are clear-cut systems where specific causes and effects are known. Yet the environment we have described, the current environment for business, is far from stable or predictable.

In critiquing "state-of-the-art" strategy models, Gary Hamel and C. K. Prahalad contend that most traditional strategy models may have "abetted the process of competitive decline." They argue that those models are a distraction from real strategic action.[52] Michael Porter also emphasizes the need for more dynamic models of strategy, ones that capture firms' actions and reactions to one another.[53] Furthermore, firm actions play a critical role in influencing industry structure and how it evolves over time.[54]

The goal of this book is to present a comprehensive, dynamic model of competitive advantage that cogently fits with today's new age of competition. Our contention is that markets are in a constant state of flux and disequilibrium, where organizational outcomes are only partly determined by strategic choice.[55] We argue that organizational outcomes emerge from interactions between firms under conditions of nonequilibrium and disorder. In that environment, strategic decision-makers play an important role in the creative evolution of the entire competitive system.

As outlined in figure 1.1, firms act and rivals react. It is in the context of this action and reaction that advantages and improved performances are obtained. Importantly, we do not assume that an advantage is sustainable; on the contrary, our research shows that any competitive advantage or success will lead to reaction and imitation, which will in turn lead to the eventual erosion of the advantage.

Many ideas presented in this book are based on our studies of actions and reactions in very diverse, mostly fast-paced competitive environments. For the purposes of our initial discussion, an action is a specific market move, such as a price cut, a market expansion, or a special promotion designed to defend or improve the firm's competitive position. In contrast, a response is a market move taken by a competing firm to counteract the initial competitive action. Table 1.3 describes action and reaction studies in terms of industries, time frame, principal variables, and methods. Information about the methods employed and the specific characteristics of each study is given in the appendix. Those diverse and dynamic studies, as well as others cited in the book, corroborate the ever-increasing competitiveness of many industries. Using that research, we have formulated an action model of advantage that has many practical implications. For managers trying to compete in the face of the perennial gale, as well as those working in more stable and less competitive environments, the action model of advantage offers great value.

Outline of the Book

Chapter 2 presents the most common economic perspectives of competition and their insights for firms to build a competitive advantage over their rivals. We examine competition and competitive advantage from the perspectives of neoclassical economics, industrial organization economics, new industrial organization, and dynamic competition. With neoclassical economics, we review different types of competition from perfect to monopolistic. With industrial organization economics, we examine the structure-conduct-performance and the more popular Porter's Five Force frameworks. We emphasize game theory in the new industrial organization perspective and introduce it as a vehicle for understanding the actions and reactions of rivals in a dynamic context. Finally, with dynamic competition, we draw on the Schumpeterian view of competitive advantage, reviewing and highlighting the more recent stream of research on actions and reactions, and Nelson and Winter's view of evolutionary economics.

Chapter 3 explores how a firm can achieve a competitive advantage over its rivals by understanding its relative market position—the first step to understanding the action alternatives available to the firm. Since a firm's relative market position involves understanding the industry structure and dynamics in which a firm competes, we examine the most popular frameworks in performing an industry analysis, including Porter's Five Forces and strategic group analyses, which help firms identify the best competitive positions and profit opportunities in an industry. We also introduce pair-wise analysis as a buildup for understanding a firm's relative market position.

Table 1.3 Authors' Studies of Action and Reaction

Industry	Time Frame	Kind and Number of Actions/Reactions	Key Variables of Interest	Method
1. High technology	1985–86	47 actions and reactions of all types	Action characteristics, response time, type, number of responders, and firm performance	Field interviews and questionnaires
2. Computer retailing	1988	25 competitive reactions of all types	Organizational resources, response time and type	Field interviews and questionnaires
3. U.S. airlines	1978–86	191 actions and 418 responses of all types	Organizational resources, actions characteristics, response time, order, number of responders, and firm performance	Archival study of *Aviation Daily*[a]
4. Brewing, telecommunications, and personal computers	1975–90	82 new product introductions and 632 imitative responses	Industry and action characteristics, response time, order, number of responders, stock market performance, and industry diffusion	Archival study of F & S Predicasts: 7,000 newspapers, business magazines, trade association publications, and business newsletters in the United States[b]
5. Software	1980–90	2,347 actions and reactions of all types	Organizational resources, industry characteristics, action frequency, response time, and performance	Archival study of F & S Predicasts: 7,000 newspapers, business magazines, trade association publications, and business newsletters in the United States[c]

(continued)

Table 1.3 (Continued)

Industry	Time Frame	Kind and Number of Actions/Reactions	Key Variables of Interest	Method
6. Leader/challenger in 41 diverse industries	1986–93	4,876 actions and reactions of all types	Action repertoires, response times, industry dethronement, financial distress, and firm performance	Archival study of F & S Predicasts: 7,000 newspapers, business magazines, trade association publications, and business newsletters in the United States[d]
7. 11 different industries	1990–96	4,600 actions and reactions of all types	Firm activity, rival activity, and firm performance	Archival study of *LexisNexis*[e]

[a] With Ming-Jer Chen
[b] With August Schomberg
[c] With Greg Young
[d] With Walter Ferrier and Cormac Mac Fhionnlaoich
[e] With Pamela Derfus

Chapter 4 focuses on how a firm can achieve a competitive advantage over its rivals by understanding its relative resource position—the second step (after industry) to understanding the action alternatives available to the firm. We explain the importance of resources and discuss different types of resources and how they relate to competitive action and competitive advantage. We also analyze a firm's sources of value and potential areas of competitive advantage using the value chain analysis and present the idea of relative resource position vis-à-vis a competitor or group of competitors to identify a firm's comparative resource position and the action alternatives it should consider. Finally, we consider both how firms build resources positions and how they should exploit such positions.

Chapter 5 introduces the action model of advantage. This model emphasizes strategy as action. We show how actions both consume and develop firm resources, and explain how they influence a firm's market position and performance. However, actions also provoke reaction, and it is in the context of action and reaction that advantages are developed and eroded. Importantly, actions include those designed to engage a competitor in direct warfare, referred to as competitive actions, and those designed to depress pair-wise competition, referred to as co-optive actions.

Chapters 6, 7, and 8 all focus on engaging a competitor with the goal of "winning the battle" or improving the firm's internal resource and external market positions. In particular, chapter 6 examines the case of the firm with limited resources and poor market position. We argue that such firms must undertake entrepreneurial actions. Entrepreneurial actions can delay reaction to the extent that they exploit competitive uncertainty and blind spots. Chapter 7 examines the case of the firm with a substantial internal resource advantage over rivals. We explain how firms can exploit such resource advantages through Ricardian actions. Ricardian actions impede competitive response because the underlying resource that makes the action possible is in scarce supply. Chapter 8 addresses the case of the market leader that has an excellent external market position. We argue that such firms can effectively delay competitive response by undertaking deterrent actions. Deterrent actions thwart response through intimidation and market power.

In contrast to chapters 6, 7, and 8, chapter 9 examines how firms can engage in co-optive actions when "winning the battle" is not an option. We consider the antitrust implications of co-optive actions both in the United States and abroad.

Chapter 10 provides practical examples of how the model can be used. Two related forms of analysis are presented: relative resource analysis and competitor analysis. They are applied to firms in the hotel and specialty coffee industries, and specific insights garnered from the analyses are discussed.

Chapter 11 summarizes our arguments and examines linkages across the resource positions presented in chapters 6 through 9. Attention is focused on firm evolution from different resource positions, and on the challenges firms with strong resource positions face to retain their resource advantages. We offer a stage model of organizational development as an integrative device to summarize and explain how firms build advantage over time. The chapter concludes with a discussion of formal mechanisms of cooperation that enhance a firm's ability to compete, as opposed to the co-optive actions designed to reduce competition discussed in chapter 9.

APPENDIX: Research on Actions
and Reactions Field Studies 1 and 2

The first two studies obtained data from chief executive officers and other executives of high-technology electronics firms and computer retailing firms. Those two industries were selected because they are emerging growth industries noted for their relatively high degree of competition and a general lack of structural barriers. The high-technology study involved 47 actions and reactions of 47 firms. The products of the high-technology firms in the samples ranged from electric switches to sophisticated electrical components for computer and space applications. The computer retailing study focused on the responses of 25 computer retailers that all marketed personal computers.

The first step in the data collection process was extensive interviewing of each firm's executive officers.[56] In the second phase a questionnaire was completed by the CEOs and other executives within the firms. The managers were asked to identify an important *competitive action* in their industry to which their firms responded. They were then asked several questions about the nature of the action and the nature and timing of their response.

Archival Studies 3 through 7

The method used in studies 3 through 6 has been labeled "structured content analysis."[57] Specifically, a series of actions and reactions were identified from extensive studies of all major industry publications. The primary data source for actions and responses in the U.S. airline industry was *Aviation Daily*, an industry journal with a 50-year history. The primary source for actions and reactions in the brewing, telecommunications, and PC industries, the software industry, and the leader-challenger study of 41 different industries was *F & S Predicasts.* That yearly data source consists of article titles, dates, and abstracts from more than 7,000 newspapers, business magazines, trade association publications, and business newsletters in the United States.

Each of the four studies had a different time period and research focus. However, in each study, several thousand news headlines and abstracts were carefully read and coded. Actions were coded into the following competitive types: pricing, marketing, innovation, legal, licensing, and product announcements. In the airline, brewing, telecommunications, and PC industries the focus was on competitive events, defined to include both an action and a response or responses. In the airline industry, a response was identified by a keyword search of each issue of *Aviation Daily*. Key words included "in responding to ...," "following ...", "under the pressure of...," "reacting to...," and the like. Thus, all actions that provoked a competitive response were included for study. Overall, the research identified 191 actions and 418 responses among airlines from 1978 through 1986. In the brewing, telecommunications, and PC industries, only new product introductions or products entirely new to the market (e.g., the introduction of light beer) were considered. Responses were identified as a matching imitation of an initial new product (e.g., all light beers). The research identified 82 new product introductions and 632 imitative responses across the three industries for the period from 1975 through 1990.

The software study examined the actions and reactions among all public software firms from 1980 through 1990. Public firms hold approximately 70 percent of the industry market share. Firms in the industry were arranged into four principal industry segments based on their largest volume of sales. Within each segment, firms were assumed to be acting and reacting toward one another. A total of 2,347 actions were identified over the study period, and the moves were sorted into the appropriate industry segments (where the firm had its largest proportion of sales). The actions within each segment were arranged in chronological order. Thus, a measure of the elapsed time between one firm's action and the next competitive action was calculated.

In the leader-challenger study across 41 different industries, a total of 4,876 actions were identified from 1986 through 1993 and arranged in chronological order. Leaders and challengers were assumed to be acting and reacting toward one another. Thus, as in the software study, a measure of the elapsed time between action and reaction was used to capture the relationship between action and reaction. Similarly, in the study examining 11 different industries, over 4,600 competitive actions were identified from 1990 through 1996. The relationships between firm activity, rival activity and firm performance were examined.

Part II

Strategic Paradigms of Competitive Advantage

Chapter 2

ECONOMIC THEORIES
OF COMPETITION AND
COMPETITIVE ADVANTAGE

Neoclassical, Industrial Organization,
Game Theory, Schumpeterian, and
Evolutionary Economics

The economics literature contains a diverse array of perspectives on competition. While the emphasis has largely been focused on the outcomes of competition for society and economic efficiency, this literature contains rich insights for firms in their quest for competitive advantage over their rivals.

The most well-known view of competition within strategy is the Porter Five-Forces model, which has its origins in the *structure-conduct-performance* (S-C-P) framework of *industrial organization* (IO) economics. The Porter model posits that competitive advantage is primarily driven by industry structure and exhibits how a firm is positioned within and influenced by that structure. From that perspective, the environment largely determines competitive advantage and performance.

However, economic theories of competition extend well beyond the S-C-P view; they are sophisticated, complex, and based on decades of theoretical and empirical research. These theories are very useful in understanding the nature of competition and the role of firm strategy and action in achieving competitive advantage. In this chapter, we review the neoclassical theories of perfect competition, monopolistic competition, oligopolistic theories of competition, and competition with strong dominant firms; the industrial organization perspective on competition from the S-C-P paradigm; the *new industrial organization* view on competition, with its emphasis on game theory models; and dynamic competition models, which include the Schumpeterian view of competition, and evolutionary economics theories. Throughout the book, we will draw on insights from this diverse array of economic theories in building our action-based approach to strategy and competitive advantage. Our purpose in this chapter is to present a summary of the academic literature within economics that deals with competition issues; a review of each of these economic perspectives on competition will give the reader a broad background on the issues involved in creating competitive advantage. An understanding of these viewpoints prepares the reader to comprehend the material presented in subsequent chapters and relate that material to alternative approaches to competitive advantage.

Theories of Competition from Neoclassical Economics

Perfect Competition

A neoclassical view of the firm focuses on a firm's technology. The firm is seen as a production function that transforms inputs into outputs, in accordance with a goal of maximizing profits.[1] The model of perfect competition is the most fundamental model of economic analysis within the neoclassical view, and serves as the starting point for most approaches to economics.

The assumptions of the model are that there are many firms, each of which is small, all selling homogeneous products. Firms have perfect information, and there are no entry barriers or other market imperfections. Firms attempt to maximize profits, and do so by setting marginal revenue (the product price, taken as given where market supply equates with market demand) equal to marginal costs. If prices initially exceed marginal cost, so that firms make a positive economic profit, entry occurs, which then drives down prices. When the market is in long-run equilibrium, prices equal marginal costs and also average costs so that economic profits are zero.[2]

There is a minimal role for firm strategy within this perspective, other than to avoid, if possible, such "unattractive" markets. However, the model of perfect competition does drive home important lessons on the strength of competitive forces in a free market economy in eroding excess profits and driving out inefficient firms, particularly in the absence of product differentiation or entry barriers.

Monopolistic Competition

The model of monopolistic competition, developed by Chamberlin (*The Theory of Monopolistic Competition*, 1938), is a variant on the model of perfect competition that allows for differentiation by firms. As noted by Chamberlain:

> Differentiation may be based upon certain characteristics of the product itself, such as exclusive patented features; trade-marks; trade names; peculiarities of the package or container, if any; or singularity in quality, design, color, or style. It may also exist with respect to the conditions surrounding its sale. In retail trade, to take only one instance, these conditions include such factors as the convenience of the seller's location, the general tone or character of his establishment, his way of doing business, his reputation for fair dealing, courtesy, efficiency and all the personal links which attach his customers either to himself or to those employed by him.[3]

In the model of monopolistic competition, firms still maximize profits by setting marginal revenue equal to marginal cost. However, successful product differentiation gives rise to excess profits, which persist at long-run equilibrium.

The Chamberlin model gives rise to a substantial role for firm strategy. Patents, trademarks, customer service, reputation, and the like can all be the source of competitive advantage; as will be discussed in the following chapter, these sources of differentiation can all be considered *resources* in the resource-based view of the firm.

Models of Monopoly or Dominant Firm

Another fundamental model within neoclassical economics is the model of a monopolist. In this instance, we have one firm in the market. This firm is assumed to be knowledgeable about the market demand curve, in other words, has information about what price each potential customer is willing to pay for its product. The monopolist then sets price to maximize its profits. In the basic model of monopoly, strong barriers to entry exist, so that the monopolist's excess profits persist in the long run.[4]

Important variants on the monopoly model allow for the potential of market entry. In limit pricing models, the dominant firm sets prices, taking into account potential entry into the market. Higher prices and subsequent profits are assumed to entice stronger and quicker entry into the market. In such models, a monopolist may be wise to lower prices from short-run maximizing levels, in order to deter entry and achieve long-run maximum profits. Such models have been extended to other tactics to deter entry, such as product proliferation, preemptive patents, and the like.[5] In the model of contestable markets, potential entry is such a powerful force that firms are forced to price at levels equal to their costs, eliminating excess profits and resulting in an outcome similar to that of competitive markets.[6] These models offer significant implications for firm strategy in the case of dominant firms, which we will explore in chapter 7.

Oligopoly Theories of Competition

The final set of neoclassical models deals with situations of small numbers of firms, highly interdependent on one another and aware of each other's actions. As opposed to models of perfect competition and monopoly, there are a variety of models with differing assumptions and outcomes. These models are sometimes referred to as conjectural variations models, as each firm makes assumptions or "conjectures" about the varied way its rivals might react to its actions. The three most common models are as follows.

1. The *basic Cournot model* (1838) considers duopoly with two identical firms. Each firm maximizes profits, defined at total revenue minus total cost. This model assumes that firms take quantity produced for rivals as given; the result is prices greater than costs and positive economic profits.
2. The *basic Bertrand model* (1883) is similar to the Cournot model but assumes firms taking other firms' prices (as opposed to quantities, in Cournot) as given. The outcome is similar to that of perfect competition, with no excess profits.
3. In the Stackleberg model (1934) a dominant firm takes the key role. This model has a leader and a follower. The leader sets quantity on follower's reaction function to maximize profits and is able to achieve positive economic profit.[7]

The models of oligopoly theory, all of which have many complex variants, provide substantial insights for firm strategy.[8] Amit, Domowitz, and Fershtman point out in detail how these models can assist firms in competitor analysis and guide formulation of strategy.[9] In addition, this can aid in forming pricing and output strategies.

Theories of Competition from the S-C-P Tradition within Industrial Organization Economics

Let us begin with a definition. Industrial organization (IO) economics can be defined succinctly as "the study of the supply side of the economy, particularly those markets in which business firms are sellers."[10] According to the economist George Stigler, a Nobel laureate, it addresses "the size structure of firms (one or many, 'concentrated' or not)...the causes of this size structure, the effects of concentration on competition, the effects of competition upon prices, investments, innovation, and so on."[11]

The field of IO took initial form with strong influence from microeconomic theory, particularly the neoclassical theories of perfect competition, oligopoly, and monopoly discussed earlier. Beginning in the 1930s, Edward Mason, considered by many people to be the father of IO economics, developed the influential structure-conduct-performance framework. The framework posits that the structure of the industry influences the conduct of the firms within that industry, which in turn determines industry performance.[12] Importantly, this framework focuses attention primarily on the industry, not individual firms.

Let us next define and explain each term in the framework in more detail. The *structure* of an industry refers primarily to the number of sellers or number of firms in that industry. At one extreme of market structure is monopoly, in which there is only one firm. At the other extreme is the perfectly competitive market, which has a very large number of small firms.

Conduct refers to the intensity of rivalry among firms in an industry. It essentially is comprised of all strategic and tactical choices of firms, including pricing behavior, product strategy and advertising, research and innovation, plant investment, and legal tactics. Among economists, pricing behavior has most often been the main focus of attention in terms of firm conduct.

Simply put, *performance* is the aggregation of individual firms' profitability and is measured at the industry level. More specifically, performance is a surrogate measure for production and allocative efficiency, progress, equity, full employment, and rate of innovation.[13]

In its simplest form, the structure-conduct-performance model argues that a highly concentrated market structure, dominated by a few large firms, will give rise to little rivalry and excessive prices and profits. On the other hand, a structure consisting of many small firms will produce a high degree of rivalry and low prices and profits.

A second major figure in the development of IO economics, especially as it relates to subsequent application to strategy, is Joe Bain. Bain extended the structure-conduct-performance paradigm by focusing on elements of industry structure beyond firm concentration. Those elements included buyer and supplier concentration, substitutes, extent of product differentiation, size distribution of firms, degree of barriers to entry, cost structures, vertical integration and diversification, the degree of government regulation, and the like.[14] Also of note is that Bain tested the structure-conduct-performance paradigm by conducting empirical studies of the impact of structure on performance.[15] Subsequent empirical work in IO largely followed Bain's, in that the linkages between structure and performance were examined, but conduct was inferred and not measured directly. Common studies had industry performance as the dependent variable and industry structural variables, such as concentration and entry barriers, as independent variables.[16]

The S-C-P model focuses on factors driving intensity of rivalry; as such, this perspective is very useful in understanding competition and competitive strategy. A large literature exists on key factors influencing rivalry or likelihood of firm tacit collusion to restrict rivalry. These include: elasticity of demand; product homogeneity; seller concentration along with number of sellers and market shares of leading firms; changes in market share over time; presence of industry groups such as trade associations; nature of the geographic market, including international competition; change in market demand over time; relationship of costs among rivals; rate of technological change; industry age; degree of diversity of firms and associated multi-market contact; barriers to entry, including size of capital and sunk costs, minimum efficient scale, and industry advertising expenditures; degree of vertical integration; and buyer concentration.[17]

More recently, IO attention has increasingly shifted from the industry to the strategic group and firm level of analysis. Richard Caves and Michael Porter, considering strategic groups, developed the concept of mobility barriers to explain differences in firm performance within an industry. For example, the presence of mobility barriers between groups prevents firms in a low-performing group from switching to a more profitable group.[18] Consistent with the structure-conduct-performance view, performance within a particular strategic group is determined primarily by structural factors such as the number of competitors.

Many studies have been done in which the firm is the unit of analysis. Firm characteristics and strategies such as size, advertising expenditures, and R&D expenditures are included with industry structural variables as determinants of firm performance. Early studies focusing on the firm placed primary attention on the relationship between firm market share and firm performance.[19] As the literature developed, the influence on firm performance of additional firm characteristics and strategies was examined. For example, David Ravenscraft, using the Federal Trade Commission (FTC) line of business data, examined the role of firm or line of business market share, capacity utilization, diversification, R&D expenditures, and advertising expenditures on firm performance.[20]

In summary, insights from IO economics have been extremely important in developing strategic management models of how firms achieve sustainable competitive advantage. The IO perspective and research tradition provide direct insights to how firms can obtain competitive advantage through positioning in the context of industry structure and pursuing strategies appropriate to that structure. However, the IO literature has limitations in producing a comprehensive theory of competitive advantage. Methodological narrowness, requiring that theory be in the form of a mathematical model with an equilibrium solution, has been an important limitation. The IO literature has suffered from a lack of attention to internal organizational factors and a general failure to measure conduct directly in empirical studies.

Whereas IO studies of the relationships between industry structure, conduct, and performance were intended to help develop public policies that promote competition, Michael Porter pioneered the application of IO concepts to strategy formulation.[21] More specifically, he viewed the structure-conduct-performance paradigm as giving managers a systematic model for assessing competition and for developing profit-maximizing strategies. However, in a significant way, Porter and other strategy writers have reversed IO's intent to erode monopoly power by recommending strategies for maximizing monopoly power.[22] Porter's key insight was that the determinants of rivalry and performance, long studied in IO, are relevant to both public policy makers and managers despite those groups' divergent objectives.

Indeed, most scholars and many practitioners of strategic management have become acquainted with the ideas of industrial organization economics through Michael Porter's 1980 book on competitive strategy, in particular, his well-known Five-Force model. Porter brought a large body of IO research into strategic management with this model, in which industry structure is the key determinant of competitive advantage.[23]

The Five-Force model can aid firms in identifying and positioning themselves within attractive industries, and we will incorporate this in a subsequent chapter. However, the IO approach to competition and competitive advantage has both contributions and limitations. One issue is that the increasingly dynamic business environment means that the industry structural factors and, indeed, industry boundaries themselves are rapidly changing. For example, local telephone companies are facing enormous change due to deregulation. New competition from wire-based, wireless, and substitute technologies, such as those offered by electric utilities and cable TV companies, has changed the very boundaries of the local telephone industry.

Using Porter's model to analyze competitive forces today and subsequently making longer term commitments based on that analysis may result in a poorly positioned firm tomorrow because of the rapid changes occurring in some industries.[24] One problem with Porter's model, and IO economics in general, is that it tends to view industries as in equilibrium and competitive advantage as sustainable. However, in today's fast-paced world, resting on the laurels of yesterday's actions, even if they were successful, is sure to result in failure tomorrow. Today's environment calls for a dynamic action orientation, with constant updating and reassessment of position and strategy.

Despite the wide use of IO concepts in strategic management, many writers have criticized IO economics as not appropriately fitting strategic management ideals. Much of the criticism has focused on lack of attention to the dynamics of competitive interaction as described in chapter 1. In particular, innovation and change can provide substantial profit, but such disequilibrium phenomena are not well captured in traditional IO models. Indeed, if environments are characterized by disequilibria and uncertainty, IO prescriptions must be viewed with caution.[25]

Porter's model becomes more useful when the forces are viewed through the lens of strategy as action. For example, the concept of entry barriers should be examined to discover actions that can be taken to promote and extend barriers. Forces determining rivalry should be examined to discover actions that can reduce rivalry. Subsequent chapters refocus these concepts from Porter and IO economics in terms of our action-oriented model—the disruptive competition of action and reaction—which is introduced in chapter 5.

However, the limitations just discussed also call for the application of new IO approaches to competition, which focus more on the rivalry between firms, and dynamic theories of competition that fit today's environment well. Recently, the IO field has shifted attention from empirical studies to theoretical work. In what is commonly dubbed the "new IO," the focus has been on mathematical modeling of competitive interaction, often through use of game theory. In addition, dynamic theories of competition have received greater attention in recent years. These theories are subsequently discussed in more detail.

The New Industrial Organization— The Role of Game Theory in Exploring Competitive Advantage

Modeling Strategy as Action

As we showed in chapter 1, rivalry, or *the frequency with which firms act and react to one another*,[26] is generally intensifying throughout the business environment. One way of modeling this action and reaction is with game theory. We now provide an introduction to game theory, beginning with the historical scenario that encouraged the development of game theory techniques.

In 1949, when the Soviet Union exploded its first atomic bomb, the U.S. nuclear monopoly ended. The Soviet bomb accelerated the nuclear arms race between the United States and the Soviet Union, and each nation would eventually arm to the point that it was capable of launching devastating nuclear attacks on the other. Many observers saw such a competitive outcome as an unacceptable dilemma; the planet could be destroyed. In fact, the predicament prompted some very distinguished scientists to suggest that the most logical solution was a surprise attack by the United States that would obliterate the enemy nation.

In a compelling book, *Prisoner's Dilemma*, William Poundstone documented this crucial dilemma. He noted that by 1950, mathematicians such as Bertrand Russell and John Von Neumann, as well as many other scientists, had concluded that there was not enough room on the Earth for two nuclear powers. A "preventive war" was thought to be the most logical and rational solution. The argument was that America should act to seize the moment and establish a world order though nuclear blackmail or even, if necessary, by surprise attack. Moreover, it was deemed crucial that such action be taken before the Soviet Union could expand its nuclear capability. Today, it is amazing that this idea was even considered. More surprising, however, is the fact that it was considered by high-level officials of the U.S. government, such as the secretary of the Navy, Francis P. Matthews, who publicly argued for the United States to become "aggressors for peace."

Clearly, each side preferred an outcome in which it was not attacked to one in which it was, but preventive war advocates feared a nuclear situation in which the enemy side could launch a devastating attack with minimal retaliation. In its December 11, 1950, issue, *Life Magazine* reported: "Talk of using the A-bomb is heard as it has never been heard before." *Time* reported the following on September 18, 1950:

> when a man knows he has a good chance to be A-bombed, nothing can stop him from wondering whether there isn't something he can do to prevent it. Very few Americans now believe that the Kremlin can be conciliated or appeased or reasoned with. Very few are content to sit back and wait for the communists to strike.

Even the *Pilot*, a newspaper of the Catholic Archdiocese of Boston, concluded that a preventive war was morally correct.

As popular as the preventive strike idea was in the early 1950s, there was concern that the United States could not win, that it did not have enough first-strike capability to destroy the Soviet Union. One worry was the number of U.S. bombs available for a first strike. (Amazingly, the U.S. government did not know how many it possessed!) Estimates ranged from no more than 50 to 688. Another concern was that the U.S. government could not accurately determine the strength of the Soviet capability. *Time* estimated that the Soviets had "more than 10 and less than 60 [bombs]—enough to give the

Kremlin a means of dreadful retaliation." Finally, the U.S. government lacked information on military targets within the Soviet Union. A 1947 article in *United States News* noted: "Russia is spread out, has no one vital nerve center. Use of enough bombs might kill a lot of people, might knock out Moscow and some steel mills, but would not win *a war* on the basis of anything now known. Such attacks are more likely to unite the Russian People." Hence, fear that a preventive first strike would not win the war was what precluded that solution, prompting instead a massive building of arsenals in the hope of deterring attack.

The nuclear arms competition between the United States and the Soviet Union is a perfect example of a prisoner's dilemma in game theory. Indeed, the prisoner's dilemma was discovered at the time when the two countries were beginning to engage in an expensive arms race. Game theory, or more specifically noncooperative game theory,[27] is the study of conflict between clear-thinking and potentially deceitful opponents who are interdependent in the sense that the outcomes of any single action depend on the behavior of the opponent. Game theory allows very precise analysis of the actions, reactions, and outcomes between opponents because players are assumed to be perfectly rational.

The game has two forms, the strategic or normal form and the extensive form. They have the following three elements in common:

1. A list of participants, or players
2. For each player, a list of strategies
3. For each combination of strategies pursued by the players, a list of payoffs received by each

An Example of a Strategic or Normal Game

Let us suppose two nations must decide whether to act and build their nuclear arsenals. Moreover, assume that building an arsenal will take several years and much of the work must be done in secret. In addition, each nation must commit to its choice without knowing what the other has decided.

Each country prefers to be stronger than the other, the obvious result if it strengthens its nuclear capability and the other does not. Alternatively, each nation is afraid of being weaker. Little will be gained if both countries build an arsenal. Power depends on *relative* military strength, and two equal military strengths cancel each other out. In fact, if both countries develop the capability with no resultant relative increase in military might, they will be materially poorer than they would have been otherwise. Even worse, once a weapon is built it tends to be used. By building nuclear capability to be more secure, both countries may in fact be worse off!

In game theory terms, this example has two players with two strategies each, so the game can be described by a 2×2 matrix. The U.S. nuclear strategies are given in the rows of the following table, and the Soviet Union's in the columns. The payoffs in each cell of the matrix correspond to the strategy pair. First the U.S. payoff is given, then the Soviet Union's.

		Soviet Union	
		Hold	*Build*
United States	*Hold*	0, 0	−100, 1
	Build	1, −100	−50, −50

In game theory terms, the strategic option of building the nuclear arsenal can be called *acting to defect*, which is viewed as a *competitive* option. In contrast, holding off on building the capability can be called *cooperation*. Both sides would prefer that neither side act to defect (reward payoff for cooperation) rather than both build for no net gain (punishment payoff for mutual defection). However, each side may well defect and build the nuclear capability either in the hope of gaining an advantage (temptation payoff) or in the fear of being the one without the bomb (sucker payoff).

Now let us replace the military players with competing business organizations: the focus of this book. Firm A and Firm B are competitors of equal size producing products for a unique segment of the consumer electronics industry. Moreover, A and B are the only players in the game and both are new to the industry. Both firms want to grow and maximize profit. Firm A is considering introducing a revolutionary product to the market that will severely hurt firm B by taking away its market. However, Firm A has learned that Firm B is considering introducing a similar new product. What should Firm A do? If Firm A defects and *acts* to introduce the product and Firm B cannot, for whatever reason, Firm A will come out the winner, having delivered a preventive knockout blow. However, if Firm B can somehow preempt Firm A by being first to the market, Firm B may come out the winner. If both firms introduce the product, they will escalate competition and both will be worse off. What should they do?

The game demonstrates that the outcomes of action (i.e., a new product introduction) depend on the reaction of rivals. If Firm A can act and Firm B fails to act, Firm A will be the winner. The reverse is true if Firm B acts and Firm A does not. However, if both firms predict that the other will act, each would be better off by not introducing the product. That is the cooperative solution, but it depends on the level of trust between the two players. Can A trust B to not act and vice versa? The answer may depend on the past history of competition between A and B and their ability to tacitly signal their intentions.

In the following chapters, in particular chapters 5 through 8, we use game theory to highlight and demonstrate key elements and relationships of our action model of advantage. We use games in both the strategic or normal form and the extensive form.

An Example of an Extensive-Form Game

The extensive form of game theory is particularly apt for examining competitive actions and reactions, as it incorporates the timing of actions and the information possessed by each player when they take action. A business decision example of the extensive form is provided in Figure 2.1.[28] An extensive-form game is similar to a decision tree. The players move sequentially, with payoffs to each according to the actual moves undertaken.

In the example, Firm A is considering the introduction of a new product. More specifically, Firm A has two choices of action in the initial period: A_1 denotes continuing with the current product line, and A_2 denotes adding a new product to that line. In the second period, Firm R has two similar choices: R_1 denotes continuing with the current line, and R_2 denotes introducing a new product. This two-period extensive game yields four possible outcomes, with associated payoffs for both players. O_1, $50 for each player, is the outcome when neither player introduces a new product. O_2, $200 for R and $-$40 for A, is the outcome when R introduces a new

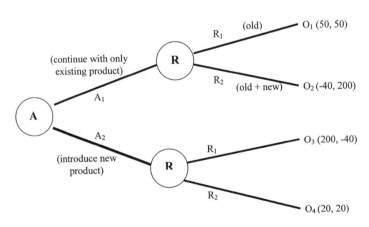

Figure 2.1   Example of Extensive-Form Game.

product and A does not. O_3 is more favorable for Firm A, $200, than firm R, −$40, because Firm A introduces a new product and Firm R stays pat. Finally, O_4 pays $20 to each firm, which is the outcome when both firms introduce a new product.

Working through the scenarios in this way can provide guidance for the firms as they try to decide the best course of action. Assuming that the set of actions and payoffs is fully known to both players and that no further actions by A are possible in a third round of the game, Firm R will clearly want to introduce a new product. Regardless of which initial action is taken, Firm R's payoff is higher if it introduces a new product. Hence, it is in Firm A's interest to introduce a new product in the first round of the game, as Firm A's payoff is higher in O_4 than in O_2. In the parlance of game theory, A_2 is a *dominant strategy* for Firm A.

Game theory—more specifically, noncooperative game theory—can be a useful tool for investigating a comprehensive model of competitive advantage in that it demonstrates the linkages between resources, competitive moves and responses, and advantage. In the remaining chapters we use game theory models to clarify those linkages.

Theories of Dynamic Competition

The Austrian School: A Schumpeterian View of Advantage

The work of Joseph Schumpeter, particularly his 1942 book *Capitalism, Socialism and Democracy*, has long influenced the field of economics. Schumpeter's views have also been increasingly influential in strategic management, particularly his notion that firms achieve competitive advantage through entrepreneurial discovery and innovative competitive action.[29]

Schumpeter's work is rooted in the Austrian school of economics. Two key features of the Austrian school are action and market process. Both are critical to Schumpeter's ideas. Murray Rothbard argued that the entire Austrian economic theory is a working out of the logical implications of the fact that human beings engage in purposeful action.[30] "Action," as used by Austrian theorists, can be understood best by contrasting actions with events. An event is something that just happens. For example, a change takes place in the world, such as a dramatic increase in demand for personal computers. An action, in contrast, causes something to happen as a result of purposeful intentions *in the natural course of events*. An example of an action is Microsoft's introduction of Windows 95, which caused a dramatic increase in the demand for personal computers. The contention is that there would not have been a dramatic increase in demand for computers without Microsoft's action. Industrial organization economists have been uncomfortable with the concept of action because "intent" is not observable. Consequently, traditional IO economists have focused almost exclusively on observable events, such as the aggregate demand for personal computers.

Market process is the second distinguishing factor for the Austrian school. Unlike traditional IO economists, who have tended to emphasize equilibrium and a static notion of competition, the Austrians view the market as a process of discovery that mobilizes dispersed and previously unidentified information. From the Austrian view, firms earn profit through entrepreneurial discovery and action. The Austrian perspective thus emphasizes the entrepreneur or manager, motivated to take action by the desire for abnormal profit. (In this book and Schumpeter's work, entrepreneurs and managers are the same and are used interchangeably.) The desire for profit spurs the entrepreneur to discover and take action on opportunities in a constantly changing environment characterized by disequilibrium and varying levels of information. However, because competitors will imitate successful actions that produce abnormal profit, the extra profit produced by entrepreneurial actions will be only temporary.

To the Austrian school, profit is not so much a result of barriers to entry or the ownership of key resources as it is the consequence and incentive of discovery and action. Hence, the key to competitive advantage is not the limitation of competitive forces, as in the Porter model, or the exploitation of scarce resources, as in the resource-based view, but rather discovery and action.

Within traditional IO economics, perhaps the most important Schumpeterian notion is that perfect competition is not the ideal market structure or that market power causes economic inefficiency.[31] In Schumpeter's view, large firms are useful and valuable because they are the most innovative. Schumpeter argued that their superior innovations would compensate for any static sacrifice in economic welfare:

> What we have got to accept is that [the large-scale establishment or unit of control] has come to be the most powerful engine of . . . progress and in particular of the long-run expansion of output not only in spite of, but to a considerable extent through, this strategy which looks so restrictive. In this respect, perfect competition is not only impossible but inferior, and has *no* title to being set up as a model of ideal efficiency.[32]

That argument inspired a long line of empirical work to test the relationship between innovation, market structure, and firm size that continues to this day.[33] In particular, Schumpeter's ideas suggest that large firms may be able to maintain their competitive advantage by being the most capable innovators. The research evidence is somewhat mixed, but generally suggests that although small firms produce more new ideas, large firms are better able to produce and distribute new products.[34]

More broadly, the Schumpeterian perspective has influenced research in many directions. As Schumpeter stated:

> But in capitalist reality as distinguished from its textbook picture, it is not [price] competition which counts but the competition from the new commodity, the new technology, the new source of supply, the new type of organization—competition which commands a decisive cost or quality advantage and which strikes not at the margins of the profits and the outputs of the existing firms but at their foundations and their very lives. This kind of competition is as much more effective than the other as a bombardment is in comparison with forcing a door, and so much more important that it becomes a matter of comparative indifference whether competition in the ordinary sense functions more or less promptly; the powerful lever that in the long run expands output and brings down prices is in any case made of other stuff.[35]

Thus, consistent with the features of the Austrian perspective, the Schumpeterian view is first of all distinctly dynamic, as opposed to the static models of competition in the IO and resource-based views. Attention centers on attainment of competitive advantage over time by taking action.[36] Second, innovation, defined broadly, is viewed as the key strategic firm variable and as much more important than price or other tactical variables.

Schumpeter's ideas about entrepreneurial discovery, action, and innovation have inspired a significant body of literature on first-mover advantages. First movers, or firms that are first to act, achieve competitive advantage by exploiting the temporary monopolistic position afforded by the imitator's lag.[37] We recently examined first-mover advantages in relation to new product rivalry in the brewing, long-distance telecommunications, and personal computer industries.[38] The results show that investors reacted favorably to new product first movers, as wealth effects were positive and statistically significant. When their moves were imitated by rivals, first movers experienced negative shareholder wealth effects. These findings support the existence of first-mover effects and the value of foreclosing or delaying response if possible.

Moreover, consistent with the dynamic Schumpeterian perspective on competition, a line of research on competitive actions and responses has produced further insights. Initially, this research took the form of case studies of actions and reactions in specific industries. For example, Richard Bettis and David Weeks examined the competitive rivalry between Polaroid and Kodak over several years.[39] More recent research has directly operationalized actions and reactions.[40] Chapter 1 provided an introduction to those studies, particularly in terms of the sample and method used in each. Specific findings from this line of research are discussed in more detail throughout the book.

In summary, the Schumpeterian viewpoint on competitive advantage has provided important insights on innovation, first-mover advantages, and competitive action and reaction. However, the approach has been limited by Schumpeter's incomplete theoretical framework. Exactly how actions lead to competitive advantage has not been developed theoretically. The following chapter discusses in more detail our action model of advantage, which builds on the Schumpeterian perspective but has elements of the IO and resource-based views as well. A key advantage of this approach is that it distinctly avoids the concepts of equilibrium and sustainability, and therefore is particularly suitable for today's, and tomorrow's, fast-paced competitive environment. The rest of this chapter provides an overview of game theory, which is used throughout the book to demonstrate components of the action model of advantage.

Evolutionary Economics: Another Dynamic View of Competition

The work of Schumpeter has also spawned a more dynamic type of research on competitive interaction. For example, Richard Nelson and Sydney Winter made important theoretical and conceptual contributions to an evolutionary theory of competition.[41] Indeed, the area of evolutionary economics is most closely associated with Nelson and Winter. Their book *An Evolutionary Theory of Economic Change*, published in 1982, is one of the most-cited books or articles within social science, and is the seminal work in this area. The work builds on the perspective of Schumpeter and focuses on innovation and technical change as constantly churning the environment.

Nelson and Winter examined strategy, performance, and survival of companies over time using a variant of Darwin's natural selection theory. In the short term, firms may pursue objectives other than profit maximization, such as "satisficing," or striving for profits to be achieved above some acceptable level. However, any firm veering too far will be weeded out of the marketplace eventually. Firms are cognizant of this harsh natural selection process and tend to learn over time how better to adapt. For example, a firm may begin with a given strategy, not at all certain that it is the superior one, and stay with that strategy unless performance falls below some threshold level. Only then will the firm change its strategy. This perspective provides useful insight into a more dynamic view of strategy.

Summary

This chapter presents multiple viewpoints on economic theories of competition and competitive advantage: neoclassical theories; the S-C-P paradigm within IO economics; the new IO view, with emphasis on game theory, and the dynamic perspectives of Schumpeterian, or "Austrian" economics and evolutionary economics. We point out that the IO view largely focuses on external factors affecting advantage, whereas game theory is introduced as a vehicle for understanding the actions and reactions of rivals in a dynamic context.

The Schumpeterian perspective is also dynamic and centers on the actions firms take and the disequilibrium of competitive markets. Within the Schumpeterian perspective, the recent stream of research on actions and reactions is reviewed and highlighted. The Schumpeterian perspective, which has both internal and external elements, is that competitive advantage is a function of firm innovation (an internal resource) and external competitive action. However, the competitive structure of the industry, especially in terms of competitive rivalry and reaction, determines the effectiveness and longevity of any firm's competitive action. The evolutionary perspective of Nelson and Winter continues this tradition of examining competition in a dynamic style.

Chapter 3

KNOWING YOUR RELATIVE
MARKET POSITION

W e discussed the new age of fast-paced competition in
chapter 1 and the most common economic perspectives on
competition in chapter 2. With this background, we now explore how a firm
can achieve a competitive advantage over its rivals by understanding its
relative market position—the first step to understanding the action alternatives available to the firm—and its relative resource position (chapter 4).
The essence of knowing a firm's relative *market* position involves understanding the industry structure and dynamics in which a firm competes
(i.e., performing an industry analysis).

To illustrate the importance of a firm's relative market position, consider the following example. Over a five-year period from 1998 to 2002,
the American Stock Exchange airline index, a stock portfolio of the major airline companies, dropped more than 70 percent. In contrast, the
American Stock Exchange pharmaceutical index, a stock portfolio of the
major pharmaceutical companies, increased more than 10 percent over
the same period, even outperforming the S&P 500 index, a stock portfolio of
the broader market, which fell about 10 percent. Much of the steep decline
in the airline index occurred after the terrorist actions on September 11,
2001, which in particular affected the airline industry. Yet the decline in
the airline index was much greater even before the terrorist actions, falling
close to 30 percent, compared to the 42 percent and 12 percent gains for
the pharmaceutical and broader indices, respectively (see fig. 3.1).[1] Subsequently, two of the major players in the airline industry, United Airlines
and US Airways, filed for chapter 11 bankruptcy protection, and the airline
industry incurred losses of more than $9 billion in the year 2002, indicative
of the difficult industry conditions.[2] Even if we examine the two industries
over a longer period and on various profit measures, the pharmaceutical

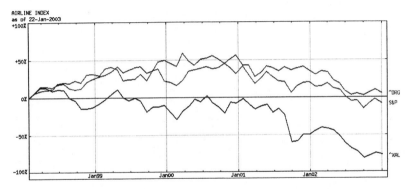

Figure 3.1 Market Returns for the Airline and Pharmaceutical Industries, 1998–2002. XAL, DRG, and S&P represent the airline, pharmaceutical, and broader market indices, respectively. Source: Copyright 2002 Yahoo! Inc.

industry still outperformed the airline industry (see table 3.1).[3] In fact, while recognizing that the airline industry is essential to any economy, many observers question the long-term attractiveness of this industry and the business models of some of its major players.[4]

Given the contrasting performance of the airline and pharmaceutical industries, we can conclude that industry membership has a significant impact on firm performance. Prior research has shown evidence to support this view. Examining firm performance from a cross-section of industries, these studies showed that industry effects account for 4 to 20 percent of a firm's performance.[5] A more recent study found that the influence of industry effects on firm performance varied according to the performance measures used—accounting versus economic profits (see table 3.1). They also found that for the vast majority of industry players— the average firms, excluding industry leaders and losers—industry effects have a greater impact on firm performance than found in previous studies, as much as 30 percent.[6] Considering that unexplained effects in all of these studies account for a substantial portion, around 45 to 80 percent, it is clear the industry effects are very important in explaining firm performance.

Certainly, our example and research evidence suggest that industry effects explain why firms perform differently. The next obvious question is: *What are these industry effects?* Hence, this chapter focuses on understanding a firm's relative market position. We first present the most established frameworks—Porter's Five Forces, complementors, and strategic groups—that explain the importance of industry structure and how firms position themselves relative to profit opportunities. Since these frameworks have traditionally focused on competition at the industry and

Table 3.1 Selected Industries and Performance Measures, 1986–1997

Industry	EVA/CE	MVA/CE	ROA
Tobacco	0.0936	3.2314	14.3979
Computer Software & Services	0.0590	4.0331	10.3530
Entertainment	0.0442	2.8240	8.4403
Personal Care	0.0281	2.8700	8.005
Medical Products	0.0276	3.0987	9.5384
Food Processing	0.0251	1.7090	8.5306
IT Consulting Services	0.0206	2.7136	6.5260
Drugs & Research	0.0065	3.3807	7.6439
Chemicals	0.0029	1.8195	7.9589
Beverages	0.0018	2.1688	5.5960
Eating Places	0.0014	2.3246	6.8867
Textiles	−0.0012	1.9392	7.4093
Building Materials	−0.0056	1.5521	5.6250
Metals	−0.0101	1.7447	—
Telephone Companies	−0.0124	1.3680	4.6181
Semiconductors & Components	−0.0126	2.0560	5.9906
Aluminium	−0.0128	1.4844	—
Paper & Products	−0.0149	1.2902	5.2342
Broadcasting & Publishing	−0.0149	1.8042	6.0059
Cars & Trucks	−0.0150	0.9473	2.1660
Computers & Peripherals	−0.0306	1.7332	3.1143
Electrical Products	−0.0327	1.3056	4.6276
Aerospace & Defense	−0.0331	1.3982	4.8390
Railroads	−0.0340	1.0257	3.7780
Airlines	−0.0416	1.1676	0.9866
Construction & Engineering	−0.0458	1.6749	—
Steel	−0.0647	1.2967	2.2646
Mean (all industries)	−0.0110	1.8930	5.5989

Notes: EVA/CE measures the ratio of Economic Value Added to capital employed; MVA/CE measures the ratio of market value of equity and debt to capital employed; and ROA measures ratio of net income to total assets.

intraindustry levels, we also introduce a pair-wise level of analysis as a build up for understanding the competitive interdependence between a focal firm and its key rival. We use the terms *industry advantage, intra-industry advantage,* and *pair-wise advantage* to reflect the respective levels of analysis. Finally, we discuss the importance of understanding industry dynamics to a firm's relative market position. Simply put, the various levels of analysis and the respective frameworks help a firm identify specific opportunities and threats and select the right position within the competitive environment. Hence, it will help a firm enhance its relative market position and in turn exploit its relative resource position, which is the focus of the subsequent chapters. Before we begin, let us briefly consider what constitutes an industry.

The most common definition of an industry is a group of firms that supplies a market.[7] Identifying industry boundaries helps firms understand the competitive pressures they face, but there is no precise way to define what constitutes an industry. Porter notes:

> Structural analysis, by focusing broadly on competition well beyond existing rivals, should reduce the need for debates on where to draw industry boundaries. Any definition of industry is essentially a choice of where to draw the line between established competitors and substitute products, between existing firms and potential entrants, and between existing firms and suppliers and buyers. Drawing these lines is inherently a matter of degree that has little to do with the choice of strategy.[8]

In sum, the preciseness of the industry boundary is not as critical as recognizing that industry structure impacts firm performance and that industry boundary is a matter of judgment that depends on the context and purpose of the analysis.[9]

Industry Advantage

Porter's Five Forces of Competition Framework

Recall our earlier example comparing the performance of the pharmaceutical and airline industries. From the perspective of an industry advantage, a firm in the pharmaceutical industry enjoys a relative market position advantage over a firm in the airline industry from simply competing in a more structurally attractive industry. Michael Porter's Five Forces of Competition is the most popular framework to explain industry advantage among scholars and many practitioners of strategic management.[10] His framework draws greatly from the ideas of industrial organization (IO) economics. Porter brought a large body of IO research into strategic management with his Five Forces framework, in which industry structure is a key determinant of industry advantage and thus competitive advantage.[11] According to Porter's framework, as depicted in figure 3.2, firms achieve competitive advantage by recognizing industry structure, positioning themselves in relation to that structure, and shaping industry structure in a beneficial manner. The analysis of the industry environment includes bargaining power of buyers and suppliers, threat of entry, effects of substitute products, and overall industry rivalry. Broadly speaking, the analysis is performed mainly from the perspective of industry incumbents and suggests that the stronger the firm's position with regard to the competitive pressures, the greater the firm's profit potential. Let us next discuss the specific competitive pressures of the Five Forces framework.

Figure 3.2   Porter's Five Forces of Competition Framework.

Buyer power depends on the balance of power between industry players and their buyers. If the balance of power favors the buyers, they have greater ability to demand lower prices and better quality and services, and to play industry players against each other, which all can undermine industry profitability. Buyers increase their leverage if the products they purchase from the industry are in large volumes, represent a significant proportion of the buyers' total cost, are unimportant to the quality of the buyers' products, and are less differentiated. Buyers also increase their leverage if they have a greater number of possible suppliers, face low switching costs, pose a credible threat of backward integration, and have full information.

Similarly, supplier power depends on the balance of power between industry players and their suppliers. If the balance of power favors the suppliers, they have greater ability to charge higher prices and to reduce the quality and services, which all can undermine industry profitability. The factors increasing the leverage of suppliers mirror those increasing the leverage of buyers.

The threat of entry depends on entry barriers, or the ability of new industry players to enter an industry. If entry barriers are low, then new entrants can easily bring new capacity and intensify competition and the fight for market share, which all can undermine industry profitability. The threat of entry increases as economies of scale, product differentiation, capital requirements, absolute cost advantages, and switching costs decrease. The threat of entry also increases if new entrants have easy access to distribution channels, limited legal and regulatory barriers, less aggressive incumbents, and do not face proprietary network externalities.[12]

The threat of substitutes depends on other industries' products that can perform the same function. Substitutes can limit the price that an industry's buyers are willing to pay, which can undermine industry profitability. The threat of substitutes increases with greater availability of close substitutes and greater superiority of the price-performance of the substitutes. For example, aluminum is increasingly becoming more of a close substitute for steel, undermining the profitability of the steel industry.

The intensity of rivalry is very often the key competitive pressure influencing industry profitability and depends on the overall state of competition among incumbents. In some industries, competition among incumbents is aggressive or warlike, whereas in other industries it is subdued or gentlemanly. Industry rivalry increases with more and equally balanced competitors, slower industry growth, higher fixed costs, lower product differentiation, lower switching costs, and higher exit barriers. Industry rivalry also increases as diversity of competitors' strategies decreases and capacity additions must be added in large increments.

Let us illustrate Porter's Five Forces framework with an industry example. Recall again that the U.S. airline industry has been a relatively unattractive and unprofitable industry. Although the framework can be used in all industry settings, this industry is a good example with which to apply the framework and to explain how all of the competitive pressures impact industry profits. A summary of the analysis is provided in figure 3.3, but let us explain in more detail the major causes of the unattractive industry structure.

First, consider the supplier power in the U.S. airline industry. While there are many suppliers to the industry, we consider only those that have

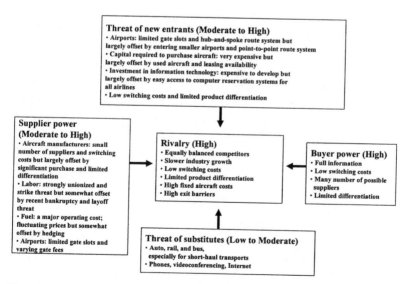

Figure 3.3   Porter's Five Forces of Competition Framework Applied to the U.S. Airline Industry.

traditionally had a major influence on supplier power such as aircraft, labor, fuel, and airports. One determinant of the bargaining power of suppliers is the number and size of possible suppliers. In regard to aircraft, this favors the suppliers, as there are a number of airlines but only two commercial (Boeing and Airbus) and two dominant regional (Bombardier and Embraer) aircraft suppliers worldwide. Another determinant of supplier power is the degree of switching costs. This also favors the aircraft suppliers as the airlines lower operational costs by flying one type of aircraft and as additional models raise, for example, maintenance, training, and flying costs. Hence, aircraft suppliers should enjoy bargaining power over the airline companies. However, this supplier leverage is largely offset because aircraft purchases represent a significant cost—over $200 million, for example, for Boeing's 777 and Airbus's A340, which are comparable models—and because the aircraft supplied by Boeing and Airbus, which largely make up the fleet of the major U.S airline companies, possess limited product differentiation. Boeing and Airbus compete fiercely to win aircraft orders. For that reason, the overall leverage with the aircraft suppliers tends to favor the airline companies, as they are able to play the two aircraft suppliers against each other and negotiate lower prices and better services.[13] Another key supplier for airlines is labor, which makes up the single largest cost for airlines. Pilots, flight attendants, mechanics, and other employees of most airlines are strongly unionized. This has historically given labor an enormous degree of leverage over the airlines. Recently, union power has somewhat diminished as airlines face extreme financial distress, which allows them to leverage the threat of bankruptcy and huge layoffs—over 100,000 employees have been laid off since September 11[14]—to obtain union concessions. For the most part, however, the unions still retain significant bargaining power because of their ability to strike, which can cripple an airline. Finally, two additional key suppliers for airlines are fuel and airports. Fuel is an easily available commodity and can be hedged, but it influences airlines, as it represents another major operating cost and prices tend to fluctuate based on supply and demand. Airports have limited gate availability, which can be a barrier to entry and growth, and levy varying gate fees according to market demand. Both aspects, however, have a relatively lesser impact on the profitability of the airlines. Overall, *supplier power* in the U.S. airline industry is *moderate to high*, mainly due to the leverage of the strong unions, which undermines industry profitability.

Second, consider the power of the buyers. Buyers basically consist of individual flyers and corporations. Corporate buyers, including government agencies and corporate travel agencies who buy tickets in bulk, have substantial bargaining power and use their enormous purchasing leverage to obtain lower prices.[15] Individual flyers do not enjoy this leverage but do benefit from full information, low switching costs, a large number of possible airline companies, and limited differentiation. Specifically, with the growth of the Internet, customers can obtain full pricing information by searching on the web sites of the airlines and online travel companies (e.g., Expedia and Travelocity). While airlines can use frequent flyer programs, advertising, and other services to promote switching costs and differentiation, customers for the most part face very low switching costs and can choose among many airlines that essentially provide the same service. In short, all of these factors encourage price competition and result in a *high degree of buyer power*, which undermines the profitability of the airline industry.

Third, consider the threat of new entrants. There are several notable entry barriers into the airline industry. As noted earlier, airport gate restrictions at many crowded airports limit entry by new airlines, and frequent flyer programs discourage customers from switching to new and smaller airlines. Hub and spoke systems provide cost advantages for carriers with larger route structures and more flights. Ownership of computer reservations systems by major airlines, such as American Airlines' ownership of SABRE, provides greater access to travel agents, who in turn provide distribution. Finally, large capital expenditures are necessary, in particular for purchase of aircraft, to enter this industry. However, a number of new entrants over the years (JetBlue as a most recent example) have been able to overcome these entry barriers. New entrants have relied on accessing less crowded airports and taken advantage of existing airports, which have built more gates on the expectation of continually growing airline travel. They have taken advantage of the low switching costs and product differentiation as customers increasingly use price as the key purchasing factor. They have entered using the less costly and sometimes more efficient point-to-point route system rather than the hub and spoke system.[16] New entrants now have greater access to computer reservations systems such as SABRE, which has been spun off as an independent company, and ability to use their own web sites as a low-cost distribution system. Finally, new entrants have lowered the capital expenditures by leasing (new and used) and purchasing used aircraft at a much lower cost than the outright purchase of new aircraft and by having a labor force made up of new employees. The labor force is a particularly important issue, as a new airline relative to industry incumbents will enjoy a significant cost advantage in labor, which we noted earlier is the single biggest expense for airlines, because airline pay structure is mainly based on years of service or seniority. In short, the airline industry has seen a number of new entrants over the years, which have increased competition and undermined industry profitability for incumbents. As such, the *threat of new entrants* is classified as *moderate to high*.

Fourth, consider the threat of substitutes. Other modes of transportation provide substitute service for short flights. For example, Amtrak's rail passenger service carries many customers in the eastern corridor—Washington, Philadelphia, New York, and Boston—and is considered a viable alternative to flying. As telecommunication technology advances, teleconferencing is becoming a substitute for some business travel. However, on the whole, airline travel will remain necessary, especially for long-haul travel, and will continue to be a vital industry for any growing economy. Accordingly, the *threat of substitutes* is classified as *low to moderate*.

Finally, consider the intensity of rivalry. Several factors stimulate rivalry among the competitors in the airline industry. The industry has a number of equally balanced competitors and is experiencing slower growth than in the past. Opportunities to differentiate airline service and increase switching costs are limited, and very few firms even attempt to compete on dimensions other than price, as noted earlier. As information on price cuts is readily available, it tends to trigger retaliation and price warfare. Most important, investment in aircraft represents a huge fixed cost and leads to high exit barriers, and once aircraft capacity is committed, the marginal cost of adding more passengers is quite low, so fare discounting and intense price rivalry are prevalent. In short, all of these factors promote fierce competition among rivals and result in *high degree of rivalry*, which undermines the profitability of the airline industry.

In summary, the U.S. airline industry is characterized by strong supplier power, very high buyer power, considerable threat of new entrants, and most prominently very high rivalry. All these competitive pressures produce an unattractive industry structure and undermine industry profitability. By applying Porter's Five Forces framework, it is easy to see why the U.S. airline industry has been historically unprofitable relative to other industries, even during good economic conditions.[17] The basic principle of Porter's framework is that the collective strength of the Five Forces determines industry attractiveness and influences the strategies available to firms in the industry and thus a firm's profit potential and its relative market position. From the perspective of industry advantage, simply put, a firm's (incumbent or new entrant) relative market position is enhanced to the extent that a firm's industry has relatively weak buyers and suppliers, high barriers to entry, few substitute products, and limited rivalry.[18]

Industry Complementors

To add to our understanding of industry profitability, we now extend Porter's Five Forces framework by introducing the role of complementors, which can be viewed as a sixth force.[19] Brandenburger and Nalebuff developed the concept of complementors and the Value Net framework depicted in figure 3.4.[20] Simply put, complementors are another industry's product or service that makes your industry's product or service more

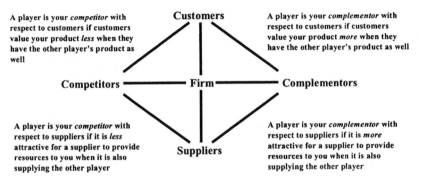

A player is your *competitor* with respect to customers if customers value your product *less* when they have the other player's product as well

A player is your *complementor* with respect to customers if customers value your product *more* when they have the other player's product as well

A player is your *competitor* with respect to suppliers if it is *less* attractive for a supplier to provide resources to you when it is also supplying the other player

A player is your *complementor* with respect to suppliers if it is *more* attractive for a supplier to provide resources to you when it is also supplying the other player

Figure 3.4   The Value Net.

attractive in the eyes of customers and suppliers. With respect to customers, two industries are complementors if the value of both industries together is greater than each of the industries individually. With respect to suppliers, two industries are complementors if the value of supplying both industries together is greater than supplying each of the industries individually. Complements are always reciprocal and very much related to network effects, where the value of or demand for a product or service increases with the performance and availability of complementors. While substitutes with improving performance and availability may have a negative impact in Porter's framework, complementors with improving performance and availability may have a positive impact on industry attractiveness.

Let us now give several examples of how complementors can increase the overall size of an industry and its attractiveness. On the buyer side, the classic example of complements is hardware and software. Hardware that improves in performance and availability increases the willingness of buyers to pay for software, just as software that increases in performance and availability increases the willingness of buyers to pay for hardware. For example, buyers value more highly video game consoles from Sony, Microsoft, and Nintendo when they have greater access to software games. Industry profits and more specifically individual success are greatly tied to the availability of popular software for the firm's respective platforms. In fact, one of the major reasons for the surprising exit of Sega, a former industry leader, is attributed to Electronic Arts's decision not to develop games for Sega's Dreamcast, its last video game console. Electronic Arts, as the number one game maker, continues to have a significant influence on industry and firm profits, and may eventually determine the biggest winner among the three big firms in choosing which platform it chooses to support in online games.[21] Similarly, the computer hardware industry profits with greater access to complements from the software industry. Producers of microprocessors such as Intel and AMD gain from greater availability of software capable of running on their chip architecture. Whenever a new operating system or application is introduced by Microsoft, computer hardware companies receive a boost in demand, and vice versa. Both the video game console and microprocessor producers can increase their overall industry size and profits with greater access to software complements.

On the supply side, the value to the flash memory chip producers (e.g., Intel and Texas Instruments) is greater when supplying both the wireless handset (e.g., Nokia and Motorola) and the electronics industries (e.g., MP3 players from Sony and Philips) compared to supplying only one industry. Thus, both the wireless handset and electronics producers are complementors and benefit, since the flash memory chip producers can reduce costs and boost innovations (e.g., in research and development) by supplying both industries rather than one industry. Similarly, Boeing can supply aircraft to the airline industry at a cheaper price when more potential buyers exist. That is, it is more attractive for Boeing to supply aircraft to numerous airline companies because it can defray the huge development costs over a number of buyers rather than one or few buyers. Although the airline companies aggressively compete with each other, the greater number nevertheless facilitates lower aircraft costs. In sum, the role of complementors adds a cooperative element to the competitive pressures of the Five Force framework in understanding industry analysis.

Intraindustry Advantage

Earlier, we established that industry matters to firm performance with an illustrative example of the airline and pharmaceutical industries and supporting research evidence. We then presented Porter's Five Forces framework and applied it the U.S. airline industry to help explain the determinants of industry attractiveness and profitability and industry advantage (or disadvantage, in the case of the airline industry). Although the U.S. airline industry has incurred losses in excess of many billion dollars over the past few years, Porter's framework does not explain how Southwest Airlines has grown and prospered in this "unattractive" environment. Because the focus of Porter's framework is at the industry level, it is rather limited in explaining the performance differences across firms within an industry. Clearly, firms within an industry vary with regard to resources and sources of competitive advantage and to performance. We will address this issue in chapter 4, which focuses on knowing a firm's relative resource position. We continue our discussion of understanding a firm's relative market position by introducing strategic group analysis to explain intraindustry competition and performance. This framework is entirely consistent with Porter's Five

Forces framework but moves our focus to an intraindustry level, where competition can perhaps be more appropriately analyzed.

A strategic group is a "group of firms in an industry following the same or similar strategy along the strategic dimension."[22] In other words, firms within a strategic group are pursuing similar strategies but differ from those outside the group on key strategic dimensions such as resource combinations, value chain activities, and scope commitments. According to the research, strategic groups are important because of their effects on competitive actions and performance. Firms within an industry face mobility barriers, analogous to entry barriers such as scale economies and distribution channels at the industry level, which explain why certain firms in a less profitable group are constrained from switching to a more profitable group within an industry.[23] The research evidence has been somewhat mixed, but more recent studies have found performance differences across strategic groups.[24] Regardless of the empirical evidence, on a practical level, strategic group analysis can be useful for several reasons. First, this framework helps to identify the closest competitors and competitive positioning of rivals. Second, it helps to understand the variance of threats and opportunities and competitive dynamics among firms within an industry. In general, it can be concluded that firms within an industry encounter different industry conditions and that firms in a particular strategic group create a favorable competitive environment for themselves compared to other firms in other strategic groups.

To illustrate, let us again examine the airline and pharmaceutical industries. Within both industries, we can identify distinct strategic groups. In the U.S. airline industry (see fig. 3.5), we can classify two distinct strategic groups: point-to-point carriers such as Southwest and JetBlue, and the network carriers such as American and United. The foremost difference in strategic posture is that the former group operates on a point-to-point route system while the latter group operates mainly using a hub-and-spoke route system. The two strategic groups also vary on other strategic dimensions such as geographic scope and services offered. In the pharmaceutical industry (see fig. 3.6), we can also identify three distinct strategic groups: generics such as Marion Laboratories and Carter Wallace; branded-generics such as Barr Laboratories and Teva Pharmaceutical; and brand-names such as Merck and Eli Lilly. Although there is some degree of overlap among the strategic groups (e.g., Pfizer and Novartis are two of the top generic producers),[25] the key difference in strategic posture is that the branded group mainly focuses on developing and patenting new drugs while the branded-generic and generic groups mainly focus on developing deviations of patented drugs and introducing drugs with expiring patents.

Let us recall also that the airline industry has been much less profitable overall than the pharmaceutical industry. However, if one examines

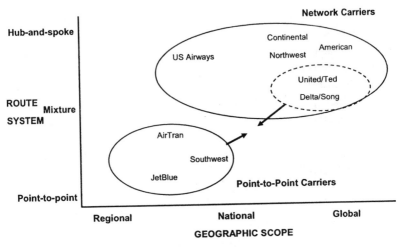

Figure 3.5   Strategic Group Mapping Applied to the U.S. Airline Industry.

performance of firms within the U.S. airline industry, some firms have clearly outperformed others. Specifically, point-to-point carriers have clearly outperformed the network carriers. For example, since 2000, Southwest, JetBlue, and AirTran have been somewhat profitable and have increased their revenues by more than $500 million in extremely difficult industry conditions, while all network carriers have been incredibly un-profitable and decreased their revenues by around $20 billion over a three-year period.[26] In fact, the point-to-point carriers are expected to continue

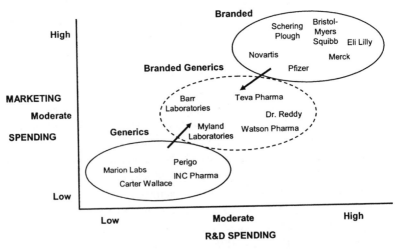

Figure 3.6   Strategic Group Mapping Applied to the Pharmaceutical Industry.

their growth and capture more market share at the expense of the network carriers, and Southwest is predicted to be the top carrier in the United States within a decade or so.[27] In short, the point-to-point carriers are in a better competitive position (or strategic group) within the industry to respond to the specific opportunities (e.g., increasing focus on low-cost efficiency and price competition) and threats (e.g., ability to endure the difficult economic environment). As a result, some network carriers have altered their strategies to better position themselves and have attempted to imitate the point-to-point carriers. For example, in 2002, US Airways's postbankruptcy strategy focused on a regional route system (or short- and medium-range routes), Delta launched "Song," and United launched "Ted," their versions of the point-to-point route system. These competitive moves by the airlines in the network carrier strategic group are mainly an attempt to take advantage of the profit opportunities and the cost advantages that the point-to-point strategic group currently enjoys. It is unclear whether the network carriers' attempts to compete directly with the point-to-point carriers and to straddle both strategic groups will be effective, as other network carriers have tried unsuccessfully to do so in the past (e.g., Continental with Continental Lite and US Airways with MetroJet). The failure of these prior efforts can be mainly attributed to the inability to make tradeoffs in activities (i.e., trying to compete in two ways at once, which degrades the value of existing as well as new activities) and the significant cost disadvantages, especially in labor, that the network carriers incur.[28] In summary, it is clear that firms within a particular strategic group are quite different from firms within another group with regard to the strategies they are pursuing, the competitive pressures they face, and their performance.

Pair-wise Advantage

We have so far presented the most established frameworks to examine a firm's relative market position from the context of a given industry structure. This is an obvious starting point since industry structure impacts the intensity of competition and thus industry and firm profits. We now move our analysis to a pair-wise advantage to capture the interdependence and fine-grained complexity of competition among industry rivals. Understanding pair-wise advantage is important for several reasons. First, pair-wise analysis enhances the industry-level analysis (i.e., Five Forces and strategic groups) as the latter fails to capture the competitive dynamics, a series of actions (moves) and reactions (countermoves), among firms in an industry. Second, pair-wise competition should be the basis for competitor analysis and examining rivalry, and to a large extent that is "how firms actually compete directly against each other."[29] Finally, pair-wise advantage is entirely consistent with the view of Schumpeterian and Austrian economics, which was discussed in chapter 2, on theories of competition—and competitive dynamics research, where firm actions are basic to understanding competitive advantage and the market process.[30]

While chapter 4 will focus on pair-wise advantage by isolating and analyzing the relative resource position of both the focal firm and its key rival, we focus here on identifying competitors and key rivals in the context of a focal firm's relative market position. We define competitors as firms that are vying with the focal firm for the same customers in the same markets (product and geographic). Following Chen's competitor analysis framework, if firms do not have common customers or markets, referred to as market commonality, then they will not have much awareness of each other or motivation to engage each other competitively. A focal firm will have a high market commonality and thus high awareness and motivation to compete with a rival if it competes directly in many markets and, more important, if it places high strategic importance on and views the rival as a significant competitive threat in those shared markets.[31]

Since primary attention should be given to competitors with the greatest degree of market commonality, we apply MacMillan, van Putten, and McGrath's competing-under-strategic-interdependence (CSI) framework to identify a focal firm's key competitors.[32] This framework is consistent with our definition of competitors as firms that are vying with the focal firm for the same customers in the same markets and with our emphasis on product and geographic market overlap in determining market commonality. The first step is to select a firm that the focal firm broadly identifies as a competitor (e.g., another firm in the same strategic group as the focal firm). The second step is to assess whether the selected firm competes directly in many markets with the focal firm by listing the major product and geographic markets that the focal firm competes in and by comparing the market overlap with the selected competitor (see fig. 3.7). This analysis can be narrow (e.g., specific product types and regional and national markets) or broad (e.g., general product segments or categories and global markets) depending on the focal firm's strategic posture and competition in the industry. The last step is to assess the attractiveness to the focal firm and reactiveness of the selected rival firm of those shared markets. In other words, does the focal firm place high strategic importance on those shared markets, and does the focal firm view the selected rival firm as a significant competitive threat in those shared markets? In sum, this framework can be used to assess whether the selected firm has high market commonality. If so, we can consider the selected firm a key competitor and then move our focus to pair-wise advantage by isolating and analyzing the relative resource position of both the focal firm and selected firm, which is discussed in chapter 4.

Focal firm: Unilever	Europe	Americas	Asia-Pacific/Africa
Foods			
Personal care			
Fabric care			

Step 1: Select a rival firm (e.g., Proctor & Gamble)

Step 2: List major product (e.g., foods, personal care, and fabric care) and geographic (e.g., Europe, America, and Asia-Pacific-Africa) markets of the focal firm

Step 3: Compare market overlaps with the selected rival firm by marking shared markets.

Step 3: Assess the *attractiveness* or how important is the market to the focal firm (market share, profitability, emotional attachment, etc. of the focal firm) and *reactiveness* or how much incentive the selected rival firm has to compete (market share, profitability, emotional attachment, etc. of the selected rival firm) of those shared markets.

Figure 3.7 Framework for Identifying Key Competitors Based on Market Commonality. Source: I. C. MacMillan, A. B. van Putten, and R. G. McGrath, 2003, Global gamesmanship, *Harvard Business Review* 81(4): 62–71. Reprinted with permission from the Harvard Business School.

Industry Dynamics

Clearly, a firm's relative market position is not as static, as firms and industries go through change. We examine firm change from the perspective of its relative resource position in chapter 4 but focus here on industry change from the perspective of a firm's relative market position. As we discussed earlier, the Five Forces and strategic group frameworks can aid firms in identifying and positioning themselves within attractive industries and groups with an industry, which produce an industry and intraindustry advantage, respectively. However, the increasingly dynamic business environment means that the industry structural factors and, indeed, industry boundaries themselves, are rapidly changing. For example, deregulation and technological innovations are driving industry change for local and long-distance telephone companies. Competition has been traditionally divided between local and long-distance providers. Now, local telephone companies can offer long distance and vice versa. Rapid changes in technology are also making traditional industry definitions suspect and creating industry convergence. New competition from wire-based, wireless, and substitute technologies such as those offered by electric utilities, cable TV companies, and Internet providers has changed the very boundaries of the local and long-distance telephone industry. Not very many years ago, the major television networks could easily count their competitors on one hand; television broadcasting was a small, highly regulated industry with tight boundaries. Currently, however, with changes in both technology and regulation, competition in the visual broadcasting industry is much more complex. Diverse new competitors (e.g., Movielink, Walt Disney's Moviebeam) have arisen and are attempting to market everything from movies "on line" to news, information, and personal services such as banking. Among companies currently in the market, or developing technology to enter the market, are cable and satellite providers, telecommunications companies, computer networking companies, and even electric utilities. These changes are completely redefining the broadcasting industry. Although many of the new services do not compete directly with the television networks, the evolution of how individuals receive signals or information from outside the home will definitely affect the broadcasting industry.[33]

Broadly speaking, industry change can be described as either evolutionary (slow and incremental with one or two structural aspects changing) or revolutionary (rapid and dramatic with many related structural aspects concurrently changing).[34] Even in today's environment of rapid technological innovations, it is debatable whether evolutionary or revolutionary change is more typical of industry change.[35] Without addressing this debate, we present here how industry change can occur, alter the opportunities and threats to a firm, and impact a firm's relative market position.

Industry change usually takes place through expected stages. One framework to explain how industries typically evolve is the industry life cycle. Analogous to product life cycles, industries too evolve and can be categorized according to the stage of development. As shown in figure 3.8, the traditional industry life cycle consists of four stages: introduction, growth, maturity, and decline. Although the life cycle varies from industry to industry, we can expect an industry to exhibit certain structural characteristics at each stage of development. Table 3.2 shows the major

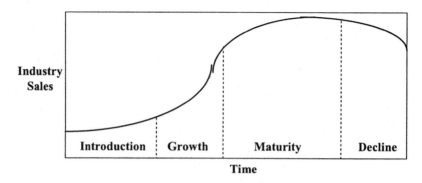

Figure 3.8   Traditional Stages of the Industry Life Cycle.

Table 3.2 The Evolution of Industry Structure and Competition over the Life Cycle

	Introduction	Growth	Maturity	Decline
Demand	Limited to early adopters: high-income, avant-garde.	Rapidly increasing market penetration.	Mass market, replacement/repeat buying. Customers knowledgeable and price sensitive	Obsolescence.
Technology	Competing technologies. Rapid product innovation.	Standardization around dominant technology. Rapid process innovation.	Well-diffused technical know-how: quest for technological improvements.	Little product or process innovation.
Products	Poor quality. Wide variety of features and technologies. Frequent design changes.	Design and quality improve. Emergence of dominant design.	Trend to commoditization. Attempts to differentiate by branding, quality, bundling.	Commodities the norm: differentiation difficult and unprofitable.
Manufacturing and distribution	Short production runs. High-skilled labor content. Specialized distribution channels.	Capacity shortages. Mass production. Competition for distribution.	Emergence of overcapacity. Deskilling of production. Long production runs. Distributors carry fewer lines.	Chronic overcapacity. Re-emergence of specialty channels.
Trade	Producers and consumers in advanced countries.	Exports from advanced countries to rest of world.	Production shifts to newly industrializing then developing countries.	Exports from countries with lowest labor costs.
Competition	Few companies.	Entry, mergers, and exits.	Shakeout. Price competition increases.	Price wars, exits.
Key success factors	Product innovation. Establishing credible image of firm and product	Design for manufacture. Access to distribution. Building strong brand. Fast product development. Process innovation.	Cost efficiency through capital intensity, scale efficiency, and low input costs. High quality.	Low overheads. Buyer selection. Signaling commitment. Rationalizing capacity.

Source: R. Grant, 2002. *Contemporary strategy analysis: Concepts, techniques, applications.* (Oxford, United Kingdom: Blackwell Publishers), p. 311. Reprinted with permission from Blackwell Publishers.

structural characteristics and the nature of competition at each stage of the industry life cycle. However, as we noted in chapter 1, in an era of fast-paced competition, product life cycles have shrunk and frequency of new products being introduced has increased. As a result, the typical progression of the life cycle has been altered to some extent in most industries.

Similarly, another framework, which directly speaks to the changes in the Five Forces of competition, proposes that industries transform through three predictable stages: trigger, experimentation, and convergence.[36] The first or trigger stage, which typically arises from a change in technology, customer taste, or regulation, alters the competitive pressures of the Five Forces, favors certain incumbent firms in a particular strategic posture within an industry, or enables new entrants or incumbent firms to do business in a significantly different way from possible before. The second or experimentation stage involves companies searching for a winning strategy, knowing that the industry is changing but unsure of the outcome with regard to the best way to exploit opportunities and minimize threats. The last or convergence stage involves a few best winning strategies as the industry structure becomes clearer and the competitive pressures of the Five Forces become more stable.

Summary

This chapter focused on performing an industry analysis, specifically from the perspective of an understanding a firm's relative market position. Appendix B provides a checklist of the key elements in performing an industry analysis. Knowing a firm's relative market position is a key first step to understanding the action alternatives available to a firm and to effectively designing strategies of action to engage the competition, which lead to a competitive advantage. Specifically, we presented frameworks from the traditional industry context, leading to an industry and intraindustry advantage. We also presented frameworks for pair-wise analysis as a buildup to understanding a firm's relative resource positions, to be discussed in subsequent chapters. Finally, we discussed how industry change occurs and impacts a firm's relative market position.

APPENDIX: Industry Analysis Checklist

1. Key industry characteristics
   a. Market size ($ and volume)
   b. Growth rate (past and future forecasts)
   c. Major competitors based on market share
   d. Industry concentration
   e. Industry performance
2. Industry advantage: Porter's Five Forces framework and complementors
   a. Threat of new entrants
   b. Threat of substitutes
   c. Buyer power
   d. Supplier power
   e. Intensity of rivalry
   f. Complementors
3. Intraindustry advantage: Strategic group mapping
   a. Identify strategic dimensions that differentiate the competitive positions among rivals
   b. Select two key distinguishing strategic dimensions and plot the firms
   c. Draw circles around cluster of firms to identify strategic groups
4. Pair-wise advantage
   a. Select a rival firm, for example, in the same strategic group
   b. List major product and geographic markets of the focal firm
   c. Compare market overlap with the selected rival firm by marking shared markets
   d. Assess the attractiveness to the focal firm and reactiveness of the selected rival firm of those shared markets
5. Industry dynamics
   a. Analyze the key drivers of industry change
   b. Analyze the stage of industry life cycle: introduction, growth, maturity, and decline
   c. Analyze the stage of industry change: trigger, experimentation, or convergence
   d. Analyze how rivals are responding to industry change

Chapter 4

KNOWING YOUR RELATIVE
RESOURCE POSITION

Gillette, which had $8.4 billion in sales and approximately $1.2 billion in net income in 2002, is an example of a company with a strong resource position.[1] Gillette's high performance and strong market position in the razor blade industry can be explained by the firm's ability to efficiently combine its unique resources to build an attractive and enviable position in the industry. Gillette's development of the high-technology razors, such as Mach3Turbo, is the case in point. Gillette's new triple-blade shaving system, at the time of writing the most technologically advanced shaving system in the world, is based on a unique combination of resources, including 35 different new patents, improved lubrication systems, and customized manufacturing processes. The razor appears to be a simple gadget with three blades mounted on small springs. However, the product is significantly more "high tech" than it may seem. Its production is based on one-of-its-kind manufacturing equipment and innovative patents. The equipment, designed by Gillette, is very complex, and it is virtually impossible for a competitor in the razor industry to understand or recreate it. Although Schick, a major competitor, has won rights to some product designs, e.g., the lubrication strip, that could help it build a competitive product, the company is lacking the key manufacturing knowhow necessary to duplicate Gillette's high-tech shaver. As a result, Gillette holds a very attractive and secure position in the industry.

Chapter 3 focused on the structure of industries and how firms position themselves relative to profit opportunities in an industry. The stronger the firm's structural position in the industry, in terms of barriers to entry, powerful buyers and suppliers, threat of substitutes, and rivalry, the greater the profit potential for the firm. However, a firm's positioning in an industry is only one half of the competitive puzzle. Firms must also match their resources with the market opportunity they face. In other words, when a market opportunity presents itself, firms must be capable of seizing it by utilizing their unique resources. This chapter examines how firms use their resources to take advantage of opportunities and defend their market position from the competition.

It is obvious that firms in every industry vary with regard to the human, physical, and financial resources they hold. We pinpointed such variety in firms' resources in chapter 3 in our discussion of strategic groups. Less obvious, though, is the importance of resource differences for understanding profits, competition, and competitive advantage. This chapter explains how firm-specific resources relate to action, competitive advantage, and performance. We use the concept of leverage to capture the relationship between firm resources and competitive action. Simply put, it means that competitive actions *should* be designed on the basis of the principle of resource strength (utilizing strengths to seize opportunities). For example, a firm with a breakthrough patent, considered a scarce resource, may introduce a new product, based on the patent, to capture 100 percent of a market; a firm with a low cost position may cut prices below rivals' and even its own costs to build market share. We will show that assessing a firm's relative resource position, that is, its position vis-à-vis the resources of other competitors in the industry, is a second step (after examining industry structure) leading to understanding the action alternatives available to the firm. We first explain the importance of resources and discuss different types of resources and how they relate to competitive action and competitive advantage. Then we introduce value chain analysis as a tool for evaluating a firm's sources of value and locating its potential areas of competitive advantage. Finally, we present the idea of a firm's relative resource position vis-à-vis a competitor or group of competitors, and employ it to identify a firm's competitive action alternatives.

The Resource-Based View

According to the resource-based view of the firm, which has become the dominant strategy perspective in recent years, the resources of the firm are the fundamental determinant of competitive advantage and performance; accordingly, resource constraints limit and resource advantages enhance a firm's performance.[2] Examples of resources are human capital, including labor and knowhow; financial capital, such as cash flow and percentage of debt; physical capital such as plant, equipment, and raw material; and social capital, such as trusting relationships and friendships among buyers, suppliers, and other stakeholders. In contrast to Porter's viewpoint, the resource-based view has primarily an internal focus on the specific resources and capabilities of the firm.

Interest in the resource-based view of the firm has paralleled interest in Porter's Five Forces model. Jay Barney defined resources as "all assets, capabilities, organizational processes, firm attributes, information, knowledge, etc. controlled by a firm that enable the firm to conceive of and implement strategies that improve its efficiency and effectiveness."[3] Because certain resources are seen as the key to sustained competitive advantage, the emphasis is on the relationship between a firm's specific set of resources and its competitive advantage. Barney contends that strategically relevant resources are those that are valuable, rare, imperfectly imitable, and have no strategic substitutes.

A resource is valuable to the firm when it helps the firm exploit specific opportunities or protect itself against key threats. Value is firm specific, as a firm's relationship to its environment (opportunities and threats) is unique. A long-term employment contract with a famous and productive scientist might be considered a valuable resource, as would Intel's many years of experience in producing microprocessors for personal computers. Competitors would be hard pressed to obtain the same valuable resource.

Resources must be rare to be of strategic use. Jim Clark's expertise and ability at spotting opportunities is an example. Not many entrepreneurs create three different billion-dollar ventures as Clark did with Silicon Graphics, Netscape, and Healtheon.[4] However, when other firms gain access to the same resource, the resource's utility in the pursuit of competitive opportunities becomes limited. For example, when Nutrasweet's patent expired, the Hollander Sweetener Company promptly entered the market, making Nutrasweet's knowhow in producing sugar-free sweeteners less rare.

Resources must also be imperfectly imitable to generate firm advantage. If other firms are able to emulate the resources, advantage will be competed away. Wal-Mart's initial geographic store location strategy in the South is an example of the strategy that is imperfectly imitable. Wal-Mart rapidly expanded its discount retailing in rural southern locations to the point that at nearly one-third of its locations, the nearest competitor was a Wal-Mart store. Later entrants in these locations, many of which had significant resources, facing the prospects of competing with a low-cost, fully operational Wal-Mart store, could not justify investment, because demand would be split between the store locations. Wal-Mart, the first mover, had ownership of all the key locations.

Barney identified three characteristics of resources that make them difficult for rivals to imitate: history, causal ambiguity, and social complexity.[5] History is a characteristic of resources that are attained over time, perhaps in a unique way. For example, Coca-Cola has over 80 years of advertising its brand name to customers. It would be hard for a soft-drink rival to match Coke's brand awareness, at least in the short run.

Causal ambiguity makes it difficult for competitors to understand how a particular resource yields advantage. The more easily a particular causal link can be deciphered, the *more* rapidly rivals will be able to imitate it. Complex organizational processes, such as creative employee incentive programs, exemplify causally ambiguous resources. It is not easy for competitors to identify the ingredients of Cannon's success in manufacturing and selling printers, which lies in the complex combination of capabilities in fine optics, precision engineering, and microelectronics.[6]

Finally, social complexity also contributes to creating resource advantages that are difficult for rivals to understand and imitate. An innovative culture fostered at Cray Computers or 3M can be easily identified as a source of competitive advantage, but it is very difficult for a rival to re-create such a culture. Similarly, the human resource management systems at Nucor or Lincoln Electric are fairly visible, but it is a challenging task for a rival to imitate them and attain the same results.

Following Barney's work on imperfect imitability, scholars distinguish between different types of resources, for example, tangible firm resources, such as patents and capital, and intangible resources, such as organizational culture and organizational processes. Table 4.1 lays out the differences between tangible resources and intangible resources and describes the indicators of such resources. Tangible resources often include the financial and physical resources of the firm. In some cases, as when the resources differences between firms are very significant (e.g., barrier to entry, mobility barrier, or isolating mechanism), tangible resources may create significant advantage because such differences may allow the dominant firm to enjoy advantages of scale, and to aggressively attack the resource-poor firm. Generally however, tangible resources of incumbent firms will not deter rivals that see a market opportunity.

Intangible resources include technological, reputational, and human resources. Technological resources, intellectual property rights, historical investments in R & D, and human capital often serve as a strong source of competitive advantages when aligned with market opportunities that require these resources. Such advantages typically arise from exclusive patents or unique, rare and valuable knowledge held by the firm and its employees. Reputational resources, such as brand name, trademarks, and established relationships with customers, suppliers, and other stakeholders, can also produce strong advantages for firms by creating switching costs for rivals. That is, rivals will have to incur extra costs to persuade customers, suppliers, and other stakeholders to switch to the rival firm's product or services. Human resources are reinforced through the education and training of employees and their experience, motivation, and skills, as well as their commitment and loyalty toward their jobs and employer. Human resources can be a powerful source of advantage but are often unstable, as employees can be lured away by rivals.

Table 4.1 Classifying and Analyzing the Firm's Resources

Resource	Relevant Characteristics	Key Indicators
Tangible resources		
Financial resources	The firm's borrowing capacity and its internal funds generation determine its resilience and capacity for investment	• Debt/equity ratio • Operating each flow/free cash flow • Credit rating
Physical resources	Physical resources constrain the firm's set of production possibilities and impact its cost position. Key characteristics include: • The size, location, technical sophistication, and flexibility of plant and equipment • Location and alternative uses for land and buildings • Reserves of raw materials	• Market values of fixed assets • Vintage of capital equipment • Scale of plants • Flexibility of fixed assets
Intangible resources		
Technological resources	Intellectual property: patent portfolio, copyright, trade secrets Resources for innovation: research facilities, technical and scientific employees	• Number and significance of patents • Revenue from licensing patents and copyrights • R&D staff as a percent of total employment • Number and location of research facilities
Reputation	Reputation with customers through the ownership of brands and trademarks; established relationships with customers; the reputation of the firm's products and services of quality and reliability The reputation of the company with suppliers (including component suppliers, banks and financiers, employees and potential employees), with government and government agencies, and with the community	• Brand recognition • Brand equity • Percent of repeat buying • Objective measures of comparative product performance (e.g., Consumers' Association ratings, J. D. Power ratings) • Surveys of corporate reputation (e.g., *Business Week*)

Human resources	The education, training and experiences of employees determine the skills available to the firm	• Educational, technical, and professional qualifications of employees
	The adaptability of employees contributes to the strategic flexibility of the firm	• Compensation relative to industry
	The social and collaborative skills of employees determine the capacity of the firm to transform human resources into organizational capabilities	• Percentage of days lost through stoppages and industrial disputes
	The commitment and loyalty of employees determine the capacity of the firm to attain and maintain competitive advantage	• Absentee rates
		• Employee turnover rate

Source: R. Grant, 2002. *Contemporary strategy analysis: Concepts, techniques, applications.* (Oxford, United Kingdom: Blackwell Publishers). p. 140. Reprinted with the permission of Blackwell Publishers.

Understanding Resources Differences: The Value Chain

As noted earlier, resources are defined as all tangible assets, human skills, and organizational processes/routines used to produce a product or service (the production function of the firm). Importantly, we contend that these resources have no *special* value beyond their cost of acquisition or development, except in action or how they are used. We are interested in a firm's relative stock of resources; that is, vis-à-vis a competitor or group of competitors. We evaluate a firm's relative position or its current stock of resources by applying a value chain analysis (to a group of competitors or a particular competitor). We also emphasize that the analysis of resources must capture more than the current expenditures or flows of resources, as it must take into account the stocks of assets accumulated over time, for example, the cumulative experience of the firm in research and development or in marketing.[7] The analysis must also reflect the specific assets of the firm, for example, technological assets, financial assets, and reputational assets.[8]

Value chain analysis starts with identifying the discrete resource activities a firm performs to deliver the product or service, such as the key value-creating activities or functions of the organization.[9] The way a firm arranges its resources to produce value will depend on its history, its strategy, the underlying economics, and the approach toward engaging the competition. Although firms in the same industry often have similar resources, subtle differences in configuration of resources among competitors can be a source of different competitive advantages and lead to diverse competitive actions.

Value chain analysis should be conducted at the business unit or market segment level of analysis since the ultimate goal is to analyze the firm's resource position relative to its competitors in the markets. The value chain is composed of all the economic value–creating activities of the firm. These activities can be conducted within the firm but may also include activities by other firms, engaged through subcontracting or alliances. Figure 4.1, drawn from McKinsey and Company, reflects a relatively simple portrayal of value-creating activities across the basic functions of the firm: technology, product design, manufacturing, marketing, distribution, and service.

Value is the amount that buyers are willing to pay for a particular product or service.[10] The first step of the analysis focuses on disaggregating the total value (e.g., 100 percent) across different activities in order to identify the principal sources of value in the firm. For example, Wal-Mart's key source of value lies in its logistical operations, whereas Nucor Steel's key source of value creation resides in its human resource management. Naturally, a firm may have multiple sources of value; for example, a firm like Nintendo enjoys advantages in game programing, technological development, marketing expertise, and management. Intel benefits from

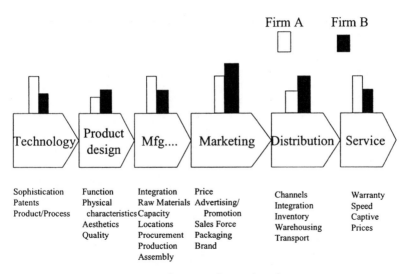

Figure 4.1   Producing Value within the Firm.

advantages in microprocessor manufacturing, technology design, and marketing. The question is: *How much value is created in each area?*

As shown in figure 4.1, the value chain is often structured in terms of inputs or raw materials, throughputs or firm-level processes that convert inputs to outputs, and, finally, outputs, which may include those processes that deliver products and services to customers. Building on the McKinsey model, Porter suggested that these value activities can be divided into primary and supporting.[11] Primary activities include all those activities. that are directly related to the success of the firm's product or service, for example, manufacturing or marketing. Support activities have a less direct and visible affect on the firm's products or services, for example, human resource management or research and development. Figure 4.2 presents Porter's modified value chain model with primary and supporting activities.

The key activities that need to be isolated in the value chain should reflect not only the firm's own competitive advantage but also the important value chain activities of its rivals. Thus, like in industry analysis, a beginning step is to define the firm's competitors (see chapter 3). Activities that should be isolated and analyzed for both the focal firm and rivals include those activities that (1) stand out because they have different economics (e.g., involve a very expensive raw material); (2) have great impact on success (costs or revenue) of a product or service (e.g., a key organizational bottleneck in the production process); and (3) represent a significant percentage of the total product or service costs. Although value chain analysis must involve careful evaluation of facts and numbers concerning each value chain area, the process is inevitably subjective and iterative.

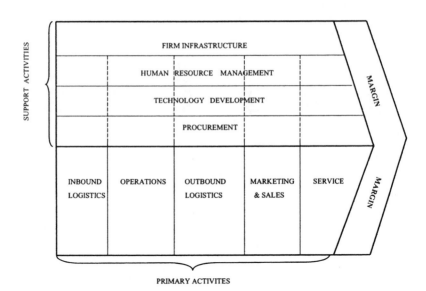

Figure 4.2   Porter's Value Chain. Source: M. E. Porter, 1980, *Competitive advantage: Creating and sustaining superior performance* (New York: Free Press), p. 37. Reprinted with the permission of The Free Press, a Division of Simon & Schuster Adult Publishing Group, from *Competitive Advantage: Creating and Sustaining Superior Performance* by Michael E. Porter. Copyright © 1985, 1998 by Michael E. Porter. All rights reserved.

Once the activities are identified, each area needs to be examined in terms of the key resources underlying the activity. An obvious beginning point would be to break down the activity in terms of tangible costs and investments. Less obvious is the analysis of the unique and rare resources that serve to support the activity, such as intangible skills and knowhow of employees, historical investments accumulated over time (e.g., years of advertising create brand identity), trusting relationships among suppliers, employees, and customers, and special organizational processes and routines that are unique to the activity or organization. Although this second category might be considered soft and subjective, it can also be connected with important tangible costs and revenue so that magnitude, value, and durability of advantage can be assessed. An important implication from this discussion is that effective value chain analysis must involve the input of knowledgeable experts from the firm or industry.

Once all the activities have been identified and broken down in terms of tangible and intangible resources, the next step in the analysis focuses on comparing the focal firm's value chain activities to that of its rival or group of rivals. Let us take for an example the value chain of Wal-Mart. Figure 4.3 reveals that Wal-Mart enjoys resource advantages over its rivals. For example, in many of its locations, Wal-Mart's nearest competitor is another

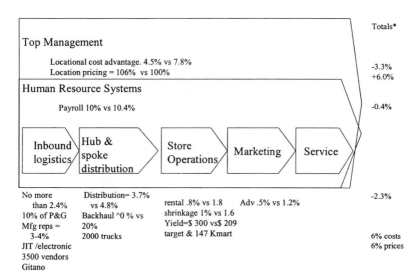

Figure 4.3   The Production of Value at Wal-Mart. Totals represent % difference between Wal-Mart and industry averages.

Wal-Mart store. At these locations, prices are approximately 6 percent higher than where Wal-Mart faces other competitors. Wal-Mart also generates around $300 per square foot, whereas Target generates $209 and Kmart only $147. In terms of costs, Wal-Mart's rental expense is a full percentage point lower than that of its rivals, and its advertising represents only 0.5 percent of sales, while the competition's advertising expense reaches 1.2 percent. The significance of these advantages to Wal-Mart is that the firm can leverage its locational advantage by charging more for its products in certain locations where it does not face competition, while in other places it can leverage its productivity and lower rental costs advantage by lowering prices to effectively engage the competition. Note that we will use this relative value chain comparison throughout the book as a way of illustrating advantages or disadvantages a focal firm like Wal-Mart might have vis-à-vis rivals. Chapter 10 specifically addresses how data for such a comparison can be gathered.

The example of Wal-Mart illustrates the value chain of a firm with multiple advantages relative to the competition. A firm with these advantages enjoys multiple options or ways of engaging the competition. Enterprise Manufacturing illustrates a company in the opposite position. In 1980, Enterprise was near bankruptcy when its new CEO arrived. In 1980 the company marketed itself as a broad-based machine tool manufacturer with multiple expertise to produce a variety of part configurations, in multiple quantities and of varying precision. Figure 4.4 illustrates the value chain configuration for Enterprise. As can be observed, Enterprise had a cost

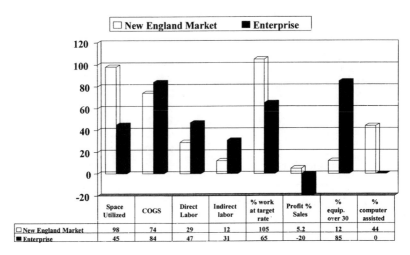

	Space Utilized	COGS	Direct Labor	Indirect labor	% work at target rate	Profit % Sales	% equip. over 30	% computer assisted
☐ New England Market	98	74	29	12	105	5.2	12	44
■ Enterprise	45	84	47	31	65	-20	85	0

Figure 4.4   Enterprise Manufacturing Value Chain.

of goods sold that was 10 percentage points higher than the average competitor in its market. Part of the cost differences can be observed in its overly high direct and indirect labor expense. In addition, the company only utilized 50 percent of its floor space and only made its target rate of $20 per hour on 60 percent of the jobs. Further, the company did not have any of the new sophisticated computer machinery that its competitors enjoyed. Indeed, 85 percent of its machinery was over 40 years old. Not surprisingly, the firm was unprofitable, with a negative 20 percent profit margin.

Our review of Wal-Mart and Enterprise highlights the different resource endowments firms may possess. As a consequence of holding resource advantages, a firm like Wal-Mart has many competitive options while resource-poor Enterprise has few. However, as we shall describe in subsequent chapters, Wal-Mart must act upon its advantages to maximize its profit potential. In contrast, Enterprise must act to build new resources advantages and/or find niches in the market with limited rivalry if it is to survive in the long run.

Summary

In chapter 3, we discussed why firms need to know their relative market positions. We argued that this position could be evaluated relative to their external industry structure and the five forces. This chapter focused on the role of firm resources, which are primarily internal to the firm. Like relative market position, the firm's relative resource position is a key step to understanding competitive advantage and to effectively designing strategies of action to engage the competition. We discussed different types of resources and their role in leading to competitive advantage. Value chain analysis was introduced to provide a technique for evaluating resources advantages relative to the competition. Having discussed relative market (chapter 3) and resource position (chapter 4), we next introduce our model of *strategy as action* and explain how firms can use action to build advantage and generate profits.

Part III

Action-Based Dynamic Model of Competitive Advantage

Chapter 5

AN ACTION-REACTION FRAMEWORK FOR BUILDING COMPETITIVE ADVANTAGE

A chieving high performance in the new age of fast-paced competition requires a new way of thinking about advantage and competition. Chapter 2 described established viewpoints on competition from economics, while chapters 3 and 4 presented the established frameworks to understanding a firm's relative market and resource position, respectively. Although each of those perspectives was noted to provide significant insights for developing a competitive advantage, each also has limitations.

This chapter introduces an action-based dynamic model of competitive advantage that is more in tune with today's fast-paced competitive environment. Let us consider the rise of Microsoft in the supercompetitive PC software industry. When IBM began to develop its own personal computer in 1980, it contracted with Microsoft to supply an operating system. Bill Gates, the CEO of Microsoft, acquired an existing operating system for $50,000 and modified it to work exclusively with IBM PCs running on Intel microprocessors. Because IBM did not want to rely on a single source of supply, it contracted with several software firms. However, Gates recognized something that few other software producers understood at the time. Gates had the wisdom to comprehend that the success of any operating system depended on the popularity of the applications programs that used it. Therefore, Gates took actions with independent software firms, imploring, nudging, and flattering them into developing a family of products that would run on Microsoft's entry, MS-DOS (Microsoft Disk Operating System). Gates noted: "Believe me, it was not IBM who made MS-DOS the standard. It was up to us to get people to focus their development on it and to get other PC manufacturers to license it." In fact, in 1984 Gates pursued developing applications for Apple's operating system. Microsoft became a dominant supplier of word processing and spreadsheet software for Apple. The early 1980s was an uncertain time, with many questions about how the PC software industry would evolve. For example, would PC manufacturers such as IBM and Apple also produce software and operating systems? Would resource-rich software leaders, such as Lotus Development Corporation and Ashton-Tate, allow a small, resource-poor firm to make inroads? Nonetheless, Microsoft acted on the competitive uncertainty to create its own future. In fact, its initial competitive actions shaped the PC software industry as we know it today. At the time of IBM's contract in 1980, Microsoft was an $8 million dollar company with 38 employees. But it grew to where virtually every PC sold is equipped with MS-DOS.[1]

Yet, Microsoft did not base its future simply on its initial operating system. During the mid-1980s, Microsoft introduced Windows, a graphics-based operating environment that ran on MS-DOS but allowed users to run several programs at the same time. Windows emulated many of the advantages of Apple's operating system, which Microsoft became familiar with while developing applications for Apple.[2] The company also introduced numerous updated versions of MS-DOS, along with applications software products, including Excel (spreadsheet), Works (multipurpose), and Word (word processing). In addition, Microsoft aggressively established subsidiaries abroad in the early 1980s, and by 1989 foreign sales exceeded U.S. sales. By 1988, Microsoft had gained market share from such major competitors as Lotus, VisiCorp, MicroPro, and Ashton-Tate. Indeed, Microsoft took a total of 54 competitive moves, both actions and reactions, in 1985—nearly five times the number taken by its nearest competitor.[3] Microsoft's advantages during the 1980s stemmed from its low operating costs, which followed from its installed base and from its people and organizational systems. As Gates commented:

> We're in the intellectual property business.... It's the effectiveness of developers that determines success.... Although the software industry was new, and we were creating the rules ... we found that the business experience these people had was very valuable.... We've always had the most aggressive approach of any software company in finding people with high IQs and bringing them in. We wanted to be known as the software company that knew how to take people right out of college and turn talent and energy into a good development engineer. That was very explicit. We also pushed to the absolute limit the number of smart people that we brought in from overseas. It was explicit that we design a development methodology that was not dependent on a few prima donnas, but that could make use of many people's talent.[4]

In the decade of the 1990s, Microsoft's position became even more dominant. In fact, in 1994 Microsoft engaged rivals with 164 competitive moves, 12 times the number of competitive moves taken by its closest challenger, Computer Associates. Moreover, Microsoft was the largest software company in the world, controlling between 85 and 90 percent of the PC operating systems market. It reported a huge $1.15 billion profit on revenue of $4.65 billion in 1994. However, by the mid-1990s Microsoft had also engaged in several controversial competitive moves that were seen, particularly by its rivals, as improperly leveraging its strong market position. Microsoft is known for aggressive pricing actions, often targeting specific rivals, hiding certain pieces of code that could help the performance of rivals' products, and announcing future products years in advance (so-called vaporware) to dampen enthusiasm for alternatives.[5] As the Internet became more indispensable, the executives of America Online, Compuserve Inc., and Prodigy argued that Microsoft was attempting to leapfrog into a dominant position in the online industry through the introduction of its new operating system, Windows 95. Microsoft was marketing an online service along with its Windows 95 operating system. In an open letter to Microsoft Chairman Bill Gates, the executives wrote:

> Bill, you more than anyone should understand the power that comes with controlling the operating system market. With dominant position comes added responsibilities. . . . Do the right thing for the industry and interests of millions of consumers. Unbundle Microsoft Network from Windows 95.[6]

The companies contended that because Windows 95 would be used by millions of customers, Microsoft would automatically obtain an unfair advantage. As a consequence of Microsoft's online plans, near monopoly in operating systems, and use of that leverage to monopolize the Internet browsers, the Justice Department's antitrust division investigated the firm and filed a complaint in 1998.[7] In the end, Microsoft settled with the government, agreeing to make it easier for personal computer manufacturers to offer and customers to install software and services of rivals. Microsoft has maintained its dominance in the market for operating systems and applications for personal computers and is striving to dominate many other markets such as the Internet, handheld devices, and video games.[8] By 2002, Microsoft had grown to reach over $7.8 billion in profits, $28 billion in revenues, and 50,000 in employees.[9]

The Microsoft example highlights the evolution of a firm from one that exploits competitive uncertainty and blind spots among rivals, to one that acts to exploit unique competitive resources, to one with a near-monopoly position. Over the course of its first 15-year rise to power, Microsoft undertook a huge array of competitive moves: 127 product introductions, 244 product announcements (some of which may have been vaporware), 55 marketing and promotional moves, and 89 vertical alliances.[10] Those moves yielded Microsoft significant competitive advantages.

This book is about competitive moves, or the actions and reactions of firms in the market. In this chapter, we explain how competitive action is related to firm resources and market position and how competitive action leads to competitive advantage in the context of competitive reaction. The chapter concludes by linking competitive action to firm evolution and development.

A Dynamic Action-Based Model
of Competitive Advantage

The action model of advantage provides a state-of-the-art picture of how firms can develop, improve, and defend their competitive advantage in the new age of fast-paced competition. Firms act, and rivals react, and it is in the context of action and reaction that competitive advantages are created and eroded over time. Figure 5.1 portrays the underlying ideas of our action and reaction framework. The roots of this framework are in Talcott Parsons's "theory of action." Parsons developed a theory of action to explain the evolution of any system, such as a business, from an existing state to an emergent state over time. For example, Parsons's theory can be used to explain Microsoft's growth from small firm to industry leader. According to Parsons, the smallest, most irreducible, and therefore the most important unit of analysis within the system is the action. For example, an action may be the introduction of MS-DOS or Windows 95, or even a

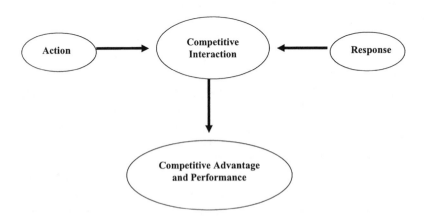

Figure 5.1   Action-Based Model of Competitive Advantage.

pricing move. Parsons's theory of action, therefore, is concerned explicitly with the selection of an action from a group of alternatives to achieve some future state. However, Parsons highlighted the problem of action choice by noting the "principle of action and reaction," whereby in any given system, actions tend to be countered by corresponding reactions. For example, Apple Computer reacted to Microsoft's initial MS-DOS operating system; a subsequent battle raged over which operating system would become the industry standard. Thus, reactions can impede the actor's progress toward some future desired state.[11] James Thompson's *Organizations in Action* advanced Parsons's framework by describing organizations as problem-solving entities capable of learning and adjusting.[12] By taking action, a firm learns about the success of its actions and the reactions of its rivals, and makes adjustments to future actions on the basis of that information.

Assume that organizations, for example Microsoft and other software producers, are problem-solving, profit-maximizing entities capable of learning and adjusting so as to improve their performance over time. Given that assumption, competitive advantage is advanced, and learning and adjustments are achieved, by taking action. Without action, any specific advantage of a firm cannot be created or exploited. Moreover, advantages are likely to erode in environments where competitors are more active or rivalrous than the focal firm.

Because actions often provoke reactions, it is in the context of action and reaction that learning occurs and competitive advantages are created. In addition, firms have choices about action, and decision-makers must choose between alternative actions on the basis of the firm's resources and the expected responses by rivals. Decision-makers must also decide whether to engage rivals with competitive actions or to work with rivals through cooperative actions. Our action model has three key components: actions and reactions, resources, and competitive advantage.

Competitive Actions and Reactions

The starting point for the action model of advantage is actions and reactions. As noted in chapter 1, a competitive action is a specific and observable competitive move, such as a new product introduction, advertising campaign, or price cut, initiated by a firm to improve or defend its relative competitive position.[13] Of the countless actions that firms can undertake, we narrow our focus to four types: entrepreneurial, Ricardian, deterrent, and co-optive.[14] We selected these four because of their close correspondence to variation in a firm's market and resource position. In other words, the appropriateness of each type of action for enhancing competitive advantage and performance depends on the firm's specific market and resource position.

Drawing from Schumpeter, we define entrepreneurial actions as ones that implement new combinations of existing resources.[15] Because entrepreneurial actions involve "new combinations," they often involve innovation and first-mover advantages. Sharon Oster defines entrepreneurial action as seizing new opportunities early. She notes that organizations with "Schumpeterian will" and the ability to undertake actions to seize new opportunities will reap entrepreneurial profit.[16] As most entrepreneurial actions do not require unique resources, rivals often can react to them easily. However, effective entrepreneurial actions delay competitive reaction by exploiting competitive uncertainty and blind spots. Such actions can include the introduction of a new product (Microsoft's MS-DOS), the selection of a new market location (Wal-Mart in the South), innovative pricing actions (AT&T Wireless combining local, long-distance, and roaming service into its pricing plans), and new ways of promoting (Pepsi's use of celebrities) or delivering products (FreshDirect's home delivery of fresh, customized grocery products). We describe entrepreneurial actions in more detail in chapter 6.

In contrast to entrepreneurial actions, which exploit uncertainty and blind spots, Ricardian actions exploit scarce, superior resources that are owned by the firm. A basic doctrine of strategic management is that firms exploit their unique resources.[17] Many years ago, David Ricardo claimed that the value created in any system is always regulated by entities that own resources versus ones that have no such facilities.[18] Thus, Ricardo highlighted the importance of scarcity and ownership of resources. More recently, scholars espousing the resource-based view of the firm have developed Ricardo's ideas further, arguing that a firm's competitive advantages are a function of its unique resources.[19] Differences in asset ownership, described more fully in chapter 7, enable some firms to undertake actions that others cannot. Hence, we define Ricardian actions as competitive actions that stem from the ownership of unique and strategically relevant resources. For example, Caterpillar's action to provide 48-hour parts delivery anywhere in the world was a Ricardian action because it stemmed from Caterpillar's singular and superior worldwide parts and dealer network. The "Pepsi Challenge" was also a Ricardian action because it was based on research demonstrating that customers preferred Pepsi's cola formula to Coke's.

Deterrent actions evolve from external market power and market leadership. The economics literature has a long history of focusing on the actions of dominant firms to defend market position. Some of the earliest work on that subject examined limit pricing—setting a lower price than would otherwise be profitable to inhibit or slow the rate of entry.[20] That literature also has examined entry-deterring actions such as extensive advertising and promotion, investment in excess capacity, the proliferation of new products, and preemptive patenting. Hence, we define deterrent actions as including, among other things, limit pricing, price predation, extensive advertising and promotion, investing in excess capacity, product proliferation, and preemptive patenting. Deterrent actions are designed to exploit market power. Those actions are described in more detail in chapter 8.

The foregoing three types of action are designed to outcompete rivals. However, when no one firm in an industry has a decisive resource advantage over the others, firms can achieve higher profit by acting collectively to limit rivalry than by engaging each other with competitive actions and escalating rivalry. A central question in industrial organization economics is whether firms will recognize their mutual interdependence and collude, most often tacitly, to achieve above-normal profit, that is, profit above what an investor normally would expect to earn from other, similar investments. Firms may recognize that they all may have low levels of profit, or may even kill each other off, if competition were to escalate uncontrollably. Hence, we use the term "co-optive" to describe actions that are designed to limit or reduce rivalry. Among the co-optive actions a firm can undertake to limit price rivalry are signaling advance information on price changes, disclosing price information and other competitive information through regular announcements, and consistently using base-point pricing. These actions are discussed in more detail in chapter 9.

A different class of formal cooperative arrangements entails pooling of resources. Examples are R & D consortiums, joint marketing arrangements, and mergers. Such cooperative mechanisms often have a primary purpose of strengthening a firm's resource position and ability to compete, but they can also reduce rivalry. They are discussed in more detail in chapter 9.

In summary, entrepreneurial, Ricardian, and deterrent actions are designed to engage rivals in competition. Co-optive actions, in contrast, are designed to avoid direct rivalry. All may lead to improvements in performance or competitive position or both.

A competitive response is the flip side of action; more specifically, it is a market move taken by a firm to counteract the initial competitive action of a rival. The combination of an action and a reaction defines a competitive event. For example, an initial price cut with a matching price reduction by a competitor, or a new product introduction with an imitative response, constitutes one competitive event.[21] Several important concepts related to dynamic competitive action and reaction and terms relevant to a competitive event are used throughout this book. Table 5.1 gives the definitions of those concepts and terms and describes their relationship to competitive advantage. We next turn to the second component of our model, relative resource position, which includes firm-specific resources and market position.

Table 5.1 Action-Reaction Concepts and Definitions

Term	Definition	Relationship to Advantage
Response lag	The average amount of time in days a firm takes to respond to a competitor's action	The longer the response time, the greater the advantage to the actor; the greater the response speed, the greater the advantage to the reactor
Response order	The average rank position in time of the responding firm among all responders in an event	The earlier a firm acts or reacts, the greater the advantage
Response imitation	The degree to which a response imitated an action; can be measured in terms of the concurrence of the action type and the response type	The less likely the imitation, the greater the advantage to the actor
Response likelihood	The number of times a firm responded to competitors' actions during a given year divided by the number of times the firm had an opportunity to respond	The less likely the response, the greater the advantage to the actor divided by number of
Magnitude of action	The extent of resources required to implement an action effectively	The greater the resources required to undertake an action, the slower the response
Scope of action	The number of competitors directly affected by the action	The greater the scope of the action, the faster the competitive response
Threat of an action	The number of customers an action could potentially steal from rivals	The greater the threat of an action, the faster the response

Relative Resource Position

Firm resources make action possible, but they also flow from action. For example, a firm with a great idea could act to introduce a new product, and thereby improve its market position or market share and enhance its profit. The firm could invest the profit in plant and equipment that enable it to achieve greater economies of scale, and then engage rivals through price-cutting actions. Thus, resources are a fundamental aspect of the action model; they make actions possible and vary over time with reinvestment of profit from those actions.

We define resources as all information, knowledge, capabilities, organizational processes, and tangible assets controlled by a firm that enable it to undertake competitive action. Moreover, we assume that resources are heterogeneous across firms. Therefore, at a given point in time, some firms will have better endowments of resources than others. Differentiation between firms should be done on a pair-wise basis: the focal firm (for example, your firm) and an individual competitor. That is, the focal firm must consider its resource position in relation to that of each and every competitor separately. In integrating resources into our model, we focus on the firm's resource position in relation to that of a particular competitor. From this pair-wise perspective, we identify two classes of resources: (1) intangible and tangible internal resources and (2) external market position. In subsequent chapters, we discuss how a firm's market position can have attributes of a firm-specific resource. Therefore, when we discuss relative resource position we include both a firm's specific resources and its market position.

Intangible resources include firm culture, structure, processes, and procedures, as well as individual skills and competencies of managers and key workers. The concept that organizational and managerial competencies are important firm resources is well established. For example, it has been argued that any discussion of firm innovation or activity must concede the important role of management knowhow.[22] The types and levels of internal competencies may be extremely diverse. Some aspects of knowledge and competency are sure to be subject to "hazards of involuntary transfer," whereas other aspects are probably highly resistant to sale or exchange.[23] For example, two crucial Microsoft resources are Bill Gates, its CEO, and the organization's ability to recruit top-quality software developers.

Internal resources also consist of the tangible and financial assets reflected in the balance sheet. Tangible internal resources are all physical assets, including plant and equipment, land, capital, patents, and raw materials.[24] Unlike knowledge and competencies, they do not leave the firm when employees resign.[25] With both types of internal resources, the focus is on the firm's relative advantage over competitors. For example, Microsoft's significant economies of scale in the development of software enable the firm to have substantially lower new product development costs than its rivals.

External market position, the second category of resources in the model, is a multidimensional concept, like firm-specific resources that includes a firm's market share in relevant markets, its reputation in the marketplace, and its experience. The importance of market position is explicit in the structure-conduct-performance model outlined in chapter 2, whereby industries characterized by few competitors, each with a high market share, have limited rivalry and high performance.

Firms with a strong market position are watched closely by rivals and are considered leaders in that they have demonstrated successful actions in the past and are able competitors.[26] In this respect, high market share is associated with historical success within the industry, a demonstration of high growth, and an accumulation of significant organizational skills. Rival managers often attribute a competitor's high market share to skilled leadership and ability. William Fellner claimed that rivals perceive a leading firm to have high relative strength because its superiority in processes, products, or sales techniques "testifies to fitness."[27] Microsoft's nearly 90 percent market share in operating systems signifies to rivals its significant market power and leadership skills.

Competitive Advantage

Theories of competitive advantage typically center on the generation of above-normal profits. With the action model of advantage, competitive advantage can be assessed by the change in market position and/or the change in profit generated by each competitive move. Thus, a firm's overall advantage can be measured by the profit generated from a stream of moves taken over time.

The Action-Based Model of Competitive Advantage

Figure 5.1 portrays the relationships between actions and reactions, resources, and competitive advantage. Competitive advantage is determined in the context of competitive resources, action, and reaction.

We have noted that actions stem from resources. It follows that a firm's relative resource position affects the type of action the firm can undertake. In particular, a firm with limited market share and no relative resource advantage has limited strategic options, whereas a firm with a strong market position and strong relative resource advantages over competitors can pursue a variety of actions. For example, Microsoft's action options in 1980 as an emerging software company were constrained by its limited $8 million customer base. In contrast, the 1994 Microsoft, the largest software producer in the world with a nearly 90 percent operating system market share and $4.6 billion in sales, had many more strategic options. Therefore, the type of action a firm undertakes is a function of its relative resource position.

As described in chapter 1, firms are not independent within their competitive environment; they are affected by one another's actions and generally are compelled to react. According to Schumpeter, some firms intentionally attempt to lead whereas others follow and imitate.[28] Both the actions of leaders and the responses of followers are essential to Schumpeter's theory; he viewed the marketplace as a mechanism through which firms experiment by taking specific actions. Firms that are successful in taking actions or seizing opportunities reap profit through the monopolistic position afforded by the imitator's lag. Thus, a firm that takes successful actions could eat away at the market of those that do not respond. No permanent equilibrium would ever be reached, however, as the visible profit of the acting firm and the loss by the nonresponder would motivate the latter to respond. Let us take, for example, Charles Schwab's introduction of trading via the Internet in 1996. Schwab was the first major brokerage firm to take this initiative and achieved immediate success as online trading accounted for close to 20 percent of its total revenues and trades within a year. However, within two years the online trading industry was glutted with a number of new players (e.g., E*Trade, eBroker, etc.), who initiated a price war by offering trades as low as 10 percent at a full-service brokerage. Soon thereafter, established brokerage firms (e.g., Merrill Lynch, Citigroup, etc.) followed suit. In a relatively short period, there were in excess of hundred firms offering online trading, and the continuation of Schwab's initial success was impeded by rival responses.[29] This clearly illustrates that in today's fast-paced environment, for every successful competitive action, there is a competitive reaction.

It follows that the effectiveness of any action depends on the speed of competitive response. In a study of new product actions and reactions in the brewing, telecommunications, and PC industries, we found that first-movers achieved significant increases in profit over laggards and that early responders did better than late responders. In addition, we found that competitive reaction cut into the profit of the first-moving firm.[30] Moreover, we have observed in industries as diverse as software, airlines, athletic shoes, and automobiles that the faster a firm responds, the greater its performance. From being near bankruptcy in the 1950s, Pepsi came to equal Coke in market share in the food store segment of the soft drink industry in 1978. In the interim, Pepsi had undertaken several actions that Coke had simply ignored. Overall, the potential advantage to the acting firm is greater when the response lag of rivals is longer.

We now turn to specific relationships between kinds of resources, types of action and reaction, and response lags. As in the preceding discussion of firm-specific resources, the propositions pertain to a focal firm and a specific competitor. We begin with the case of the firm with limited relative resources and market position.

Avoiding Rivals with Entrepreneurial Actions

Consider first the case of the firm that has both an internal and external resource disadvantage in relation to a competitor. This is analogous to the situation of an entrepreneurial firm or an established firm in need of a turnaround. Such a firm must avoid competition to prevent losing a head-on battle with a more resource-rich rival. In general, we argue that the firm's best option is to discover and seize new opportunities that the rival will not immediately perceive or counter. The outcome from such an act of discovery, as viewed in Austrian terms, cannot be attributed to any particular tangible resource, nor can any tangible resource guarantee discovery.

When Wal-Mart acted to set up discount retailing stores in rural southern locations, it was behaving in a way that was unheard of before that time. The inspired entrepreneurial hunch that leads to entrepreneurial action—to seize an opportunity where others see none, to notice opportunity for innovative products or services that others fail to discern—is, from the Austrian perspective, motivated by the lure of profit.

By taking actions when others are uncertain, resource-poor firms may avoid competitors. Hence, when a focal firm with limited resources is up against a stronger rival, it will seek to avoid direct competition. Therefore, firms with resource disadvantages and a poor market position are more likely to undertake entrepreneurial actions than other types of actions.

Arguing the case of the entrepreneurial firm, Richard Rumelt contended that "uncertainty is the central issue." That is, resource-rich competitors could easily duplicate any action taken by the firm with inferior resources, but the uncertainty surrounding the entrepreneurial action delays competitive response. In early 1980, Bill Gates of Microsoft was playing on the competitive uncertainty surrounding the development of the software industry. Clearly, many larger firms could have outcompeted Microsoft at the time. Gates, however, had his own belief about how the industry would develop and acted to make his vision a reality. Given Microsoft's small size and the uncertain nature of the industry, competitors probably did not pay much attention to the company's initial actions. Competitive response to entrepreneurial actions may be delayed because rivals are either uncertain of the payoffs or unaware that the action has occurred. Thus, entrepreneurial actions delay competitive reaction because of the high level of competitive uncertainty surrounding the action. The uncertainty results in information asymmetries among rivals, which when resolved lead to an action that could be perfectly and quickly imitated. Entrepreneurial actions can delay competitive response when taken under conditions of uncertainty. Thus, the greater the competitive uncertainty surrounding the action, the greater is the delay in reaction.

Engaging Rivals with Ricardian Actions

The second case concerns the firm with specific relative resource advantages. Such a firm may well lack the market position to engage rivals with deterrent actions but has resource advantages that enable it to engage rivals with Ricardian actions. Microsoft was in that position in the mid-1980s, when it introduced many upgraded products and exploited its human resources and cost advantages in product development. The task for such firms is to link a specific resource appropriately with a suitable Ricardian action. In the case of Microsoft, the resources included software designers, economies of scale in development and marketing, and brand recognition, and the actions included moves to introduce new products, upgrade products, and cut prices. The roots of this resource-action link can be found in the strategy literature, which has long argued for a fit between the resources being exploited and the competitive strategy being employed.[31] By taking Ricardian actions, the firm exploits specific resources for which it has a unique advantage over rivals. Such resources make a potent set of actions available to the firm. In an effort to enhance their competitive advantage and exploit their unique resources, firms with relative resource advantages are more likely to undertake Ricardian than other types of actions.

From a resource theory point of view, the resources must be scarce and heterogeneous across firms to produce advantage. As Richard Rumelt defined scarcity, "extra profit commanded by this [particular] factor is insufficient to attract new resources into use."[32] In short, rivals may be motivated to imitate but are prevented or blocked from imitation because of their inability to secure in a timely way the resources needed for action. Take, for example, Microsoft's offering of its Windows operating system for $20 per unit. Microsoft could offer the system at such a low price because of the company's economies of scale in marketing and software development. Apple, which does not have those economies of scale, has higher unit costs and is therefore unable to respond to this low price effectively without substantial loss. Therefore, Ricardian actions can delay competitive response by exploiting scarce resources; the greater the scarcity of the resource, the greater is the delay in competitive response.

Engaging Rivals with Deterrent Actions

The third case concerns the firm with a strong market position. Industrial organization scholars have paid significant attention to the role of the dominant firm and especially the strategies such firms can use to maintain and exploit their dominance.[33] By undertaking deterrent actions, the firm exploits market power. For example, in the mid-1980s, NutraSweet held a dominant position in the low-calorie artificial sweetener market because it possessed the worldwide patents for aspartame.[34] In 1985, the new Holland Sweetener Company (HSC) prepared for market entry since

NutraSweet's patents would expire in Europe and Canada in 1987 and in the United States in 1992. Subsequently, HSC did enter the European market in 1987. NutraSweet had to decide between an aggressive or accommodating response. Perhaps with an eye toward establishing an entry-deterring reputation, especially for its larger U.S. market, NutraSweet responded very aggressively to HSC's entry, severely cutting its prices and putting HSC into a bleak position.

Dominant firms may also undertake entrepreneurial actions and Ricardian actions, but in an effort to maintain and defend their competitive advantage, firms with strong market positions are more likely to undertake deterrent actions than other types of actions.

Deterrent actions delay response through intimidation. For example, dominant firms can set a lower price than would otherwise be profitable so as to intimidate rivals and deter their response. Moreover, dominant firms can carry out extensive advertising and promotion, raising the stakes for rival firms and affecting their behavior. Dominant firms can also delay rivals' actions by investing in excess capacity, flooding the market with products, and preemptive patenting. In addition, a dominant firm can deter response by establishing its credibility and commitment to fight, which can critically influence a rival's behavior. Microsoft's aggressive pricing and "vaporware" actions fit into that category. Thus, deterrent actions can delay response by exploiting intimidation and market power; the greater the reputation of the dominant firm for intimidation and market power, the greater is the potential delay in competitive response.

Winning the Peace: Avoiding Warfare with Rivals

In the final case, no firm has a resource advantage and the market positions of competitors are comparable. Take, for example, competition in the lead-based antiknock gasoline additives industry. In 1973, the U.S. government altered emissions regulations and thereby significantly reduced demand for the lead-based compounds. Normally a sharp reduction in demand in an industry with large fixed and sunk costs would result in intense price competition. However, firms in this industry successfully engaged in co-optive activities that stemmed or limited price competition. Their actions included quoting prices on a uniform-delivered-price basis, announcing price changes well in advance of effective dates, and including in contracts to customers the right for the customer to receive any discounts extended to other customers. Apparently the firms cooperated because they had relative parity in terms of resources and market share. More generally, whenever no one competitor has a decisive resource advantage over any other, firms that tacitly act to limit rivalry among

Table 5.2   The Basic Components of the Action Model of Advantage

Type of Action	Key Resource	Strategic Intent	Chapter
Entrepreneurial	Entrepreneurial discovery	Delay response by exploiting uncertainty	6
Ricardian	Factor of productions	Delay response by exploiting scarce resource ownership and scarcity	7
Deterrent	Market share and reputation	Delay response by exploiting market power and intimidation	8
Co-optive	Parity	Avoid rivalry through tacit coordination	9

themselves all achieve higher profit than they would if rivalry were intense. Therefore, firms with no decisive resource advantages over rivals are more likely to undertake co-optive actions than competitive actions.

When two firms are similar in terms of resources, the challenge for both firms is to achieve the superior profit that is a function of less intense warfare, for example, when both firms can somehow keep their prices high. To coordinate actions successfully across competitors, firms need to be very aware of each other's actions and sensitive to one another's strategies. Tacit communication is the key legal mechanism for achieving such coordination. For example, a firm may use market signaling (e.g., press announcements or public listing of prices) to alert rivals to changes in prices and other competitive moves. Signaling of intentions creates a nonthreatening environment that lessens the possibility of an outbreak of war. When rivals can read one another's signals and trust one another to behave as signaled, they will be less tempted to engage in secret price cutting. An open atmosphere will be created in which cooperation can be maintained.[35] In sum, co-optive actions whereby firms signal and communicate their intentions and expectations may lead to co-optive reactions and less intense rivalry.

Table 5.2 summarizes the basic components of the action model of advantage. In subsequent chapters we examine various aspects of the model in detail: entrepreneurial actions in chapter 6, Ricardian actions in chapter 7, deterrent actions in chapter 8, and co-optive actions in chapter 9. We now turn to an examination of the key process aspects of the action model of advantage.

Process Aspects of the Model: Building Competitive Advantage

The model just outlined highlights relationships between relative resources and actions, and between actions and competitive reactions. Resources allow action and action provokes reaction. Delayed reaction accrues advantage to the acting firm. Advantage is defined in terms of change in market position and improved profit. Given the assumption that organizations are problem-solving, profit-maximizing entities capable of learning and adjusting, it is reasonable to predict that firms will reinvest profit from actions to enhance and improve their respective resource positions over time. In addition, investments in some resources—namely ones that produce value, are rare and in short supply, and are inimitable—will be preferred over alternative resource investments. Moreover, if no investment is made, attritional effects of rival action will erode a firm's resource and competitive position.[36] Finally, firms will evaluate feedback about the effectiveness of each action to adjust actions in future rounds of competition. Figure 5.2 portrays the learning and adjusting feedback process.

An evolutionary version of the model takes the time component one step further by explaining how firms grow and develop. We introduce this extension now to illustrate the applicability of our action model in diverse organizational settings, and to show how a firm's action alternatives are a function of its resource position over time. Scholars have long argued that organizations evolve in systematic ways and that their evolution can be segmented into stages.[37] We can consider our action model as the three-stage model of evolution depicted in figure 5.3. The stages are startup or turnaround, growth, and maturity.

The first stage addresses the small firm, new venture, or firm in need of a turnaround that has limited resources and a poor competitive position in relation to rival firms. This firm must rely on entrepreneurial discovery or the managers' capability to exploit uncertainty and blind spots by taking entrepreneurial actions. As the entrepreneurial actions are carried out and to the extent that competitive response is delayed by uncertainty, the weakly positioned firm can improve its market position and profit, and therefore reinvest profit to improve its relative resources. It may soon be in a position to exploit specific resource advantages instead of uncertainty and blind spots. That is, it may become a more formidable competitor.

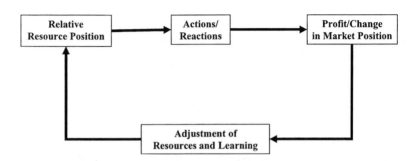

Figure 5.2   Action-Based Process Model of Competitive Advantage.

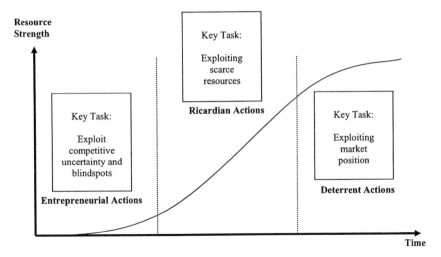

Figure 5.3   Action-Based Model of Organizational Evolution.

As the firm evolves from the startup or turnaround stage to a high-growth stage, its attention will shift away from entrepreneurial discovery and entrepreneurial action to the exploitation of specific resources through Ricardian actions. That transition may require different management capabilities, perhaps a shift from entrepreneurial discovery to the management of core competencies. In any case, managers must design Ricardian actions based on the specific resource advantages held by the firm. Of major concern is which competitors the firm should target. By exploiting scarce resources with Ricardian actions, the firm can impede response by rivals and improve its relative competitive position and profit, perhaps to the point of industry leadership.

Becoming the market leader may again lead to a shift in the firm's orientation, perhaps away from exploitation of specific resource advantages through Ricardian actions to defense of market position with deterrent actions. The task for a firm in this stage is to defend its market leadership against attack. Deterrent actions in defense of position might include limiting output, acting with predatory pricing, buying out competitors, and securing sources of material.

In summary, the three-stage model of organizational development suggests that firms with limited relative resources and poor market position can improve their resources and position by exploiting uncertainty with entrepreneurial actions. Firms with specific resource advantages can make further inroads on competitors by taking Ricardian actions, and market leaders can defend their position with deterrent actions. Of course, a firm with a dominant industry position and strong relative resource advantages will have more action alternatives than a firm without such resources.

Moreover, such resource-rich firms may simultaneously undertake all three types of competitive action, an alternative not available to the firm in a poor market position that lacks resource advantages. The challenge for a dominant firm is to avoid becoming too defensive in orientation and ceding its advantageous positions to challengers because of lack of aggressiveness. We return to this issue in chapter 8.

Summary

This chapter presents the action model of advantage. The model, which is based on actions and reactions between firms, provides a state-of-the-art picture of how firms can build, improve, and defend their competitive advantage in the new age of fast-paced competition. In the model, competitive advantage is accrued by taking action. Importantly, without action, any specific advantage a firm may have cannot be exploited. Moreover, any resource position will erode in an environment where competition is active.

Overall, our model shows that firms with no resource advantages and poor market position must rely on the skills and competencies of managers to undertake entrepreneurial actions. Entrepreneurial actions delay response by exploiting uncertainty. Firms with resource advantages exploit those advantages with Ricardian actions. Ricardian actions delay response because the firm owns the scarce resources on which the action is based. Market leaders exploit their market share advantages by undertaking deterrent actions. Deterrent actions delay response because the leader has market power and the ability to intimidate. Finally, the best strategy for firms with comparable resources may be to seek a cooperative relationship. These resource positions and the corresponding actions are discussed in detail in the following four chapters.

Chapter 6

AVOIDING RIVALS WITH ENTREPRENEURIAL ACTIONS

Exploiting Competitive Uncertainty and Blind Spots

F ieldTurf Inc.'s rise as a major player in artificial turf for athletic playing surfaces came from its innovative and aggressive competitive moves. In 1997, Field Turf, led by a skillful, innovative, and experienced founder, "revolutionized" the artificial turf industry with entrepreneurial actions. FieldTurf's actions included developing a new turf made of long synthetic fibers woven into a base made of sand and recycled rubber pellets—giving it the look, feel, and drainage of real grass and causing fewer injuries—and targeting it to low-profile fields (e.g., indoor soccer and high school fields). Gradually, the new turf started to sell itself, including to high-profile fields (e.g., college and professional football fields). It was a significant improvement over the traditional AstroTurf, sold by the industry leader Southwest Recreational Industries, Inc., which had dominated with about three-fourths of the U.S. market. Shortly, Southwest responded and introduced its own version of the new turf but was slowed considerably by FieldTurf's legal actions citing patent infringement. Southwest and other rivals, who were blind to and uncertain of the wisdom of FieldTurf's entrepreneurial moves, were somewhat slow to respond at first, providing a window of opportunity for FieldTurf to become one of the industry leaders. During the years it took rivals to respond, privately held FieldTurf grew from $1.7 million in 1997 to $50 million in 2000; it recently reported a 60 percent sales increase in 2002 alone.[1]

Enterprise Manufacturing was nearly bankrupt in 1980 when a new CEO arrived. Enterprise was a general-purpose contract machine shop operating in the very competitive New England market. The machine shop market in New England was extremely price sensitive, with hundreds of suppliers competing for a shrinking base of customers. Recall also from chapter 4 that Enterprise's resource position was poor relative to other

New England competitors. Although he was relatively inexperienced in the machine shop industry, Enterprise's new CEO realized that the company needed to broaden its base outside New England and that it must specialize in some way to survive in the long run. From his experience in the heavy-duty pump industry, the CEO perceived an opportunity for a machine shop totally dedicated to serving the needs of that single industry. Accordingly, the manager creatively changed the name of the company from Enterprise Manufacturing to Enterprise Pump Shafting and began to market its services solely to the pump industry. Enterprise developed a series of promotional letters, which it mailed to major pump manufacturers across the United States, and was the first company ever to advertise its services as a pump shaft manufacturer in the *Thomas Register* and other trade magazines. The promotional letters and advertisements noted that Enterprise was the *only* machine shop in the nation totally dedicated to the pump industry and that with such dedication it could better serve pump customers. Many local New England competitors thought Enterprise's actions were foolishly daring. However, the campaign brought Enterprise customers from across the United States. The repositioning enabled Enterprise to avoid the very competitive New England market and subsequently improve its financial performance. Years later, when other competitors began to imitate Enterprise's actions, Enterprise created a new division to service the motor industry—Enterprise Motor Shafts.[2]

Entrepreneurially opportunistic, Sam Walton, and his business success, is well known. But Wal-Mart's initial actions in small southwestern towns have been less publicized. Walton initially focused his operations in small towns with populations of 5,000 to 25,000. Larger rivals, such as Kmart, Target, and Sears were blind to Wal-Mart's actions because they viewed such territories as incapable of supporting a large discount operation. By the time rivals reacted, Wal-Mart had gained a near monopoly in the small towns and had developed the skills and resources necessary to compete in big cities.[3]

These examples illustrate how firms with limited resources can enhance their market position and performance by undertaking clever entrepreneurial actions that exploit competitive uncertainty and blind spots. Competitive uncertainty delays rivals' responses because of skepticism about the action's outcome, whereas blind spots keep rivals from perceiving the action. In the FieldTurf, Enterprise, and Wal-Mart examples, information asymmetries allowed the first mover to act without immediate reaction. Southwest, which had been the dominant industry leader, and other rivals were blind to the opportunities of developing an innovative artificial turf and targeting low-profile fields, as carried out by FieldTurf. Pricing was the only competitive weapon for machine shops in New England, so rivals were very dubious about Enterprise's move to specialize.

In the rural retail markets, industry leaders such as Kmart were blind to the potential of the small towns.

Chapter 5 introduced two categories of resources—intangible and tangible internal resources and the firms' external market position—and corresponding actions: entrepreneurial, Ricardian, deterrent, and co-optive. This chapter examines the business situation in which a firm has no significant resource advantages over competitors and a poor market position. Such is often the predicament of small firms, new ventures, or even large firms in need of turnaround. In many cases, firms without resource advantages are in the third or fourth position in their respective industries. That is obviously not an enviable position; such firms are generally at a distinct competitive disadvantage in relation to well-endowed rivals that are probably capable of matching almost any move the inferior firms make.

Firms in this unhealthy position must rely on the knowledge and skills of managers to create a competitive advantage. If they are to survive, their managers must explore and discover opportunities created by disequilibrium in the marketplace and implement entrepreneurial actions to exploit those opportunities. We define entrepreneurial actions as actions that seize new market opportunities by combining existing resources in new ways. In other words, entrepreneurial actions involve implementing new combinations of current and ordinary resources in innovative ways. Importantly, entrepreneurial actions emphasize market opportunities, not resource advantages.

Entrepreneurial actions such as those undertaken by FieldTurf, Enterprise, and Wal-Mart can enhance financial health and improve market position because they exploit competitive uncertainty and blind spots. Exploiting the uncertainty and blind spots of one's competitors enables a manager to take action with limited fear of rapid competitive response. Even though our focus is on firms in constrained positions, such actions can be taken by any firm, not just ones with limited resource advantages and poor market positions. We discuss such combinations of resource positions and actions in chapter 11.

Figure 6.1 portrays the relationships between relative resource position (especially knowledge), entrepreneurial action, and competitive advantage (performance) explored in this chapter. The figure is a subset of the action model of advantage presented in chapter 5. In this chapter we first review the notion of disequilibrium, and how disequilibrium can lead to discovery and profit for the alert manager. Next, we discuss the meaning of discovery and the profit incentive of discovery. We also review some of the key management skills and knowledge necessary for discovery. Attention is then turned to the different types of entrepreneurial action that translate disequilibriums into profit. We explain how entrepreneurial actions can delay competitive response and how delay is related to competitive advantage.

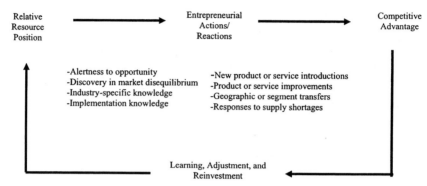

Figure 6.1   Entrepreneurial Actions and Competitive Advantage.

Market Disequilibrium and the Knowledge Problem: Sources of Competitive Uncertainty and Blind Spots

During the twentieth century, many economists and management scholars have explained market and business phenomena in terms of equilibrium models. More specifically, they have defined competitive advantage, and such strategic behaviors as pricing and innovation, in terms of market equilibrium. Take for example the perfectly competitive market with one commodity. Considering the market price for the commodity, the scholars begin with the assumption that it is the price at which the quantity supplied equals the quantity demanded. Underlying that assumption is the notion that the market has already achieved equilibrium. For the most part, when these scholars observe discrepancies between market data and the expected values of their equilibrium models, they suggest a more complicated equilibrium model.[4]

Our goal is not to develop a complete critique of equilibrium models but rather to highlight one key objection raised by the Austrian school of economics. The objection is that by focusing on equilibrium, economic and strategic management theory has ignored the equilibrium process itself. On the whole, the unstated premise of equilibrium scholars is that the forces for equilibrium are strong and virtually instantaneous and therefore the process of equilibrium is unimportant. Yet, as we noted in chapter 1, the rapid pace of competitive activity in the global business community today—the disruptive competition—is driving market disequilibrium.[5] As we shall document, disequilibrium creates variation in knowledge among market participants, which can be a source of opportunities for alert managers.

Consider a market in which two prices prevail for the same commodity in different parts of the market. For example, prices were different between the general purpose and specialized segments of the machine tool market in the Enterprise case and between the metropolitan and rural discount retail outlets in the Wal-Mart case. Equilibrium theorists would deny such a possibility, arguing either differences in the quality of the commodity or the presence of mobility barriers that separate the markets. In equilibrium theory, one barrier might be lack of awareness about pricing, which the theorists consider costly to eradicate. Another view, however, more consistent with the Austrian school of economics, suggests that different prices for the same commodity are the result of differences in knowledge among managers of which they are unaware. That is, some managers are more knowledgeable than others, and not all managers are aware of the difference. Following the work of Hayek, Kirzner referred to this variation in knowledge among market participants as the "knowledge problem."[6]

Suppose Paterson Machine Company, a Cincinnati general purpose machine shop, has been supplying drive shafts to a large pump company, also located in Cincinnati, for $15 each. Following company tradition, the pump company solicits quotes from all local vendors on a yearly basis. Paterson's price usually is the lowest. Enterprise, a New England special purpose machine shop, sells the same shaft for $13. Clearly the pump company could buy the shaft for $13, but in fact pays $15 because it does not know about the lower price. The pump company is unaware that the shaft can be purchased at less cost.[7]

When the pump company receives a special promotional letter from Enterprise stating the shaft price of $13, the pump company quickly switches from Paterson to Enterprise. Paterson is unaware or ignorant of Enterprise's action. Moreover, even after Paterson does become aware of Enterprise's prices, it remains optimistic that other buyers will not switch. Therefore, Paterson keeps its prices high.

Another view is that there are two separate markets or strategic groups, perhaps a local versus a national group, or a general purpose versus a special purpose group. In particular, the presence of two sets of prices for identical products indicates that firms paying a high price, such as the pump company buying from Paterson, overlooked the possibility of buying for less from Enterprise. In addition, firms selling at the lower price, for example Enterprise, overlooked the possibility of selling at a higher price in other markets, for example at $14 or $15 per shaft in Cincinnati. Furthermore, some buyers in the higher price market might be refraining from buying, going without the product, even though the product is available in the other market at a lower price. Some participants in the lower price market may be refraining from selling because of the lower price, even though they could find potential buyers who are willing to pay higher prices, such as the pump company in Cincinnati paying $15. The point here is that the market contestants failed to grasp potential opportunities because they had inaccurate knowledge about what others might have been prepared to do. These errors highlight the knowledge problem, that market contestants are sometimes unaware of what others might be willing to pay or do; the contestants lack crucial market knowledge.

The importance of the knowledge problem is that it creates competitive uncertainty and/or blind spots among competitors. Competitive uncertainty is due to participants' inability to predict the outcomes of competitive events with confidence. Blind spots are due to decision-makers' lack of accurate information to make their predictions.

Competitive uncertainty and blind spots create profit opportunities that attract alert, profit-seeking entrepreneurs. Little is known about exactly how profit opportunities attract entrepreneurial attention, but there can be little doubt that profit is a powerful motivator of entrepreneurial action. The lure of profit is what encourages the entrepreneur to exploit knowledge problems to discover opportunities and act. As Kirzner argues:

> This entrepreneurial element in human action is what responds to the signals for pure profit that are generated by the errors that arise out of the dispersed knowledge available in society. It is this yeast that ferments the competitive-entrepreneurial discovery process, tending to reveal to market participants more and more of the relevant information scattered throughout the market. It is this entrepreneurial competitive process that thus grapples with the basic knowledge problem.[8]

Our use of the term "entrepreneur" is consistent with that of Schumpeter and the Austrian school and refers to any individual who goes through the entrepreneurial discovery process and subsequently takes entrepreneurial actions. The entrepreneur can be an owner, a manager, or even a team of managers. As Schumpeter noted: "It is leadership rather than ownership that matters."[9] In the Austrian view, the most important feature of the market is the entrepreneurial discovery process.[10]

The Meaning of Discovery

A firm that has high profit is generally viewed as having achieved it by the deliberate deployment of resources. Indeed, recall from chapter 4 that the resource-based view of the firm contends that a firm's competitive advantage and high profit stem from the ownership, and marginal contribution, of productive resources. What is often overlooked, however, is that a firm's highly productive resources are probably the result of some entrepreneurial discovery. Fundamentally, the act of discovery involves the seizing of a perceived, available opportunity.

The outcome from an act of discovery is not attributable to any particular resource, nor can any tangible resource guarantee discovery. The outcome of a discovery depends on the skills of the creator in conjunction with chance. When FieldTurf discovered a new artificial turf for athletic surfaces and implemented the discovery by marketing first to low-profile fields such as high schools and municipal fields, it was executing an action that had not been taken before. When Enterprise defined a new specialized segment of the machine tool market, it acted in a way that no other company had tried. When Wal-Mart set up discount retail stores in rural southern locations, it was behaving in a previously unheard-of way. The inspired entrepreneurial alertness that leads to entrepreneurial action—to seizing an opportunity where others see none, to noticing opportunity for profit that others fail to discern—is as creative as Michelangelo's sculpting of *David.*

An example of such discovery and creativity is found in FreshDirect. Despite the numerous failures, such as Webvan, Kozmo.com, and Urbanfetch.com, in the home delivery business model, FreshDirect has developed an operating strategy of home delivery of food products that seems to be working. FreshDirect's cofounders, Jason Ackerman and Joseph Fedel, have imitated Dell's model in computer products to food products. Just like Dell, FreshDirect has used the Internet to use a make-to-order business model, providing fresh, high quality, and customized food products at a lower cost. Its model works like this. A typical grocery store carries approximately 25,000 different packaged food products, which generate about 50 percent of sales, and 2,200 perishable food products (e.g., meat, seafood, product), which generate the other 50 percent. Alternatively, FreshDirect offers 5,000 perishable food products, which generate approximately 75 percent of sales, but only 3,000 packaged food products, which generate about 25 percent of sales. It takes all customer orders via the Internet by midnight, purchases all the perishable items the following morning from suppliers and just enough to meet the previous night's orders, and processes them by 4 p.m., when the deliveries begin. On average, it may carry one day of inventory, while the traditional grocery store carries a week of inventory for perishable products. Furthermore, the perishable orders are customized and fresh, providing greater value to customers. To reduce costs on packaged food products, FreshDirect carries only limited sizes and lets suppliers have exclusive access, which enables it to negotiate lower supplier costs. In summary, FreshDirect's margins are much higher compared to rivals from the efficiency gains in the supply chain and from greater sales in perishable food products, which generate higher margins. Ackerman and Fedel saw the need for good-quality fresh foods rather than the delivery process and convenience, which were the emphasis of the failed delivery startups.[11]

Whereas credit for the act of exploiting productive resources goes to the owners of the resources, credit for innovation goes to the discoverer "whose alertness brought the discovered item to his or her notice,"[12] just as first-finder's logic prevails when the finder of an unowned object is considered the rightful owner.

However, we stress that such alertness alone is not a sufficient condition for profit. That is, alertness is not deployed; alertness to opportunity must be followed by the act of seizing the opportunity. The early writings of Joseph Schumpeter recognized this point: "thorough preparatory work and special knowledge, breadth of intellectual understanding, [and] talent for logical analysis . . . may under certain circumstances be sources of failure."[13] Schumpeter claimed that although most people readily perceive the opportunity, few are "in a position to do it. Most people see it but they want someone else to lead." He highlighted the need for discovery *and* action.

In a study of patent success, Jeffrey Timmons concluded that about one tenth of 1 percent of patented "good ideas" result in financial gain for the inventor.[14] He noted that inventors invent, but it is entrepreneurs who are driven to seize opportunities through action. In short, an opportunity is often necessary for success, but it is not a sufficient condition. The entrepreneur is the catalyst who translates the opportunity and idea into action. As the marketing guru Ted Levitt commented: "Ideas are useless unless used."[15] Discovery must be followed by action.

Types of Knowledge Needed by Managers

We have explained how disequilibrium causes variation in knowledge, or knowledge problems, which, in turn, can be exploited by the alert entrepreneur. Let us now consider what types of knowledge are the most valuable to managers who are attempting to exploit disequilibrium and identify opportunities.

Opportunity-Specific Knowledge. Not all discoveries and actions are effective. Scholars are just beginning to recognize that managers must have opportunity-specific knowledge, knowledge about a particular opportunity.[16] Jeffrey Timmons claimed that often managers fail as entrepreneurs "they lack enough experience in specific market areas and in business."[17] As a result, they lack knowledge about the rules of thumb and benchmarks that can guide them in recognizing a good opportunity and ignoring the rest.[18] Donald Hambrick found that nearly 80 percent of U.S. managers believed product and service quality would be a fundamental source of business opportunity in the year 2000, but barely 50 percent of Japanese managers agreed. The Japanese managers were much more oriented toward opportunities in innovative products and services. Hambrick concluded that American managers would continue to play catchup with their Japanese counterparts because the Americans were not sufficiently focused on specific new market opportunities.[19]

Indeed, Gary Hamel and C. K. Prahalad reported that top management's agenda in the United States was dominated by issues of restructuring and downsizing. They found that less than 1 percent of management time was devoted to future opportunities and concluded: "If senior executives don't have reasonable detailed answers to the 'future' questions, and if the answers they have are not significantly different from the 'today' answers, there is little chance that their companies will remain market leaders."[20] They recommended that managers seek opportunity-specific knowledge—such as what products and services customers will require in the future, what competencies will be needed to produce future products or services, and in what way future products and services will be marketed. Such knowledge can be acquired in part by conducting careful industry analysis. Successful entrepreneurs develop new ideas through market studies, strategic planning, industry-specific experience, and talking with customers. The information gained can result in a superior ability to perceive opportunities, or a knowledge advantage.

Several interesting studies have investigated where managers find opportunities. For example, one study of 82 entrepreneurs found that most of them recognized rather than sought out opportunities, and that most found those opportunities in fields where they had work experience and industry-specific knowledge.[21] In a study of nearly 3,000 new ventures, 43 percent of the entrepreneurs developed their new venture idea for the industry in which they were working.[22]

Both of these studies emphasize the importance of industry-specific experience in identifying effective opportunities for action. More than anything else, industry-related experience gives the entrepreneur a sense of what will and will not work. Jeffrey Timmons reported that in 95 percent of the new firms he studied, the founders launched the venture in the same market or industry where they had acquired the bulk of their relevant experience.[23]

Competitor-Specific Knowledge. The discoverer must also be skilled at predicting competitor actions and reactions, as rapid competitive response may reduce the effectiveness of entrepreneurial actions. By knowing in advance the way rivals are likely to behave, managers can design actions that will not prompt quick responses. In chapter 10 we provide much more detail on how to do a competitor analysis. Here, however, we note that one can predict the actions and reactions of rivals by considering their competitive beliefs, intentions, and past history of action. For example, studies at the University of Maryland's Smith School of Business have shown that competitors respond fast if they have a bountiful supply of resources, are externally rather than internally focused, and are run by younger rather than older managers. Other researchers have found that small competitors respond more slowly and are less responsive overall than large competitors. In addition, they have found that small firms' responses are less visible.[24]

As we noted earlier, Ming-jer Chen has developed a framework for competitor analysis based on two key dimensions: market commonality and resource similarity.[25] By *commonality* Chen means the degree to which competitors compete in the same markets for the same customers. Resource similarity refers to the extent of resource overlap between two firms. Chen argues that those dimensions are the key drivers of competitive behavior. He explains how firms become aware of each other in terms of commonality and similarity, and that their motivation to attack or respond is based on the level of those overlaps. Importantly, he contends that a given set of conditions may have an asymmetric effect on the way a firm attacks and responds. More specifically, the conditions that increase the likelihood of a competitive response may not increase the likelihood of the attack itself. Chen argues that of the two factors, market commonality, or market overlap, is the key predictor of attack and response. We return to these points in chapter 10.

From a prescriptive point of view, Chen's model suggests that increases in market commonality between firms will decrease the likelihood of attacks but increase the likelihood of responses.[26] Chen also argues that resource similarity between competitors influences the likelihood of attack and response. Because attackers will be leery of rivals that have strong retaliation capabilities, the likelihood of attack will decrease as resource similarity between competitors increases. However, the likelihood of response will increase with resource similarity.

Consider Chen's framework in the context of the firm with no or limited resource advantages and a poor market position. According to Chen's argument, such a firm could delay response by engaging competitors that are in diverse, noncommon markets and have dissimilar resources. In fact, such firms will probably be uncertain about or blind to the creative actions of a new rival.

Implementation Knowledge. Being able to recognize opportunities and predict competitors' actions and reactions will not lead to effective action; the manager must also have a keen sense of timing and the ability to implement actions successfully. That may be especially true for managers of a firm without resource or market position advantages. The "window of opportunity" is constantly opening and closing with changes in the marketplace, technology, and competitors' actions and reactions. If the manager delays action implementation, a portion of the opportunity window is lost. In software production, for example, a firm's new product introduction rate is related positively to profitability—the faster products are introduced, the greater is the profit.[27] Fast decision-making on the part of company managers is also linked positively with profitability.[28] Hence, there is significant support for the idea that a firm's advantage can be enhanced by implementing actions quickly.

Interestingly, the fast-acting organization implements changes differently from the slow-acting organization.[29] Fast-acting firms plan for comparatively less improvement between actions. They make only incremental changes in new products or services, new advertising campaigns, and so on but make changes more often. In total, fast-acting firms take *more* actions. In manufacturing, fast-acting firms plan for smaller lot sizes and shorter product life cycles. Time-based companies also focus on the entire system and its main sequence. They generate a continuous flow of work, change upstream practice to relieve downstream problems, and invest in reducing time overall. In addition, fast-acting organizations emphasize multifunctional teams and decentralization to improve speed. Joseph L. Bower and Thomas M. Hout contend that fast-acting organizations, especially big ones, work hard at heightening everyone's awareness of how and where time is spent. They make the key parts of the cycle visible to and understandable by all employees through training. All are aware of key functions and interfaces between functions.[30] As Bower and Hout note:

> Fast-cycle companies differ from traditional organizations in how they structure work, how they measure performance and how they view organizational learning. They favor teams over functions and departments. They use time as a critical performance measure. They insist that everyone learn about customers, competitors, and the company's own operations, not just top management.[31]

The slow-acting organization, in contrast, improves function by function, works in departments or in batches, focuses on reducing bottlenecks to speed work, and invests to reduce costs. In highlighting the importance of speed, George Stalk and Thomas M. Hout reported that the average product development period is 5 to 8.5 months in fast-acting firms and 20 to 30 months in slow-acting firms.[32] Relatedly, research on the U.S. airline industry found that small firms can execute actions faster than large firms.[33] Herb Kelleher, the former CEO of Southwest Airlines, recently said,

"If we think and act big, we'll get smaller. If we think and act small, we'll get bigger."[34]

Types of Entrepreneurial Action

Now that we have examined disequilibrium, discovery, and the specific types of knowledge that foster the discovery process, let us consider what it is about entrepreneurial actions that increase the likelihood of success. Recall that previously we defined entrepreneurial actions as ones that implement new combinations of current and ordinary resources in innovative ways. Remember, entrepreneurial actions are not resource based but opportunity driven. Organizations with "Schumpeterian will" and the ability to seize new opportunities will reap entrepreneurial profit.[35] Two key characteristics of successful entrepreneurial action are creativity and moving first.

The range of first-moving innovative entrepreneurial actions can be quite diverse. Joseph Schumpeter claimed that entrepreneurs create competition with the introduction of new commodities, new technologies, new sources of supply, and new types of organization. More recently, Carl Vesper identified a set of new venture strategies that parallel Schumpeter's claims.[36] Vesper's actions included new product or service introductions, product or service improvements or efficiency enhancements, geographic or segment transfers, and responses to supply shortages. The following sections explain how each type of entrepreneurial action can lead to advantage.

New Product or Service Introductions. The introduction of a new product or service is probably the most obvious type of entrepreneurial action. Certainly, both large and small firms introduce new products or services, but a study of 8,000 innovations showed that small firms produced the majority, or 55 percent, of new products or services.[37] Coca-Cola's Vanilla Coke, a product line extension, is an example of a new product offering, and Nextel's DirectConnect, a unique two-way walkie-talkie feature in wireless phones, is an example of a new service offering. In a recent study of new product and service introductions in the personal computer, brewing, and telecommunications industries, we found that the first firm on the market with a new product had significantly greater stock market gains than competitors that did not introduce the product or competitors that later copied the product.[38]

Ted Turner is a prime example of an entrepreneur who introduces a new service. Indeed, an Atlanta billboard characterizing Turner proclaimed: "I was cable before cable was cool." Turner's background in advertising prepared him to identify opportunities in the communication business. Armed with a belief that information technology was an opportunity and having a strong desire to prove his worth, Turner created the first independent local television station (TBS) to broadcast by satellite, as well as the Cable News Network and CNN2.

Turner is preoccupied with action. He once commented: "Do you want to do it? Are you committed to making it work? Then it will, or at least it'll have the only chance it ever had. The reason nothing gets done in this country anymore is that there are so many committees. It just has to be you. Like McDonald's says, 'You're the one.'" Turner's dedication of the Cable News Network captured his intensity:

> To act on one's convictions while others wait,
> To create a positive force in a world where cynics abound,
> To provide information to people where it wasn't available before,
> To offer those who want it a choice,
> For the American people, whose thirst for understanding and a better life
>   make this venture possible....
> I dedicate the New Channel for America, The Cable News Network.

Christian Williams, in his biography of Ted Turner, concluded that Turner will "remake the world of commercial television."[39] In sum, the example of Ted Turner and the introduction of new television services illustrates well the combination of discovery and entrepreneurial action.

Product or Service Improvements. An alternative to introducing a completely new product or service is to modify and improve a current product or service. Indeed, it has been argued that the most common entrepreneurial action is to do what competitors do, but better or more efficiently.[40] One example is Southwest Airlines. It engaged in entrepreneurial actions that improved airline efficiencies, lowered prices, and increased demand.

Two other examples are Under Armour and Wal-Mart. Kevin Plank, with the introduction of Under Armour athletic underwear, is an example of an entrepreneur who undertakes product improvement actions. Plank was a football player and business major at the University of Maryland. Plank got the idea for the improved athletic underwear after having to change his undershirts several times during practice and after some of his football teammates suffered serious heat exhaustion during summer practice. He and the other players were mainly wearing cotton T-shirts, which tended to soak up sweat and become heavy with moisture and uncomfortable. He wanted athletic underwear that fitted tightly, stretched, was light, and did not hold moisture, but none existed in the marketplace. With that specific knowledge, he started Under Armour in 1996 and turned it into market leader in a niche apparel segment, referred to as "compression performance apparel," against industry giants such as Nike and Reebok. He found the right fabric, contracted out the manufacturing, and then targeted equipment managers at college and professional athletic teams to use his products. As a result of his targeted marketing, Under Armour built a loyal following among athletes and received a great deal of inexpensive advertising. Under Armour has now broadened its distribution to select retail chains. Since it started, Under Armour's sales have expanded to $55 million by end of 2002 and are expected to reach over $100 million by end of 2003. It still holds the number 1 position, with 67 percent market share in compression performance apparel.[41]

Plank has continued to focus on entrepreneurial actions and product improvements as Under Armour has added new products and offered improvements. For example, it has introduced a line of compression underwear for other weather conditions and other compression active wear, including T-shirts in a polyester fabric with a cotton feel; a men's underwear line with items such as boxer briefs, boxer shorts, and sport briefs; and polo shirts and tank tops designed specifically for golf and basketball.[42]

Wal-Mart's approach to discount retailing consisted of a series of incremental improvements in traditional methods and is seen as a highly efficient alternative to small town retailing. Wal-Mart's concept was based on the variety store franchised by Ben Franklin that Sam Walton and his brother opened in Newport, Arkansas.[43] Over a 17-year period, Walton built up a chain of 16 variety stores in rural Arkansas that were considered Ben Franklin's most successful franchises. But competition by discount stores increasingly worried Sam and eventually led him to search for retailing alternatives. Despite the conventional wisdom that full-line discount retailing required a population base of at least 100,000, Walton became convinced that discounting could work in small southwestern towns. "If we offered prices as good or better than stores in cities that were four hours away by car, people would shop at home."[44] Because Ben Franklin was not interested in his ideas, Walton set out to build his own discount chain. By 1970 he had expanded his chain to 30 discount stores. However, the cost of goods sold—almost three quarters of discounting revenues—skyrocketed. As Walton described: "Here we were in the boondocks, so we didn't have distributors falling over themselves to serve us like competitors in larger towns. Our only alternative was to build our own warehouse so we could buy in volume at attractive prices and store the merchandise."[45] With warehouses strategically arranged to accommodate its discount stores, Wal-Mart's operations mushroomed. Thus, Walton's actions included opening large discount retail stores in rural locations with populations of less than 100,000 and selectively locating the stores within convenient proximity to centralized supply depots. Walton was also innovative in the kinds of products sold and in his guaranteed everyday low pricing.

Geographic or Segment Transfers. Entrepreneurial actions designed to copy and transfer effective actions from one geographic region or market segment to a new region or segment can also be very successful. For example, the McDonald brothers developed the McDonald's hamburger chain in California, but Ray Kroc had the foresight to purchase the operation and expand it nationally. California Pizza is another example of a regional concept that has been expanded nationally through entrepreneurial action. Finally, Alfred Steele positioned Pepsi in the food store segment of the soft drink industry in the early 1950s just as supermarkets were emerging as an important retail outlet. At that time, Coke was focusing on traditional retail outlets.

When Alfred Steele took the reins at Pepsi, most employees thought he was brought in to liquidate the organization. In 1950, Pepsi was near bankruptcy and Coca-Cola commanded 70 percent of the soft drink market. However, Steele defined his strategy as "Beat Coke." Legend has it that Steele, previously employed at Coca-Cola, was personally intent on knocking out Coke because of a dispute with Coke's management.

As an experienced soft drink executive, Steele perceived the supermarket segment as a growing opportunity. He also knew that Coke believed the U.S. market was mature and would realize little growth. With that information, Steele directed Pepsi's energies toward the supermarket segment, motivated bottlers, cut prices, and began aggressively advertising "the Pepsi generation." Very slowly Pepsi gained momentum, ultimately overtaking Coke in the supermarket segment of the soft drink industry in 1975.

Responses to Supply Shortages. Selling umbrellas on a rainy street corner and opening a restaurant near a busy intersection are examples of entrepreneurial actions that respond to shortages of supply. Many experts have argued that the entrepreneurial task is to identify something that is in short supply and find a way to provide it.[46]

All of the preceding examples illustrate the relationship between knowledge and entrepreneurial action. Entrepreneurial action is the vehicle or the mechanism by which entrepreneurs achieve. Let us now turn to the relationship between entrepreneurial action and advantage.

Entrepreneurial Action/Reaction and Competitive Advantage

We observed in chapters 1 and 5 that firms are not independent; they are aware of one another's actions and are generally compelled to react. Therefore, even if firms have the necessary opportunity and skills, the effectiveness of an entrepreneurial action still depends on the extent of competitive *reaction*. Reacting to the entrepreneurial actions of firms with limited resource advantages and a poor market position is theoretically easy for more established competitors, as the entrepreneurial actions are generally not based on resource advantages. To avoid reactions, however, the action-oriented manager must focus on exploiting the competitive uncertainty and blind spots created by knowledge problems.

In a seminal article, C. K. Prahalad and Richard A. Bettis coined the phrase "dominant logic" to refer to "the way in which managers conceptualize the business and make critical resource allocation decisions."[47] They contend that few organizational events are totally unique. Consequently, managers process information about specific events through their present knowledge systems, called "schemas." Schemas represent a manager's viewpoint of how competitors will behave and how the business environment operates; they are cognitive systems of beliefs, theories, and propositions that have developed over time on the basis of a person's experiences. Schemas enable people to categorize and evaluate efficiently the importance of specific events. The dominant logic of a firm or industry is the combined or aggregate set of managers' schemas in that firm or industry.

The dominant logic of a firm or industry may not be a perfect representation of the relevant organizations or business environment. Indeed, some schemas are relatively inaccurate perspectives of the world, especially as environmental conditions change. The dominant logic may not have incorporated recent innovations or changes. Faulty dominant logic can lead to knowledge problems, and resultant competitive uncertainty and blind spots can delay competitive response to entrepreneurial actions. Michael Porter claimed that action outcome uncertainty and blind spots are "areas where a competitor will either not see the significance of events at all, will perceive them incorrectly, or will perceive them very slowly."[48]

Examples Based on Game Theory

We can examine the importance of competitive uncertainty and blind spots in the context of entrepreneurial action and reaction with a simple game theory model. Figure 6.2 is an extensive game modeling the options and payoffs for a firm with a limited relative resource position and a poor market position. We assume that this firm must compete against one or more larger and comparatively richer rivals through entrepreneurial actions to survive in the long term. The firm has the choice of three initial entrepreneurial actions, denoted A_1, A_2, and A_3. Assume for the purposes of this example that the scenario being considered involves the introduction of a new service improvement, such as a free car wash after auto service.

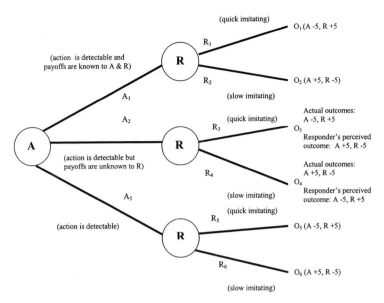

(quick imitating)

O_1 (A -5, R +5)

R_1

(action is detectable and payoffs are known to A & R)

R

R_2

O_2 (A +5, R -5)

A_1

(slow imitating)

A_2

(quick imitating)

Actual outcomes:
A -5, R +5

R_3

O_3

Responder's perceived outcome: A +5, R -5

A

R

(action is detectable but payoffs are unknown to R)

Actual outcomes:
A +5, R -5

R_4

O_4

Responder's perceived outcome: A -5, R +5

A_3

(slow imitating)

(quick imitating)

R_5

(action is detectable)

R

O_5 (A -5, R +5)

R_6

O_6 (A +5, R -5)

(slow imitating)

Figure 6.2   Entrepreneurial Action/Reaction and Advantage.

A Timely Response. In A_1, the action is easily detectable by rivals, and the payoffs of the new action are clear to both players. Once this action is taken, the rival firm has two options, R_1 and R_2; R_1 is a quick matching response, and R_2 is a slow response.[49] Each set of actions and responses has an associated outcome, reflecting payoff for both players. The combination A_1-R_1 yields outcome O_1. A quick response to the entrepreneurial action of launching new service (A_1) produces a negative result for the acting firm and a positive result for the responding firm, largely because of the resource imbalance between the firms. With greater resources, the responding firm is capable of quickly exploiting the new service action that it recognizes as beneficial or adding value for customers. A slow response yields outcome O_2, which is positive for the acting firm and negative for the responding firm. In the case of A_1, which is easily detectable and for which the payoffs are known to both players, the responding firm will choose the quick response, with a negative outcome for the acting firm.

An example of an entrepreneurial action that prompted a swift competitive response can be seen in the battle between Amazon.com and Barnes & Noble in the book retailing industry. Founded in 1994, Amazon.com shipped its first book in July 1995 and eventually became the leading online book retailer. Barnes & Noble, the leading traditional book retailer, had been aware of online book retailing and was watching Book Stacks, which launched its web site in late 1994 before Amazon.com. However, as Amazon.com continued to grow and racked up sales in several million dollars within a year, Barnes & Noble responded quickly by launching its own transaction-oriented web site in 1996. Predictably, Amazon.com's entrepreneurial action and continued growth incited Barnes & Noble to go on the offensive, launching its full web site by 1997, becoming an exclusive bookseller for AOL's Marketplace, offering personalized book recommendations, and reducing prices by 20–30 percent. Those actions effectively slowed the advances of Amazon.com and forced it to respond in kind. Amazon.com also introduced its personalized book recommendations, added an additional 1.5 million titles, and reduced prices even further than Barnes & Noble on some books.[50]

Competitive Uncertainty. As shown in figure 6.2, the firm can alternatively choose entrepreneurial action A_2, for which the outcomes associated with the corresponding response choices are identical to those of A_1. However, in this instance we assume there is asymmetric information about the payoffs. Large rivals would be capable of responding instantaneously to the firm's action as in A_1, but in A_2, the acting firm knows the true payoffs of the new service, offering and the responding firm believes the payoffs are the reverse. In other words, in the responding firm's view, there is high uncertainty surrounding the action A_2. The responding firm does not clearly see the benefit of the action. It therefore will choose R_2, and delay its response, at least temporarily, which results in a positive outcome for the acting firm.

An example of uncertain payoffs occurred in the case of Wal-Mart's action in the rural Southwest. Sam Walton recognized that traditional large retail outlets such as Kmart and Sears did not believe that small (5,000 to 25,000 people) rural towns in the South would support a discount retailer. With years of retailing experience in the South, he believed otherwise. Kmart, Target, and Sears did not recognize the value of Wal-Mart's southern location strategy because it was at odds with industry logic on how to compete as a discount retailer. Entrenched rivals did not counter Wal-Mart's actions because they were uncertain of the payoffs.

Blind Spots. In the preceding two examples, firm responses were determined by the level of uncertainty surrounding the action. The third choice for the acting firm, A_3, is to focus on blind spots. The potential responses and payoffs for A_3 are identical to those in the first two cases. However, because in this instance the move occurs in a blind spot, it is not initially detected by the responding firm. By the time the responder discovers the move, a quick response (R_1) is no longer possible, and R_2 and O_6 result.

When Alfred Steele was hired as the new CEO of Pepsi, he knew that Coke was vulnerable in the supermarket segment of the soft drink industry. Coke believed the U.S. market to be mature and was focusing its attention overseas, so it was blind to domestic opportunities. Accordingly, Pepsi was able to design a set of entrepreneurial actions to gain share in the super-market segment of the soft drink industry. These actions included using celebrities in advertising, adopting innovative advertising slogans, and developing new product introductions. In addition, Pepsi built an aggres-sive distribution network that effectively fought for shelf space in super-markets. If Coke had not been blind to Pepsi as a competitor, those actions would have been easy for Coke to counter.

Coke was blinded also by its own self-image; it considered itself invin-cible and the guardian of the industry. So persuasive was this belief that Coca-Cola executives were prohibited from using the word "Pepsi" in corporate headquarters.

Considering the game theory model and examples, we can see how a firm with a poor market position and limited resource advantages can undertake entrepreneurial actions to exploit uncertainty and blind spots. Clearly uncertainty and misperceptions are major issues. That is, the re-sources necessary to carry out an entrepreneurial action are readily available among competing firms, as in the case of Barnes & Noble's re-sponse to Amazon.com, but the uncertainty surrounding the action can delay competitive response. Response may be delayed because rivals are either uncertain of the payoffs associated with the entrepreneurial action or are unaware that the action has occurred. Hence, entrepreneurial ac-tions that potentially delay competitive reaction are those surrounded by high levels of competitive uncertainty, which results in information asymmetries among rivals. Without information asymmetries or imper-fections in the perception of market opportunities, profit would be elimi-nated almost immediately through competition. In summary, successful entrepreneurial actions delay competitive response by creating uncer-tainty; the greater the competitive uncertainty surrounding the action, the greater is the potential delay in reaction.

Signal Jamming:
Creating Uncertainty

Firms always face uncertainty; they never have perfect information. However, a firm can influence the level of uncertainty a particular rival faces. Consider the case in which one competitor, Paterson in the example of the Cincinnati pump shaft market, is uncertain as to its own future profitability and uses current profit level to decide whether to act aggres-sively or to seek business elsewhere. If profit is low, Paterson may decide to deploy its scarce resources elsewhere. Another firm, such as Enterprise, which is aware that Paterson is making the decision, perhaps through private contacts with the customer, may engage in such actions as secret price cuts that are not fully observable by Paterson but serve to reduce its current profit. From Enterprise's perspective, the corresponding reduction in its own current profit may be offset by future gains if Paterson is induced to seek market opportunities elsewhere. If those moves were made public, Paterson would probably cease to view the level of its current profit as an accurate guide to its future prospects.

Consider the following game model in which the competition between Paterson and Enterprise unfolds in two stages.[51] Assume Enterprise has two pricing options as it attempts to sell shafts to the pump producer. It can offer its product at the current Cincinnati market price of $15 per shaft, or it can *secretly* offer it at $13. However, if Enterprise earns the pump producer's business by secretly offering the shaft for $13, it would reduce its profit by $2 per shaft.

In addition, assume Paterson is uncertain as to the future profitability of its general purpose machine shop. One estimate, if Enterprise opts for the $15 price, is that there is some chance that Paterson will earn $1 per shaft in each stage of competition, but also some chance that Paterson will lose $1 per shaft in each stage. If the order is for 1 million shafts, Paterson may earn or lose $1 million.

If Enterprise secretly offers its shaft product to the pump company at $13 per shaft, Paterson will definitely lose $1 per shaft, or 1 million, in stage 1. Paterson has no way to discover in stage 1 whether Enterprise has priced at $15 or secretly cut its price to $13.

Faced with losing $1 per shaft, or $1 million, in stage 1, Paterson must decide in stage 2 whether to act more aggressively or exit the market and deploy its resources elsewhere. Given that the best predictor of Paterson's future profit is its stage 1 profit, the $1 million loss, Paterson may be reluctant to commit to more aggressive behavior that could lower profit even further in stage 2. If Paterson decides to exit the industry, Enterprise stands to earn much higher profit, which could substantially exceed what it would normally earn in stage 2 if Paterson remained a competitor. As long as Paterson does not learn about Enterprise's secret price cuts, Enterprise has an incentive to cut prices secretly. The secret moves will create uncertainty for Paterson, forcing it to exit the industry. This example illustrates well how a firm can create competitive uncertainty for a rival.

Characteristics of Competitive Action and Response

Our discussion has shown the importance of competitor analysis or attempting to predict how a rival will act and respond. However, many managers fail to understand that the characteristics of their own actions will influence the extent of competitive response. Three dimensions of action can affect the degree of reaction: scope, threat, and radicality.

Scope. The scope of an action refers to the number of competitors that can be potentially affected by the action. Some moves affect only one competitor, whereas others have much wider effects. Actions affecting many competitors are more likely to provoke a response, at least by one firm, than actions affecting only one or two rivals. In addition, action scope is determined by the rivals' physical proximity to one another.

For example, the hundreds of personal computer retailers in the Washington, D.C., area frequently promote their actions in the *Washington Business Journal,* a weekly publication of the *Washington Post.* When Micro Systems, a computer retailer, advertised innovative "in-the-home" service contracts, the news was disseminated quickly. Competitors could see fairly easily that this entrepreneurial action would be successful; in other words, there was little competitive uncertainty. Many rivals therefore matched the service agreement offer in the very next issue of the publication. Rivals beyond the scope of the action were not knowledgeable of or were blind to the action, and therefore did not respond.

In contrast, few rivals were aware of a word-of-mouth price campaign by Computer Age. Computer Age marketed its low-priced computers to, and through, new graduate students and freshmen at the local university, where news of the promotion traveled quickly. Most rivals were blind, or actually deaf, to Computer Age's actions, and therefore did not respond.

Threat. Although an action can potentially affect many competitors, it may represent a more direct threat to some rivals than to others. Actions targeted at select customers or competitors may be of limited scope but pose a large threat. Pepsi initially gained share against Coke by taking relatively nonthreatening actions within a narrow scope, the supermarket segment of the industry. Coke was hardly aware of Pepsi's inroads. Pepsi's invention of the Pepsi Challenge, however, was a direct threat.

Pepsi developed an in-store marketing program challenging consumers in blind taste tests to select their preferred cola: Pepsi or Coke. With the success of its initial campaign, Pepsi publicly announced it would take the Pepsi Challenge nationwide in 1977. In the 1980s, John Scully, the president of Pepsi USA, used the success of the Pepsi Challenge to urge bottlers to go for Coke's "jugular." The threatening nature of Pepsi's action forced Coke to respond. Coke finally formally recognized Pepsi and responded aggressively with its own set of actions, including price cuts and increases in advertising. The rivalry between the two intensified, and Pepsi's supermarket share gains halted.[52]

Radicality. The final action dimension to consider is radicality, defined as the extent to which the action departs from previous competitive moves in an industry. As radicality increases, less information is available for judging the potential success of the action. When PETSTUFF, a pet supply store, refused to sell pets, rivals laughed—"A pet store without pets!" When PETSTUFF began to offer free clinics where pet owners could bring unwanted animals to meet people looking for pets, rivals "could not understand and were uncertain of the benefits." While its competitors hesitated, PETSTUFF built a strong customer base. People (and eventually an acquiring competitor, PetsMart) obviously valued the services PETSTUFF offered, even if the actions taken were too radical for competitors to comprehend initially.[53]

Rival's View of the World

The impacts of scope, threat, and radicality of action must be considered in terms of a rival's belief structure, or how the rival views the world. For example, Coca-Cola viewed itself as "Mother Coke," the industry leader, invincible to challenges. Similarly, Kmart did not believe a discount retailer could be successful in small, rural southern towns. In the construction equipment industry, Caterpillar believed the most effective way to run a global organization was through standardization and centralization. All of those beliefs were effectively challenged by upstart rivals. If a firm has narrowly defined competitive boundaries, it may be *blind* to, or fail to recognize, the actions of firms outside the boundaries. For example, Caterpillar defined its industry boundaries as the developed world and was therefore vulnerable to Komatsu, an up-and-coming Japanese producer that was building market share in less developed countries. In the early 1970s, Coors defined its brewing business as regional and ignored the growing national beer market. Before long, Coors faced competition from several national brands in its local region. Similarly, ABC, CBS, and NBC defined their boundaries so narrowly that cable TV, with operators such as Turner Broadcasting, grew without challenge.

In attempting to identify how a rival has defined its industry boundaries, a focal firm should consider how rivals determine where the industry begins and ends, the customer groups it seeks to serve, and the technology it seeks to exploit. Importantly, those factors must be considered over time for each competitor. Apple Computer initially dismissed IBM as a personal computer competitor because Apple was shipping more PCs each month than IBM had shipped in total.[54] However, IBM still became the industry standard.

Typically firms focus on current competitors, especially when those competitors have been rivals for many years. For example, Caterpillar considered its competitors to be familiar domestic firms, International Harvester and John Deere, and for the most part totally overlooked

Komatsu. In contrast, the upstart Komatsu directly targeted Caterpillar, the industry leader.[55] Generally firms concentrate on rivals that are most similar to themselves in resources and goals and ignore ones that are very different.[56] Xerox focused on its U.S. rivals, IBM and Kodak, rather than new emerging rivals, Canon and Minolta. IBM and Kodak were very similar to Xerox in resources and goals, whereas Canon and Minolta were culturally different and used different strategies.[57]

Sometimes incumbent firms do recognize upstart rivals but underestimate their capabilities and strategies. First, incumbents may monitor the wrong kinds of information about upstarts. They often monitor the most visible aspects of competitors, such as balance sheet information.[58] Firms have been found to pay more attention to rivals' competitive pricing, strategic plans, market position, and new product plans[59] than to their organization, structure, culture, and intent. Such focus may lead to inaccurate assessments of a rival's capabilities. By studying only visible capabilities and limited financial data, an incumbent firm could conclude that a disadvantaged rival is not capable of competing when in fact it may have significant invisible assets.

Second, a firm may misjudge a challenging rival's actions. For example, the incumbent firm may apply traditional critical success criteria and not notice how those criteria have changed over time. Wal-Mart, Turner Broadcasting, Pepsi, Komatsu, Nike, and Honda all revolutionized their industries by creatively destroying entrenched beliefs about how to run the business. In each of those cases, incumbent firms recognized the challengers but discounted them as viable foes. Chapter 10 offers a model and a set of techniques to help gather information on rivals' intentions, past actions, and resources.

Timing of Competitive Actions and Responses

The advantage created by entrepreneurial actions is generally temporary. Figure 6.3 outlines the life cycle of an effective action, from launch through exploitation and finally to imitation by rivals. As rivals imitate, the action's advantage will evaporate. Even if the firm's initial actions are shrouded in competitive uncertainty, as those actions succeed, they are likely to become known. Therefore, entrepreneurial firms should think about strings of action.

Domino's Pizza built an initial advantage over rivals by being the first to offer home delivery in one half hour or less with a free product guarantee. Rivals at first scorned that tactic but eventually imitated it. Once most pizza retailers offered home delivery, Domino's initial advantage was gone. Domino's second action was to offer a giant pizza, the "Big Foot"; its third

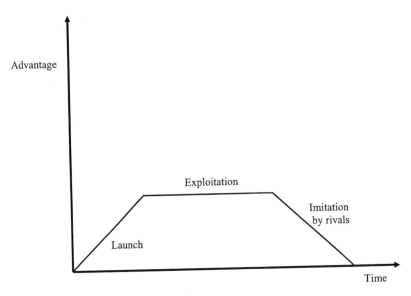

Figure 6.3   Action Life Cycle.

was to distribute direct mail coupons; and its fourth was to give its customers handy magnets for easy access to Domino's phone number. Only through a string of actions could Domino's maintain its advantage and keep rivals off guard. Figure 6.4 outlines strings of entrepreneurial actions for first movers, fast seconds, and laggards.

Creating Resource Advantage

In this chapter, we have introduced the concept of entrepreneurial action. Entrepreneurial actions are especially suited for resource-poor firms who should most avoid direct competition with stronger rivals. We argued that entrepreneurial actions can be most effective in generating profits by exploiting competitive uncertainty and blind spots. Nonetheless, entrepreneurial actions do not create direct competitive advantages for a firm other than perhaps first-mover advantages. And if entrepreneurial actions generate profits, competitive response can be expected. As a consequence, firms with limited resources must also think about creating resource advantages that can provide a better defense against the competition.

In chapter 4, we noted that resource heterogeneity is a central assumption of the resource-based view. As such, any theory of building new resource advantage must first focus on making the firm's resource endowment different from that of rivals. We introduced the value chain as a way to consider resource differences among firms. Thus, the process of creating new resource advantages must begin with the decision-maker

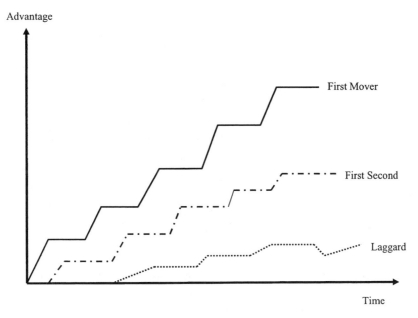

Figure 6.4   Strings of Entrepreneurial Actions.

evaluating his or her firm's arrangement of resources along the value chain relative to the competition. We refer back to chapter 4 and the example of Enterprise Manufacturing's value chain in comparison to other New England machine tool companies. From figure 4.4 in chapter 4, you may recall that Enterprise had a high cost structure, including high direct and indirect labor costs relative to the competition, outdated machinery, and a broad-based assortment of expertise. Relative to the New England competition, Enterprise did not have an advantage, except that its was relatively efficient in the manufacturing of drive shafts.

In our continued illustration of Enterprise in this chapter, we described how Enterprise explored the shafting market outside of New England in the Mid-west, where customers were less price sensitive. However, this in itself is not defensible because other New England manufacturers could imitate the same moves. Thus, Enterprise must also explore ways to work on its cost structure and in the selection of business to focus on. By changing its name to Enterprise Shafting, the company signals its intended speciali-zation. But the firm must also cut costs and invest in new manufactur-ing technology so that it can competitively price its products as the competition increases.

Acting to alter the stock of resources to create a resource advantage can occur anywhere along the value chain (inputs, throughputs and outputs) or in combination of areas and can involve the investment in or devel-opment of tangible and or intangible resources. Often such changes are viewed as exploratory and experimental until the results of such actions prove feasible. For example, the new CEO of Enterprise realized the need to cut costs and therefore laid off all indirect employees. By specializing in shafts only, the firm explored emphasizing the product that best exploited the existing expertise of its workers, thus moving the average rate per hour from 60 percent of target to 100 percent. Enterprise then invested the first profits from these new changes in advanced computer-controlled machine tools, dramatically increasing the use of computer technology while also lowering the age of its equipment. The company experimented by using its vacant space to offer free inventory of shafts for its customers in the Midwest, which allowed the firm to better schedule production and further cut costs through larger production runs. As a result of these exploratory actions, Enterprise developed into a low-cost producer of drive shafts. Figure 6.5 compares the value chain of Enterprise before and after its new CEO arrived and reconfigured the value proposition.

Generally speaking, firms can adjust their resources through two types of actions. They can acquire resources in factor markets, as Enterprise did by purchasing new equipment. Or they can internally develop advantages, as Enterprise did by specialization and through its inventory program. The changes were a result of the CEO's insight into new markets and a deep appreciation of the poor resource position of the firm. The firm's entrepreneurial actions repositioned the firm in a vacant niche, and allowed management to generate profits that could be used to build new competitive advantages in costs, equipment, and shaft expertise.

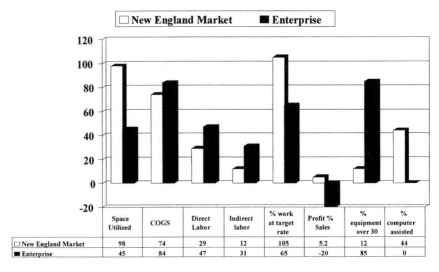

	Space Utilized	COGS	Direct Labor	Indirect labor	% work at target rate	Profit % Sales	% equipment over 30	% computer assisted
New England Market	98	74	29	12	105	5.2	12	44
Enterprise	45	84	47	31	65	-20	85	0

Figure 6.5a   Enterprise Manufacturing Value Chain.

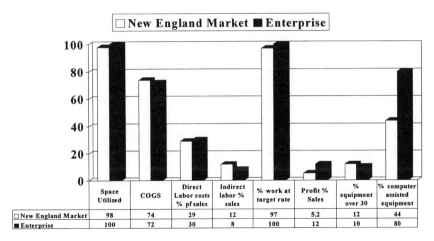

	Space Utilized	COGS	Direct Labor costs % pf sales	Indirect labor % sales	% work at target rate	Profit % Sales	% equipment over 30	% computer assisted equipment
☐ New England Market	98	74	29	12	97	5.2	12	44
■ Enterprise	100	72	30	8	100	12	10	80

Figure 6.5b   Enterprise Shafting after Reconfiguring Resources.

Nucor provides another example of a company that undertook both factor market actions and internal development actions to develop new competitive advantages. Ken Iverson of Nucor was searching for new opportunities to grow in the mature steel industry. He decided to buy the license for a new continuous casting process from a German developer that was unproven. However, Iverson also developed and combined a number of internal processes and capabilities to go along with this new continuous casting process (e.g., guaranteed employment, group incentive contracts, training of farm workers, etc.). The combination of this purchase of the new casting technique and the development of new organizational processes allowed Nucor to dramatically alter its stock of assets relative to integrated steel mills, and the firm also achieved a lower cost position relative to other minimills. Nucor investments have all been focused in the area of throughputs that resulted in a portfolio of accumulated assets that yielded a decided advantage in terms of lower unit costs. For example, Nucor combinations of resources yielded it as much as a $44 per ton cost advantage relative to integrated mills.[60]

Acquiring new resources or reconfiguring existing resources through internal adjustment can occur simultaneously in multiple areas of the value chain. For example, a firm could simultaneously purchase or train R&D scientists, develop low-cost production capability through the acquisition of high-technology plant and equipment, develop an extensive distribution system, and create a high-quality customer service center. The children's game producer Nintendo is an example of a company that created such extensive *broad-based* resource advantages in the early 1990s. During the 1980s, the children's video business grew rapidly, but none of the firms could carve out a sustainable position. In fact, there were numerous failures as heavy competition quickly eroded profits. Nintendo changed the game by conceiving a new value proposition. For example, it acted to hire internal software producers, instead of subcontracting, to develop new games (Mario); developed a low-cost capability and chip technology to produce proprietary hardware for children's video games; created a security chip in each game that made it difficult for outside software producers to copy; and developed a customer service center and a extensive field sales force. Thus, Nintendo created multiple new resource advantages along the entire value chain that allowed the firm to dominate the video market throughout the late 1990s.

Summary

This chapter examines how firms with limited resources and a poor market position can undertake entrepreneurial actions to improve their competitive position and advantage. We explain that disequilibrium in the marketplace is a source of opportunity for the alert manager. However, such managers must also be skillful in opportunity identification, competitor analysis, and implementation to take entrepreneurial actions successfully. Piecing the model together, we can see that the knowledge and skills of the discovering manager must be used to make entrepreneurial moves. Opportunity without action is simply forgone opportunity. Managers must be knowledgeable about market opportunities and competitors and be able to act within the window of opportunity. Entrepreneurial actions include developing new products or services, improving products or services, making geographic transfers, and satisfying shortages of supply. Firms with inferior resources and market position have no choice but to delay competitive reaction by exploiting uncertainty and competitive blind spots until they generate the profits to build more enduring resource advantages. Firms can build new resource advantages by acquiring resources in factor markets and/or by reconfiguring internal resources and policies.

Chapter 7

ENGAGING RIVALS WITH RICARDIAN ACTIONS

Exploiting Ownership of Superior Resources

In 1995 eBay, Inc., launched its web site for Internet auctions and pioneered the person-to-person trading community. By being a first mover, eBay has developed a strong brand name and large customer base of buyers and sellers, creating a network effect—value increases with greater number of users. Hence, buyers and sellers prefer to use eBay's web site because buyers have a greater number of sellers to choose from and sellers have a greater number of buyers to sell to. As a result, eBay has essentially become synonymous with Internet auctions. Nevertheless, because of eBay's great success and low entry barriers, a number of competitors have attempted to battle with the online auction giant eBay. Many considered Amazon.com's entry into the business in early 1999 a very serious competitive threat. At the time, Amazon was considered to be another successful Internet company, which started out selling books and diversified into CDs, videos, and other items. In fact, Amazon ranked number 1 in brand recognition among e-commerce web sites, while eBay ranked third.[1] However, eBay's experience and superior competitive position in Internet auctions have proved too formidable for Amazon. Before Amazon's entry, eBay launched a series of preemptive moves, such as engaging in a marketing alliance with AOL and establishing a verified user program, insurance program, and feedback forums.[2] In the end, Amazon failed to make a significant competitive threat as it could not overcome eBay's strong network effects of a large customer base. More recently, eBay has started to emphasize fixed-priced transactions by pursuing corporate sellers, such as Disney, IBM, and Xerox.[3] While this action places eBay in more direct competition with Amazon and other online retailers, it also allows eBay to further leverage its large customer base while still acting as a virtual marketplace and performing only a transaction role. And so eBay continues to be one of the few remaining and profitable dot-com companies, reaching revenues of over $1 billion, profits of $250 million, and profit margins of 20 percent, and to dominate, with 85 percent of the Internet auctions marketplace by the end of 2002.[4]

Pepsi instituted the Pepsi Challenge in the state of Texas in 1975, and in 1977 the campaign went national in supermarket locations around the United States. Customers took a blind taste test of Coke versus Pepsi and were asked "Which cola tastes best?" The challenge was based on Pepsi's scientific research, which revealed that 58 percent of cola drinkers preferred Pepsi's cola taste to that of Coke. Pepsi's move was aggressive but was soundly based on its research and its superior cola formula. Indeed, Coke could not match Pepsi effectively without changing its formula. Ten years went by before New Coke was introduced, which many people believed tasted like Pepsi. When Coke introduced New Coke, Pepsi called a holiday for its employees; after many years of eyeball-to-eyeball competition, Pepsi claimed that Coke had blinked. Some observers at the time claimed that Coke's New Coke taste campaign might have been dropped if the company had not been so intent on seeking revenge and hurting Pepsi.[5]

Wal-Mart's location advantage in the Southwest is unique. By establishing stores in small southwestern towns, Wal-Mart preempted rivals such as Target and Kmart. Those firms could not justify a response because customer density in most areas would support only one store. By the time they recognized Wal-Mart's success, the first mover had already locked up key locations. Wal-Mart's growth resulted in significant economies of scale and lower costs due to its centralized distribution system. Because Wal-Mart's store location strategy was based on a concentric distribution system that cost millions of dollars to develop, rivals could not duplicate Wal-Mart's cost advantage quickly.[6] When Wal-Mart moved into larger towns and competed with its rivals directly, it retained that cost advantage. As of this writing, Kmart, perhaps Wal-Mart's principal competitor, is reeling. It is closing nearly 10 percent of its current locations, 192 of 2,300 stores, and cutting approximately 6,000 jobs.[7] One indicator of Wal-Mart's competitive advantage is the fact that in 1993, Kmart was earning only $147 per square foot of floor space while Wal-Mart was generating over $300 per square foot. In markets where Wal-Mart has been extremely aggressive, competitors such as Kmart, Bradlee's Inc., and Caldor Corporation have filed for bankruptcy, and Jamesway Corporation, Ames Department Stores, Inc., and Filene's Basement Corporation are weak and losing money.[8]

The preceding examples illustrate how firms with superior resources can enhance their market positions and performance by undertaking competitive moves that exploit those scarce resources. Such competitive actions do not provoke responses because rivals lack the resources necessary to respond effectively. A strong brand name and a large customer base, leading to strong network effects, prevented rival Amazon from imitating eBay's initial success in Internet auctions and also provided an advantage for eBay's entry into fixed-priced transactions. In the second case, realizing that the majority of consumers preferred Pepsi's taste, Coke could not respond effectively without changing its formula. Indeed, the very formula that had made Coke successful originally became something of a liability in light of Pepsi's taste campaign. Finally, Kmart lacks the distribution economies of scale that Wal-Mart has developed, a disadvantage proving deadly in head-to-head competition.

Chapter 5 introduced the relationship between a firm's relative internal resources and external market positions and its competitive action: entrepreneurial, Ricardian, or deterrent. Chapter 6 concerned firms with limited resources, those without significant resource advantages and in a poor market position. Success for those firms depends on managers' creativity in developing entrepreneurial actions. We argued that entrepreneurial actions delay response by exploiting competitor uncertainty and blind spots.

Unlike the firms discussed in chapter 6, the firms we examine in this chapter have a superior resource advantage. The task for managers of firms in this healthier position is to formulate and implement what we call Ricardian actions. Recall from chapter 5 that Ricardian actions are competitive actions that directly engage rivals and stem from the ownership of resources. Firm resources can include tangible factors of production such as plant and equipment, land, capital, patents, raw materials, and financial assets reflected on the balance sheet, as well as intangible resources such as firm knowledge and culture. The focus here is on relative resources or resource areas where the firm has an advantage over competitors. Ricardian actions, such as the network effects of eBay, Pepsi Challenge, and the concentric distribution strategy of Wal-Mart, lead to enhanced financial health and to an improved market position because rivals lack the resources needed for an effective response. For example, Amazon lacked the strong customer base required in a trading community that would enable it to respond effectively to eBay's Internet auctions. When scientific consumer research revealed that Pepsi's taste was preferable, Coke's response options were to change its formula to something completely new or to imitate Pepsi. In fact, some suggest that Coke's introduction of "New Coke" failed because it tasted just like Pepsi. Kmart could match Wal-Mart's low costs only by investing hundreds of millions of dollars into new distribution centers—money it did not have—eventually forcing bankruptcy.

In contrast to that in chapter 6, much of the material in this chapter may be familiar to many readers. In particular, we draw from literature on competitive advantage that is based on both industrial organization economics and the resource view of the firm.[9] We first review David Ricardo's ideas about the relationship between ownership of scarce resources and competitive advantage and profit. We then define Ricardian actions in more detail and compare them with the entrepreneurial actions discussed in chapter 6. Alternative kinds of resource ownership are reviewed and related to two types of Ricardian actions: low-cost and differentiation actions. Through the use of game theory we demonstrate how Ricardian actions, backed by the ownership of key resources, can be effective in delaying response. Finally, we discuss the conditions under which Ricardian actions can maximize the delay of a competitive response.

David Ricardo and Ricardian Rents

A basic doctrine of strategic management is that firms exploit their unique resources.[10] Many years ago, in his *Principles of Political Economy*, David Ricardo highlighted the scarcity and ownership of physical resources. In Ricardo's world, the owner of a resource benefited from the productivity of the resource, and his or her income, or rent, was not necessarily restrained by growth in either competition or population. In fact, the owner was likely to gain as competition and demand grew.[11] We now turn to Ricardo's thesis to understand the nuances of resource ownership and relative resource advantage.

In Ricardo's world, the landlord or the owner of scarce resources was a unique beneficiary in society. Workers received wages and capitalists made profit, but owners of scarce resources earned rent. Rent was not just the price paid for the use of the scarce resource, such as interest paid for capital or wages paid for labor, but was a special return that had its origin in the fact that not all resources are equally productive.

Let us consider Ricardo's well-known example of the two farms. On one farm, the soil on the landlord's fields is very fertile. With the labor of 100 persons and a set amount of equipment, the landlord can raise 2,000 bushels of grain. On the second farm, the landlord's fields are less fertile. With the same amount of labor and the same equipment, the second landlord can raise only 1,000 bushels of grain. Ricardo argued that the difference is due simply to a technical fact of owning a scarce resource, fertile land. However, it also has a significant economic consequence for the owner, in that grain is cheaper to produce per bushel on the fertile farm than on the less fertile farm. Because the costs of producing the grain are different, an economic advantage accrues to the landlord who produces 1,000 more bushels from the soil than his or her competitor. It is this difference in inherent costs that gives rise to Ricardian rents. As long as demand is high enough to justify tilling the less fertile soil, raising grain on the more productive farm will certainly be profitable. Of course, the greater the difference in productivity between the two farms, all else being equal, the greater the economic rent and competitive advantage will be.

This principle is straightforward, but Ricardo added an important insight to the argument. For Ricardo, population and economic activity were constantly expanding, necessitating cultivation of additional land. Hence, as demand for grain expanded with population growth, an increasing amount of less and less fertile land would be put into use, and the cost of grain would have to rise. As the selling price of grain went up, the first landlords would receive ever-higher profit per bushel. Indeed, landlords on the most fertile land would become increasingly better off as less productive soil was brought into use.[12]

Let us now translate Ricardo's farming example to that of a present-day organization. Consider a firm that has introduced a new product with great market potential. The firm has invested significant financial capital to acquire state-of-the-art plant and equipment, developed first-rate organizational processes to produce the product efficiently, and invested heavily in human capital. This firm is a first mover, as it is introducing the new product and developing its capabilities first. Assume that customer demand is significant and the plant quickly expands to full capacity. The company benefits from economies of scale and economies of learning. It moves quickly down the learning curve, lowering unit costs substantially from the initial product introduction phase.

Soon, customer demand outstrips supply, and competitors react with imitations. However, imitators with less experience and lower volume (i.e., a weaker relative resource position) have higher unit costs. The first-moving firm meanwhile is investing to expand capacity, develop new products, and further reduce costs. All other things being equal, the first mover that is capable of expanding capacity, achieving economies of scale, and moving down the learning curve ahead of rivals will achieve the same kind of Ricardian rents as the farmer with fertile land. For a firm, the rents stem from ownership of superior plant, equipment, and organizational knowledge. That combination of resources gives the firm a more efficient capability than its less-endowed rivals. With increasing demand, prices will rise to cover the costs of the less efficient producers, generating greater profit for the first-moving firm. Even if market demand were to level off, the first-moving firm would be more efficient than less experienced imitators that produce a lower quantity of product.

Considering the preceding example, we define Ricardian actions as competitive actions that directly engage rivals. The success of the action in delaying rival reaction stems from the ownership of superior resources. The dominance of eBay in online transactions is considered a Ricardian action because it was based on the company's ownership of a large customer base. Amazon and other rivals have had great difficulty in winning a significant market share in online auctions because of eBay's strong network effects. In contrast, eBay has had greater success in pursing corporate sellers for fixed-price transactions because of its superior resource of a large customer base of buyers and sellers. The Pepsi Challenge is considered a Ricardian action because it was based on research demonstrating that customers preferred Pepsi's cola formula to that of Coke. Wal-Mart's move to establish stores in small towns was also a Ricardian action because it stemmed from the company's singular and superior distribution system. Kmart, the nearest competitor to Wal-Mart, lacked the financial resources to acquire the same type of distribution system.

Ricardian Actions

This chapter examines exploitation of a superior resource position. Let us recall that our analysis of resource position is pair-wise, or between a local firm and a specific rival. We take the resource positions of each as given. That is, our focus here is not on how a firm builds such a resource position but instead on how a firm can use superior resources to engage competitors effectively with Ricardian actions. Importantly, superior resources do not yield advantage without action. For example, a sophisticated piece of equipment (similar to fertile soil) may become relevant only when it enables the firm to undertake some action against rivals (e.g., produce and sell grain). Hence, the managerial task is to link the superior resource appropriately with the suitable Ricardian action.

Our emphasis on the importance of matching resources and actions echoes the arguments of strategy researchers who have stressed the fit between resources and strategy. For example, Michael Porter, in his seminal book *Competitive Strategy*, contended that firms with lowest cost production capability should seek to be the lowest cost producers, implying low-price actions, whereas firms with differentiated advantages in production quality, service, or innovation should seek to differentiate themselves with actions that emphasize quality, service, or innovation. Porter implies that firms failing to achieve a fit between resources and actions would be "stuck in the middle." Consistent with this perspective, we classify Ricardian actions as ones that stem directly from a firm's ownership of superior resources. For example, low-cost actions are Ricardian if the firm has large-scale plant and equipment cost advantages, whereas premium price actions are Ricardian if the firm has high-quality products. Those two options follow directly from a firm's income statement, in that income is a function of sales minus costs. A firm can maximize profit by increasing sales and revenue while holding costs constant, or by lowering costs while holding sales and revenue constant.

In pursuing cost actions, a firm's goal is to exploit and enhance its cost leadership position. In pursuing differentiation, firms undertake actions that exploit and enhance their commanding brand image. Few firms actually have such highly focused action strategies. That is, low-cost firms often take differentiation actions, and differentiator firms often take cost actions. Toyota is a integrated low-cost producer of automobiles but is also well-known for its innovation and high-quality manufacturing of automobiles. In many industries the market leader exploits both differentiation and cost actions. General Motors, Dell Computer, FedEx, and McDonald's all use both types of actions. However, those actions are Ricardian if only they stem from the ownership of scarce resources and the acting firm has a strong resource advantage.

The Ricardian actions discussed in this chapter can be understood best by contrasting them to the entrepreneurial actions of chapter 6. Ricardian actions are deliberate outcomes of plans to exploit unique resources. When taking Ricardian actions, firms can choose between emphasizing lower costs or differentiating and improving products, but a few select firms can choose to integrate both cost and differentiation advantages. Entrepreneurial actions are more spontaneous, based on opportunities created from market disequilibrium. Ricardian actions conform to the criteria of economic efficiency or utility. For example, a firm will arrange its assets and resources to maximize customer value or to minimize its costs and thereby its prices. In so doing, it takes Ricardian actions to maximize advantages over competitors by achieving the lowest cost or the greatest differentiation. Entrepreneurial actions, in contrast, have no such maximum. Credit for Ricardian actions belongs to the owner of the resource, whereas credit for entrepreneurial actions goes to the discoverer whose alertness perceived the opportunity. Finally, Ricardian actions are based on present-day resources or resources known at the time of the action. The future results of Ricardian actions are therefore predictable, as each Ricardian action unfolds from known resources. The discovery process is much more uncertain and difficult to predict. Indeed, the outcomes from entrepreneurial actions cannot be predicted from past events and, as was discussed, depend on competitive uncertainty and blind spots. Table 7.1 lists the key differences between entrepreneurial and Ricardian actions.

Figure 7.1, a subset of the action model of advantage presented in chapter 5, portrays the relationships among resources, Ricardian action, and competitive advantage examined in this chapter.

Low-Cost Resource Advantages

Low-cost resource advantages enable a firm to engage competitors with aggressive low-price actions. Michael Porter argues that low-cost firms

Table 7.1   Key Distinctions between Entrepreneurial and Ricardian Actions

Category	Entrepreneurial Actions	Ricardian Actions
Goal	Avoid rivals	Engage rivals
Source	Opportunity based	Resource based
Intent	Spontaneous, based on opportunities created from disequilibrium	Deliberate outcome of plan to exploit resources
Criteria for evaluation	No guidance on conformance; newness	Conform to criterion of economic efficiency or maximization
Credit	Credit goes to discoverer	Credit goes to owner of resource
Outcome	Unpredictable	Predictable

succeed because rivalry can "only continue to erode profits until those of the next *most* efficient competitor are eliminated and because the less efficient competitors will suffer first in the face of competitive pressures" (emphasis added).[13] Low-cost resources include economies of scale, economies of learning, and efficiencies in capacity utilization, product design, and input costs.

Economies of Scale.   Economies of scale are achieved when the scale of production of a good or service increases and the unit cost of the product or service decreases. More specifically, when an increase in the amount of inputs employed in the production of some good or service results in a more-than-proportionate increase in total output, economies of scale are present. Economies of scale can be obtained by investing in plant and equipment, standardizing products and services, or implementing innovations in

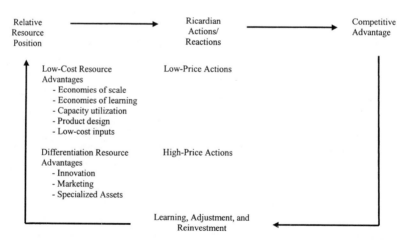

Figure 7.1   Exploiting Advantage by Ricardian Actions.

products and processes. They can also be brought about by spending large amounts of money in purchasing, advertising, R & D, and distribution so as to spread costs over a greater sales volume. Scale economies are important in industries such as steel, automobiles, cigarettes, household detergents, beer, and soft drinks. For example, Henry Ford sought to build economies of scale with the well-known Model T. Investing in large-scale plant and equipment and specializing in one model and one color enabled Ford to be the lowest cost automobile producer. Wal-Mart is a modern-day example of a company that has significant economies of scale. It minimized its distribution costs by building its discount stores around distribution centers that effectively service the needs of Wal-Mart stores within each area. The more discount stores the centers can service, the lower are the total distribution costs.

Financial capital and first-mover advantages are often important in achieving economies of scale. Establishing Wal-Mart's centralized distribution system required capital not only for building centralized inventory warehouses but also for developing an efficient transportation capability. Wal-Mart's trucking fleet is the second largest in America, exceeded only by that of the U.S. Postal Service. Any rival attempting to duplicate Wal-Mart's advantage would require billions of dollars of investment. In addition, rivals such as Kmart were incapable of changing their store location and distribution strategy because of fixed investments and geographic mobility barriers.

Scale economies are often gained by investments in large specialized assets, such as a high-technology auto plant, that a challenger would have to invest heavily to match. If prices stay high and the challenger is able to expand production, it too can achieve low costs. However, if the investment in specialized assets is risky, perhaps because demand is uncertain or the established firm prices its products or services aggressively (close to its costs), the challenger will be deterred.

Economies of Learning. Investing in human resources and organizational coordination to promote economies of learning and improved knowhow is another way to lower unit costs. Economies of learning arise from cost reductions through repetition. Repetition reduces costs by decreasing the time needed to complete a task and by increasing overall coordination. Efficiencies through learning can be linked to organizational structure that maximizes coordination between functions and to human resource policies that promote job stability and productivity. Clearly, employee turnover must be low if the firm is to benefit from learning. Typical measures of learning are cumulative volume in, time or experience in, and cumulative investment in a particular activity.[14] Lincoln Electric Company produces electric arc welders and exploits economies of learning by focusing on productivity. Employees are paid exclusively on productivity and quality and therefore work extremely hard to maximize quality output. Employees also have very long tenure, which promotes and enhances learning.

Lincoln Electric promotes learning by emphasizing volume in production, high personal incentives to make employees productive, programs for employee retention to enhance learning, and a frugal organizational structure that promotes coordination and efficiency.[15]

Achieving economies of learning requires standardization, repetition, and volume. Moreover, in many cases it may require significant capital, a new product or service, or a new mechanism of manufacturing a product or delivering a service. Economies of learning often depend on first-mover advantages. When initial production or service volume is low and the cost of producing the new product or service is high in relation to that of other products, services, or technologies, the costs of learning will be very steep at first, and rivals may view the first-moving action as too risky to imitate. The result is that the first mover's initially steep learning costs level off and decline. As volume increases, knowhow expands and costs decline further.

The challenge for managers is to capture these benefits fully as they accrue, cutting price to increase volume further and move down the learning curve faster than later-responding rivals. In 1909, when his lowest priced car was $850, Henry Ford announced that he would soon sell a Model T Ford for $400. Ford believed his low price for the Model T would give him the volume necessary to gain the experience that would cut his costs substantially. Ford was so successful that steel arriving at one end of the plant would be transformed into a completed car four days later. Inventories were cut by half, and labor expenses were reduced by more than 60 percent. By 1925, the price of the Model T was less than one-fifth what it had been in real dollars in 1909. Ford's market share had increased from 10 to 40 percent.[16]

A firm just beginning to descend the learning curve will be at a cost disadvantage in relation to the firm that has already moved down the curve. Of course, if the firm with learning experience and lower costs keeps its prices high, the less experienced firm may have incentive to move down the curve faster in an attempt to duplicate the learning advantage of the first mover. Hence, the experienced firm must keep the price of its products or services at or below that charged by less experienced rivals. By maintaining competitive prices, the experienced firm can increase volume and experience while thwarting competitive reaction.[17]

Efficient Utilization of Capacity.   The capacity to produce a good or service often involves fixed costs. When the demand for a product or service is low, capacity is underutilized and total unit costs increase. When the demand for a product or service is high, output can be pushed to the extreme, with people working overtime, machines running faster, and normal maintenance being postponed, and costs increase. Therefore, the ability to adjust and manage capacity to meet variations in demand can provide a major cost advantage for firms. Nucor's ability to increase profit despite the depressed state of the U.S. steel industry was due largely to its speedy cuts in fixed operating expenses. Nissan Motors also has been successful in capacity management. Nissan enhanced capacity utilization through modular auto design that promoted greater flexibility, and focused production on 18 basic auto frame designs that Nissan found satisfied 80 percent of its users.[18]

Achieving efficient capacity utilization requires capital investments in flexible technologies, processes, structures, and procedures, as well as management talent that are responsive to changes in demand. Sometimes flexibility comes at the expense of efficiency, as when the firm trades specialization for flexibility. However, if demand may vary substantially, flexibility may provide greater efficiency in the long term. In some industries, changes in demand and technological developments such as flexible manufacturing systems and mass customization have made efficient capacity utilization a more important low-cost resource than economies of scale.

In fact, in such industries, obsolete plant and equipment that once lowered costs through economies of scale could now be a liability and the source of higher fixed costs due to fixed investments.

Efficient Product Design. Designing a good or service to exploit new technology can yield significant increases in productivity, thus lowering total unit costs. For example, the conversion of television sets from a vacuum tube design to a solid state design with modular subassemblies resulted in a 50 percent reduction in the cost of television set components. IBM's first PC printer cost more than $5,000 to build when introduced in 1983 and had more than 150 component parts. After redesign, the IBM Proprinter had only 62 parts, required 3.5 minutes of production time, and offered greater speed and reliability.[19]

Improved efficiency in product design generally requires significant capital investments. For example, the costs associated with designing and developing new models of automobiles escalated dramatically in the 1980s. The new Ford Mondeo cost $6 billion, and the GM Saturn cost $5 billion. Consequently, smaller producers such as Saab, Rover, and AMC/Jeep were unable to develop new models without seeking mergers with larger firms. Similarly, in the software industry the cost of developing a new operating system is in excess of $500 million. The industry leader, Microsoft, spreads the development costs of new operating systems over its installed base of millions of customers, hence can entice its customers to upgrade to the latest Windows version with a low $20 price. In contrast, Apple Computer, which has a much smaller installed base but faces the same development costs, cannot price as effectively because its unit costs are much higher, for example $150 per current customer. Recently, Apple has failed to recognize its cost disadvantages and has had disappointments with "low-cost" products.

Low-Cost Inputs.   Low-cost inputs stem from low labor rates, ownership of or contracts with low cost suppliers, and special relationships with suppliers. Where labor costs are important, efficiencies can be achieved by avoiding unionization or by contracting with labor in areas where it is cheaper. The airline industry has great differences in labor rates among competitors because of union relations and productivity. For example, labor costs at United Airlines, which has had a history of weak union relations and lower productivity, are almost 50 percent of revenues, whereas those at Southwest Airlines, which has had a history of stronger union relations and higher productivity, are only 36 percent of revenues.[20] Often wage rates vary across geographic locations. For example, in labor-intensive industries such as clothing, footwear, handtools, and even animation drawing and programing, U.S. manufactured goods and services are at a significant cost disadvantage to equivalent goods manufactured and services by firms with low-cost labor operating in less developed countries.

When inputs represent a significant percentage of total costs, a cost advantage can be achieved by the acquisition of low-cost sources of supply. For example, Kodak gained a major advantage over other film producers by integrating into film-related chemicals. Because Kodak profitably supplied the chemicals to other film producers, it could be certain its costs were lower than those of its competitors. Moreover, by supplying raw materials to its competitors, Kodak knew exactly what its competitors were attempting to achieve.

Vertical integration generally requires significant capital and first-mover advantages. Widespread integration by rivals might result in limiting or eliminating potential sources of supply. Moreover, to the extent that rivals enter into a bidding war for a supplier, the price may be bid high enough to offset any vertical integration benefit.

Locking up a source of supply by long-term contract also often requires first-mover activity. For example, Pepsi achieved a six-week advantage over Coca-Cola by its early contracting with Nutrasweet for aspartame. Pepsi used that window to market its Diet Pepsi soft drink effectively as the only product on the market with aspartame. In addition, a firm can have a special relationship with suppliers that enables it to cut costs. For example, just-in-time inventory management enables firms to cut inventory costs by working closely with suppliers for on-time delivery. In fact, Japanese firms (e.g., Toyota in automobiles and Toshiba in electronics) that pioneered such efforts have cut costs and improved delivery times.

In many ways, the actions firms take to secure resources are important competitive actions—for example, acting to build plant and equipment ahead of competitors, or to secure a critical input at the lowest possible cost. However, competition for the acquisition of a low-cost resource will ultimately determine the value of the resource to the organization. If competition for a resource is high, the price will be bid up, and the relative value of the resource will, in general, decrease.[21] Ultimately, the resource must be used to take an action that rivals cannot easily emulate if it is to provide value. We now turn to a discussion of Ricardian price actions that explains the value of low-cost resource advantages clearly and concisely.

Ricardian Actions to Exploit
Low-Cost Resource Advantages

The game theory example in figure 7.2 pertains to a firm with strong relative cost advantages (e.g., economies of scale, learning effects, etc.) over a competitor. Those advantages yield the company the lowest costs in the industry. The firm is considering lowering its price 20 percent, to just above its own costs, to achieve further economies of scale and learning in manufacturing and raw material purchasing. The lower price is expected to attract some of the rival's current customers. This action is noted as A in figure 7.2. If the rival chooses not to respond (R_1), the outcome (O_1) will be enhanced advantage due to increased volume and lower unit costs for the actor and a loss for the nonresponder. The rival can try to counter the initial action with a matching price cut (R_2). Even though the responder's costs are higher than the actor's, the outcome (O_2) will be better for the responder than O_1. However, if this response triggers subsequent price cuts by the actor in a second round (A_3), perhaps to a level equal to its own costs, the outcome (O_3) will be worse for the responder than if it had not initially responded. In other words, this pricing battle is one the responder cannot hope to win without achieving an equal cost advantage.

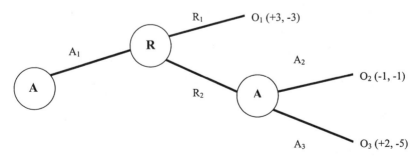

Figure 7.2   Ricardian Action/Reaction and Advantage.

The low-cost actor has a strong overall cost advantage in the pricing war, and the responder's best option is to refrain from prompting escalation of the conflict until it improves its cost structure.

Let consider the competition in the microwave oven industry as an example of such a battle. The microwave oven was invented in the United States more than 40 years ago. Nonetheless, if one buys a microwave oven today, the odds are one in three that the oven was produced 10,000 miles away in Korea by Samsung. Yet it was only in 1979, when U.S. producers were making millions of microwave ovens, that Samsung got its start, producing a few very crude ovens. In fact, Samsung's first microwave oven melted on the test stand. Today, Samsung makes more than 80,000 ovens per week. This story is even more amazing when one considers the competition Samsung conquered—no less than the likes of General Electric and major Japanese producers such as Matsushita. In the early stages of the industry, competition was between General Electric and several Japanese firms, but the Japanese firms had a distinct cost advantage.

> The Japanese weren't dumping. Their plants and product designs were so efficient they could indeed land microwave ovens in the United States cheaper than those coming off GE's new assembly line. Moreover, GE's share was falling even as the world market grew. Other U.S. producers had declined even more. The shift had almost all gone to the Japanese.[22]

That was when Samsung appeared on the scene with only one goal: low-cost production. Viewing the market as global, Samsung invested heavily in product design and efficient large-scale manufacturing. Interestingly, GE was investing in new microwave plant and equipment at the same time as Samsung. However, with early orders from J. C. Penney, Samsung was able to get its cost per oven down to $155. That figure was dramatically lower than GE's cost of $218. The actual sources of the cost differences between the two producers were amazing. For example, GE's labor cost per oven was $8, and Samsung's was 63 cents. Overhead was $30 per oven at GE and 73 cents at Samsung. GE's management costs totaled $10 per oven, and Samsung's were only 2 cents per oven. GE only had two options in responding to Samsung's pricing: invest heavily in an attempt to lower manufacturing costs or subcontract production directly from Samsung. Soon GE announced that it would stop U.S. production of microwave ovens. "From now on, GE would be doing the sales and service side of the product; Samsung, the manufacturing."[23] Samsung was the winner and is now the leading producer of microwave ovens worldwide.

In describing the low-cost strategy, Michael Porter notes that the low-cost firm can earn high profit in an industry despite the presence of strong competitors.[24] By virtue of its low-cost position, the acting firm can still earn profit after its rivals have competed away their profit in price battles. Porter also notes that the lowest cost position guards against buyer power because buyers can bargain prices only as low as those of the next most efficient producer. The low-cost producer also has greater margins for dealing with powerful suppliers.

Differentiation Resource Advantages

Differentiation advantages are more complex than low-cost resource advantages that enable firms to achieve competitive advantage by pricing low. Michael Porter contends: "A firm differentiates itself from its competitors when it provides something unique that is valuable to buyers beyond simply offering a low price."[25] According to Porter, differentiation leads to higher performance to the extent that the price premium achieved exceeds the additional costs of providing the unique product or service. As in the case of cost advantages, the underlying drivers of differentiation must be based on scarcity, so that the differentiation action will be difficult to replicate. Resource advantages that serve as a foundation for differentiation can be broadly classified as advantages in innovation, marketing, and ownership of specialized assets.

Innovation. Developing a product or service that is different often requires innovation. For example, in the tire industry, Firestone and Goodyear dominated for years because of their innovations in bias-ply radial technology. Lim Kunstoff Technology has been promoting innovations in liquid injection molding technology. In tire cord, American Viscose led in rayon, then DuPont in nylon, then Celanese in polyerts. Now DuPont is again ahead with Kevlar.[26] Polaroid was successful in extending its lead in instant photography to the next generation of products through innovation, until digital cameras became the vogue. These examples illustrate that the ability to innovate can be a powerful resource. Three critical characteristics of innovation are R & D spending, R & D process, and R & D property rights, which for the most part capture the variation in a firm's resource position related to innovation.

Consider the former industry leader, Polaroid, which has a virtual monopoly on the production of the instant camera from the 1960s to the 1980s. Assume that a challenging firm such as Kodak hopes to enter that industry segment on the basis of an uncertain innovation that could produce a new and improved instant camera. Kodak does not have access to Polaroid's current technology because of patent protection. Each company decides how much money to spend on developing the innovation. The R & D phase lasts a certain length of time, and the amount of dollars invested determines the intensity of the development effort.

Let us assume that there is no "spillover" in R & D. Therefore, if only one company is successful in developing the new technology, the other will not have access to it. Also, the probability of success for either company is independent of the R & D effort of the other.

If Polaroid is successful in its R & D efforts but Kodak is not, Polaroid will earn profit on the new generation of products of, say, $5 million. Kodak will earn no return and will lose its entire investment in R & D. If only Kodak is successful, it will replace Polaroid as the leader in the instant photography segment of the industry. Kodak will earn $5 million, and Polaroid will receive no return. If both companies are successful in developing the new product, intense competition will drive both companies' earnings to zero. Finally, if neither company successfully develops the technology, Polaroid's leadership position will continue and Kodak will earn no returns.

The preceding example illustrates a high-stakes battle involving capital investments in R & D and chance. It is riskiest for Kodak. Kodak faces not only the possibility of R & D failure and total loss, but also, if successful, the risk of Polaroid's success and intense competition. Polaroid faces similar risks, but if both Polaroid and Kodak are unsuccessful, Polaroid will at least continue to hold its leadership position. If both firms start their investments at the same time and have similar R & D capabilities, the probability of success will be a function of R & D spending.[27]

In addition to R & D spending, organizational expertise plays a key role in the innovation process. For example, 3M's practice of encouraging its scientists to use their time on individual "pet projects," allowing them to manage and partially own those projects if successful, is a unique part of 3M's culture and structure. Gillette's ability to manage the innovation process is also more than a simple matter of dollars. Schick won rights to produce Gillette's Sensor twin-blade razor but has been unable to duplicate the product's performance. Gillette has designed and developed unique equipment to produce the Sensor that makes it impossible for rivals to imitate. Sidney Winter has argued that an organization's knowledge or expertise can serve as a key scarce resource as long as the knowledge is (1) tacit rather than definable, (2) not readily observable, and (3) complex as opposed to simple.[28]

Knowledge and expertise that meet those criteria will be scarce and difficult for rivals to duplicate. By using the relative innovation experience of each competitor, we can modify the probability distributions for Kodak and Polaroid in the game model outlined previously. Assume Polaroid is much more experienced in R & D because of its industry leadership position. The experience can either cut Polaroid's R & D costs and provide the same probability of success, or it can be used to hasten the R & D process, providing a timing advantage to Polaroid. Kodak, without such experience, can only rely on R & D spending. The advantage clearly goes to the more experienced Polaroid, as it either lowers its R & D cost or increases the speed of development. This game theory model reflects what actually happened in the Polaroid example outlined in the beginning of this chapter.

Acting to acquire property rights for an innovative good or service can also be a critical method of achieving differentiation and blunting competitive reaction. The importance of property rights and innovation has been recognized since the British Parliament passed the 1623 Law of Monopolies, which secured patent law as we know it today. Property rights have important legal meaning to their owners in that, if a right is breached by a rival through imitation, the property right owner can seek a remedy in a court of law. The four types of property rights are patents, copyrights, trademarks, and trade secrets. Their value as a competitive source of differentiation varies substantially, depending on several factors.

Patents are an exclusive right to a new product or process. Patents are the outcome of some inventive activity that is both new and useful. Patent laws vary by country, but in the United States a patent can be valid for 17 years. Polaroid's development of the Land camera and the SX-70 in instant photography is an example of effective innovation involving patents. In contrast, Schick was successful in overcoming Gillette's patents on its Sensor safety razor. The logic behind patent law is that in creating innovations, organizations generally expend resources. Often there are several false starts, which can be very expensive. For example, in the pharmaceutical industry only about 10 percent of drugs actually reach the market.[29] However, if rivals could imitate successful innovations without facing the development costs, there would be little incentive for innovation. The patent system was developed to prevent this so-called free-rider problem. The goal of the patent system is to enable the innovator to reap sufficient profit to cover the expense of innovation and innovation failures.

Copyrights provide exclusive production and marketing rights to the creators of artistic works. They are similar to patents in establishing ownership but pertain only to intellectual property. Copyright law in the United States is predicated on the 1710 Statute of Anne in English common law that gave protection to the rights of writers, artists, and composers. Today, copyrights are also granted to software developers. Copyrights are distinct from patents and trademarks in that the property right is protected for the life of the developer plus 50 years. A copyright relates to the *form of expression* rather than the subject matter; thus copyrights apply to the expressions of artists, writers (including software developers), and composers. John Grisham, author of *The Firm* and *The Client*, was sued for violating the copyright of another writer with his book *The Chamber*. Trade sanctions have been proposed against several Asian countries for violation of copyrights in the production of compact disks, software, and books.

Trademarks are words, symbols, or other indications used to distinguish a firm's goods or services. They are often the basis of brand recognition. Well-known trademarks include Nike, Nutrasweet, NBC, Apple, IBM, and Coca-Cola. A trademark can be "any word, name, symbol or distinguishing device, or any combination thereof, adopted and used by a manufacturer or merchant to identify goods and distinguish them from those manufactured or sold by others."[30] An important qualifier for a trademark is that the name, insignia, or mark be used commercially. Trademarks are granted for 20 years by the U.S. Patent Office.

Trade secrets often relate to formulas, recipes, and processes, and their protection from copy is less well defined. Good examples of innovative formulas are Coca-Cola's original cola, McDonald's french fries, and Starbuck's coffee. Trade secrets are proprietary information used to gain an advantage in manufacture or commercialization of products or services. Because such "inside" information is often available to employees as they carry out their work, it is difficult to protect despite copyright laws. Indeed, after Steve Wozniak left Hewlett-Packard to start Apple Computer with Steve Jobs, there were claims and counterclaims about the proprietary ownership of trade secrets and software concepts between the two firms.

The support of creative activities, including the development and commercialization of formulas, trademarks, and works of art, often involves substantial front-end costs. That is, once the investments are made, they are irretrievable. To justify such investments, the developer expects some degree of protection from competitive reaction. That is the idea behind intellectual property rights laws. However, in reality, defending property rights is difficult and expensive.

Property rights can act to deter competitive reaction but are by no means effective in all cases. Indeed, in some industries, such as semiconductors, electronics, and biotechnology, and in some countries, especially many Asian countries, intellectual property right laws are relatively easy to circumvent. Simply filing the documents necessary for competitive protection often provides information that aids competitive imitation.

Marketing. Offering a different product or service requires customer communication. Potential customers are always looking for ways to understand and become knowledgeable about the goods they acquire. Judging important characteristics of a product or service through inspection is often difficult, and characteristics of many products or services can be discovered only through experience. Knowledge is developed over time by trial and error. That situation is a classic game theory model for the producer of the good or service. For example, the producer has an option of offering a product that cuts the customer's costs or one that enhances the customer's operating satisfaction in relation to commodity products on the market. Both options require a price higher than those of other products.

The customer can select either the high-priced product or a low-priced commodity-type product. If the features of the product that allow it to lower the customer's costs or enhance the customer's operating satisfaction cannot be detected by inspection, the low-priced traditional commodity product will be selected even though the customer may be better off with the higher priced product. Therefore, the challenge for the producer is to find some credible way of signaling the product's superior features. Among the actions the producer can take to make the product more credible are offering a warranty, developing a reputation for quality through effective advertising or word of mouth, offering money-back guarantees, or providing a high-quality environment where the service is offered.

Market signaling and reputation are very important for services and products in which quality is difficult to measure even after the purchase. For example, in banking and law firms, the quality and reliability of the organization cannot be ascertained easily even after a relationship has been established. Therefore, those types of organizations rely on investments to produce symbols of prosperity and security, such as office decor, proper attire, status symbol partners, and perceptions of size.

Signaling is most important for product or service advantages that can be experienced only after purchase. Advertising will be effective in signaling such advantages because commodity producers of goods and services will not expect repeat purchases. Advertising a national product can be expensive. For example, the advertising budgets for Coca-Cola and Budweiser are approximately $500 million per year.

Extensive advertising and reputation building through packaging and other symbols or signals generally yield high brand recognition. Effective brand names inform customers of performance characteristics associated with the good or service. When products or services with strong brand names provide superior quality to customers over time, customers become loyal repeat purchasers and do not easily switch to a competitor's product or service. Marlboro, McDonald's, Mercedes Benz, Nike, and Coca-Cola are brand names well recognized around the world. Such brand names are scarce organizational resources that are very difficult and expensive for rivals to duplicate.

Specialized Assets. A common source of differentiation for a firm is a specialized asset. We have already examined property rights in discussing innovation. Specialized and scarce assets in the form of modern plant and equipment designed for a special product or ownership of a special input may also be a source of differentiation. Long-term contracts that tie up the most favorable distribution system may confer differentiation as well. For example, Coke and Pepsi had significant advantages over challenges, such as Dr. Pepper and Seven-Up, through the ownership of their franchise bottling and distribution systems in the soft drink industry.

A firm can obtain specialized assets in two ways, by acquiring them in the open market or developing them internally. The ability to acquire specialized assets or resources in the open market depends on their scarcity and mobility. A resource is immobile when it cannot be purchased without losing its value in the course of the acquisition.[31] In particular, even if a resource is mobile per se, it may still lose its value during acquisition because of transaction costs. Transaction costs are greatest for highly specialized assets.[32]

The alternative to buying the asset is to develop it internally. We have already explained that rivals have difficulty replicating actions that are based on unique organizational knowledge and routines. For example, GM's attempt to imitate the Toyota-style team-based production techniques used in its NUMMI joint venture at Fremont, California, at the GM Van Nuys plant just 400 miles away involved complex learning and adjustment problems that remained unsolved for more than two years.[33]

Like acting to acquire low-cost resources, acting to innovate, market, or acquire specialized assets can be considered a critical competitive action. Indeed, the game models we used to explain innovation as a race and marketing as signaling capture this idea. Competition for resources will determine the resources' ultimate value. Nonetheless, our primary focus is to take resource positions as given and to explore how managers can use the resources to undertake Ricardian actions that impede competitive reaction.

Ricardian Actions to Exploit
Differentiation Resource Advantages

Having described forms of differentiation, we next illustrate how a differentiated firm can exploit its position. Reconsider figure 7.2, but now from the perspective of the firm with a relative resource advantage in high-technology plant and equipment, which yields products superior in quality to those of a less well-endowed rival. The firm with the differentiation resource advantage is considering acting to introduce a one-year product warranty in place of the standard 30-day warranty, while maintaining its current price. To do so is advantageous for the firm because its products are of such high quality that they rarely require repairs. The new one-year product warranty is expected to attract some of the rival's current customers. This action is noted as A_1 in figure 7.2. If the rival chooses not to respond (R_1), the outcome (O_1) will be an increased advantage for the actor and a loss for the nonresponder. The rival can also try to counter the initial action with a matching one-year warranty of its own (R_2). If the actor does not take subsequent action (A_2), the outcome (O_2) will be better for the responder than O_1, but will increase its costs substantially because it lacks the ability to produce such a high-quality product. That is, its products will have more warranty claims because they are of inferior quality. However, if this response triggers a subsequent extension of the acting firm's warranty to two years (A_3), the outcome (O_3) will be worse for the responder than if it had not initially responded. Therefore, this battle is one the responder, which lacks the differentiation resource advantage, cannot hope to win. The actor has a strong advantage in this warranty war, and the responder's best option is to refrain from prompting escalation of the conflict until it improves its resource position.

In the preceding example, the firm without the resource advantage lacks the necessary resources to engage successfully in a warranty war. From a resource-based perspective, resources must be scarce and heterogeneous across firms to produce advantage. Rivals may be motivated to imitate but are prevented or blocked from imitation because of their inability to secure in a timely way the resources needed for action. They lack the resources and capability to match the high quality of the actor's product or service.

American Express's planned exploitation of its unique information-processing capability is an example of a Ricardian action. The *New York Times* reported that American Express's best chance for success in the hotly contested credit card market is for it to exploit information technology, in which it has "undisputed advantage in the area of personalized rewards." More specifically American Express plans to introduce a new rewards program to its cardholders based on its unique "ability to manipulate vast amounts of information it collects on what card holders purchase."[34] That is, American Express will provide rewards tailored to individual cardholders. Monthly statements no longer will come stuffed with offers made indiscriminately to all cardholders. With the new introduction, particular rebates and rewards will be offered only to individuals who are likely to find them appealing. American Express will make the determination by analyzing each individual's buying patterns. For example, a monthly statement showing a charge for a United Airlines flight to Europe might offer a 23 percent discount on the next United flight. Barry Hill, vice president for product development, noted: "Although there's a flurry of rewards programs out there now, they are fairly crude. The new program will allow us to vary the pricing, vary the discount, vary the reward option, right down to the personal level."

As the article argued, "to run a personalized rewards program requires collecting card-holder data on a scale that American Express—and not Visa or MasterCard—is capable of." American Express owns and manages what is known as a closed-loop network, whereas Visa and Mastercard employ decentralized banking systems and their information is scattered throughout those systems. Visa and MasterCard, therefore, will need substantial time to react to the American Express action because they lack the key resource. While both Visa and MasterCard were eventually able to follow American Express's lead in exploiting information technology to personalize rewards, they have relied much more on exploiting affinity cards or reward cards that offer perks of their affiliated partners, for example, frequent flyer miles from an airline or cash rebates from an automobile manufacturer. To date, all three credit card rivals are continuing to exploit information technology capabilities such as using wireless chips that will allow users to pay anywhere for anything.[35]

Predicting Competitive Reactions

The principle behind Ricardian actions, and indeed their appeal, lies in the fact that they are based on relative resource advantages the acting firm singularly possesses. Ownership of a scarce resource and its exploitation through Ricardian action, along with a positive customer demand, create the opportunity for high profit and an improved market position for the acting firm. However, any successful action that is accompanied by abnormal profit will create an incentive for other firms to attempt to respond and imitate. Several complex factors can be used to predict competitive reaction. We examine three related variables: the degree of resource imbalance between the acting firm and potential responders, the degree to which the action threatens one or more competitors, and the degree to which competitors are interdependent for the same customer and resources.

Degree of Resource Imbalance

The greater the resource imbalance between the acting firm and competitors or potential responders, the greater will be the delay in response. Greater resource advantages enable the firm to undertake more significant Ricardian actions, which cause greater response delay. For example, we have found in our studies that response was slower after Ricardian actions, requiring unique resources than after actions requiring fewer and more general resources. Table 7.2 details the relationship between Ricardian actions and the speed of response in four industries. In a study of Ricardian new product introductions and imitative responses in the telecommunications, PC, and brewing industries, we found significant delays in responses associated with Ricardian actions. In fact, the average response time after Ricardian actions was 995 days, 577 days, and 1,630 days,

Table 7.2   Ricardian Actions and the Speed of Response in Four Industries

	Electrical Manufacturing	High Technology	Computer Retailing	Domestic Airlines
Percentage of moves that were Ricardian	81	44	15	16
Response time to Ricardian actions	271 days	540 days	47 days	34 days
Response time to tactical actions	124 days	165 days	24 days	8 days

respectively. Those figures compare favorably with the listing in table 7.2 of average response times after tactical actions, which require fewer resources. In the same study we found that the speed of imitative response was related inversely to radicality of the Ricardian action, or the degree to which the action departed from industry norms. As the radicality or innovativeness of the Ricardian action increased, the speed of competitive response was reduced. Moreover, the greater the resource differential between acting and responding firms, as measured in terms of marketing expenditures, the greater was the delay in response.

In today's competitive environment there appears to be no perfectly safe ground, as even patented products and processes are being imitated. For example, one study found that across 12 industries, patents were judged effective for 65 percent of pharmaceutical inventions, 30 percent of chemical inventions, 10 to 20 percent of inventions in petroleum and metal products, and less than 10 percent of inventions in electronics, instruments, metals, and textiles.[36] In addition, a survey of 650 R & D executives showed that for both products and processes, the nonpatent strategic advantages of being an innovator were more important than patent protection.[37] Edwin Mansfield and his colleagues found that about 60 percent of successful patented inventions were imitated within four years.[38] A far-reaching study of unpatented new products showed that R & D costs of imitating unpatented new products exceeded 50 percent of the original innovator's R & D costs in 86 of the 127 industries. Moreover, duplication costs exceeded 75 percent of the first-moving firm's costs in 40 percent of the industries studied.[39] Because information about patented products is made publicly available to rivals, such products may require fewer resources to duplicate than unpatented products, for which information may be more expensive to obtain.

Degree of Threat

A Ricardian action may evoke a response even when the responder is at a significant resource disadvantage. In particular, if the acting firm directly confronts and threatens a rival firm, some reaction can he expected regardless of its appropriateness or effectiveness. Amazon eventually responded by offering its on online auctions to challenge eBay's dominance. After eBay threatened Amazon by entering the fixed-priced format and offering surplus new goods of corporate sellers, Amazon responded by offering used, refurbished, and new goods of independent sellers on its web site.[40] Wal-Mart's opening of almost 300 stores per year meant that it would soon directly threaten its rival Kmart, eventually driving Kmart into bankruptcy. In our studies of Ricardian new product introductions in the telecommunications, PC, and brewing industries, we found that as the perceived threat of a new product introduction increased, that is, as the degree to which a new product introduction directly threatened a rival increased, the speed of competitive reaction also increased, despite the resource difference between competitors.

Chapter 6 introduced the notion that resource-poor firms can exploit action uncertainty and competitive blind spots. Such strategy is also appropriate for firms with relative resource advantages. Resource-rich firms that want to avoid threatening weaker rivals and forcing them to respond and escalate conflict should take Ricardian actions that exploit uncertainty and blind spots. A Ricardian action such as introduction of an innovative product might be viewed as so radical that rivals will want to take a wait-and-see attitude before attempting to develop the resources necessary to respond.

Degree of Competitor Interdependence

The extent to which firms are interdependent in the marketplace is another important predictor of response. Interdependence is defined as the extent to which the actions of one firm directly affect or influence the behavior of its rivals. For the most part, firms are not independent in the market.

They feel each other's actions and, whatever the reason, are prone to react. In some markets, interdependence is very high, and every action is felt directly by one or more rivals. In other markets, the degree of interdependence is not as extreme. The greater the market interdependence between rivals, the greater is the likelihood of competitor reaction, regardless of the resource imbalance between rivals or the threat of the action to rivals.

The degree of competitive interdependence is influenced by two very important factors: growth in customer demand and the number of competitors. Customer demand can be measured by the growth in industry sales. When industry growth is high, competitors are less likely to feel each other's. That is, under conditions of high demand, everyone in the industry can benefit from less rivalry. Consequently, the response to a Ricardian action taken in a high-growth industry will be slower than the response to a Ricardian action taken in a low-growth industry. In our studies of new product rivalry in the telecommunications, PC, and brewing industries, we observed that response times were longer when industry growth was high. Relatedly, we observed that competitors perceived actions as less threatening in high-growth industries, which is perhaps why reactions were slower. As growth slowed, as happened in the PC industry particularly, actions and reactions increased in frequency and speed, and rivalry increased dramatically. In fact, response time dropped from an average of 34 days to just 1 day![41]

The number of competitors in an industry also influences the degree of interdependence between firms. As the number of competitors increases in a market or industry, so does the likelihood that the actions of one firm will affect the others. Again, in our studies of Ricardian actions in the telecommunications, PC, and brewing industries, we observed that competitive response became faster as the number of competitors in the industry increased. And managers indicated that as the number of firms in their industry increased, so did the likelihood that a competitive action would threaten their business.

Hence, despite the advantages a Ricardian action offers, managers must be cognizant of how their actions will affect and be reacted to by rivals. The likelihood, speed, and magnitude of response will be a function of the resource imbalance between rivals, the degree of competitive threat, the degree of competitor interdependence, and the rivals' ability to predict each other's behavior. An understanding of those variables will aid the manager in formulating and implementing effective Ricardian actions.

Value Chain Position and Ricardian Action

The competitive dynamics research on which this book is based has explained firm performance by focusing on characteristics of observable market-based moves, including aggressiveness, speed, radicality and simplicity. Earlier in this chapter we discussed the connection between resources and action and the need for a good fit. For example, and as noted in chapter 6, when firms are at a disadvantage in terms of their relative resource position (vis-à-vis competition) they should seek to avoid confronting rivals with market actions. Presumably, such firms would not hold the resources to effectively compete. In contrast, as we show in this chapter, when a firm has a specific resource advantage, the firm should directly engage the competition with Ricardian actions, which exploit firms' specific resources. Ideally, rivals will have difficulty responding to Ricardian actions because they will lack the necessary resources to respond. Importantly, we argue that for resources to have value, they must be exploited by taking market actions. Thus, from our point of view, merely holding a resource advantage does not in itself confer any special value to the firm.

Nucor, with its significant cost advantage, can price its products at the level of the competition and earn greater profits than the competition (because of the lower costs of its resources). Or it can lower its prices below those of the competition and generate new customers (increase market share) and still keep profits high, depending upon its cost advantage. Again, Nucor is exploiting a low-cost capability, as reflected in its resource endowments. If Nucor failed to do either of these two alternatives it would not maximize value. In this context, value is realized by taking actions that create favorable reply from customers—a low price that generates more sales, and Nucor's low cost of production (resource advantage).

There is also a relationship between the level of resource advantage and the scale of action. More specifically, the greater the level or degree of resource advantage, the greater the potential for scale of action and for exploiting advantage. Andy Grove from Intel describes how the Japanese producers of DRAMs used a 10 percent rule to drive Intel out of the DRAM business. At the time, DRAMs had become a commodity business, and the Japanese were the low-cost producers. The 10 percent rule meant that the Japanese would cut prices 10 percent on every one of Intel's customers until Intel gave up on that customer. Intel eventually exited the DRAM business.

Often firms enjoy multiple advantages in resources. Consider the video game producer Nintendo, which in the early 1990s had advantages in software production, low-cost manufacturing capability for hardware, security chips for its software, customer service center, and extensive sales force. Nintendo could engage the competition on the basis of one single area of advantage (e.g., pricing of its game station), or it could take on the competition in multiple areas (e.g., new game introductions, marketing promotions, etc). Therefore, the greater the scope of a firm's advantages across the value chain, the greater the potential for alternative types of action. In other words, the firm with multiple resource advantages may engage the rivals in multiple areas. Figure 7.3 portrays the value chain position of a firm such as Nintendo. As can be observed, a firm with such a broad set of advantages can effectively engage the competition on a number of dimensions. Resource poorer rivals may have a difficult managing such a battle.

Summary

This chapter examines the case of firms with relative internal resource advantages over rivals. We focus primarily on resources that can be owned

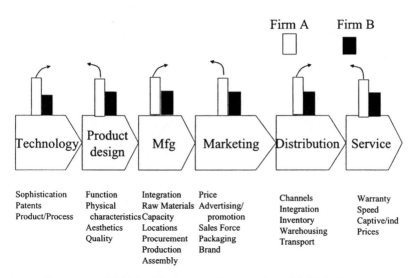

Figure 7.3   Multiple Advantages—Engage along Multiple Fronts.

by the firm and are in short supply. The goal of Ricardian actions is to engage a competitor directly. We demonstrate that when scarce resources are linked effectively to appropriate Ricardian actions, competitive response can be impeded and delayed. Nonetheless, managers must understand their competitive environment and how their Ricardian actions will influence rivals. The greater the advantage and the greater the scope of advantages across the value chain, the more effectively a focal firm may engage the competition.

Chapter 8

DEFENDING AGAINST RIVALS AS A DOMINANT FIRM

The Role of Deterrent Actions

For almost 100 years, American Telephone and Telegraph Company (A T & T) had a monopoly in providing long-distance telephone services. In the late 1960s, the long-distance market was opened to competition, and A T & T responded aggressively to new competitors such as MCI by sharply lowering prices. Despite the subsequent divestiture of its local Bell System companies in 1984 and the deregulation of the industry in 1996, which allowed long-distance and local telephone companies to compete in each other's markets, A T & T has been able to maintain its leadership in the long-distance market, holding steady with market share of about 35 percent in 2003. Its closest rival, MCI, has less than 20 percent of the market.[1]

General Motors has dominated its industry since 1931, when it moved past Ford Motor Company to become the number 1 U.S. automobile maker. Between 1976 and 1983, GM products accounted for nearly 60 percent of domestic auto production; over that period, GM engaged in aggressive product proliferation, fully occupying the available product space to discourage entry, and established a ubiquitous, exclusive distribution network that constituted a considerable entry barrier.[2] Although GM's market share has eroded in recent years and Toyota has surpassed Ford to number 2 in market share, GM is still the number 1 domestic auto manufacturer with around 27 percent of the U.S. market in 2002.[3]

These two examples illustrate that industry leaders can act to defend their positions and maintain long-term dominance. Whereas chapter 6 detailed how firms with limited resources can act by undertaking entrepreneurial actions, and chapter 7 described how firms with superior resources can exploit and enhance their advantages with Ricardian actions, this chapter examines how firms with dominant market share can exploit and protect their market power advantage. Table 8.1 highlights key distinctions among the entrepreneurial actions discussed in chapter 6, the Ricardian actions discussed in chapter 7, and the deterrent actions discussed in this chapter. Dominant firms are strong enough to fight and win head-on battles with fringe competitors and new entrants. These "Goliaths" have the enviable, but not easy, task of fending off the fledgling "Davids" of the marketplace. Goals for firms in dominant market positions are to deter market entry and protect their superior relative resource advantages.

Recall from chapter 5 that the three central components of the action model of advantage are resources, competitive action and reaction, and competitive advantage. Figure 8.1 shows the links of the model discussed here. This chapter examines how dominant firms protect their advantage through deterrent actions and reactions, which we define as competitive moves made from a position of market power. Only dominant firms can make deterrent moves. Moreover, deterrent actions and reactions are specific moves that firms take to both exploit and protect their strong market positions.

We use the term "deterrent" to describe actions based on a critical resource component, strong market position, or high market share. The term is not meant to suggest that dominant firms should engage in tactics

Table 8.1   Key Distinctions among Entrepreneurial, Ricardian, and Deterrent Actions

Category	Entrepreneurial Actions	Ricardian Actions	Deterrent Actions
Goal	Avoid rivals	Engage rivals	Deter rivals
Source	Opportunity based	Resource based	Market based
Intent	Spontaneous, based on opportunities created from disequilibrium	Deliberate outcome of plan to exploit resources	Deliberate outcome of plan to defend resource platform
Criteria for evaluation	No guidance on conformance; newness	Conform to criterion of economic efficiency or maximization	Conform to the criterion of long-term profit maximization, but not economic efficiency
Credit	Credit goes to discoverer	Credit goes to owner of resource	Avoid credit
Outcome	Unpredictable	Predictable	Predictable

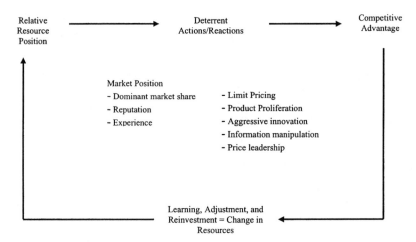

Figure 8.1   Exploiting Advantage by Deterrent Actions.

that improperly restrict competition. We do not think deterrent actions, as we use the term, are unethical or illegal. Indeed, the final section of this chapter explores in some detail the antitrust proscription of illegal monopolization of an industry to help managers distinguish between deterrent actions, which properly take advantage of strong market positions, and actions that constitute illegal monopolization of an industry. However, firms with strong market positions should anticipate close antitrust scrutiny and frequent legal challenges, particularly in the form of private antitrust suits initiated by competitors.

We first explore the market position resource advantage. The notion of market share as a resource is explained, as are reputation and experience—additional resources that often accompany market leadership. Next, we describe deterrent actions that slow the rate of competitive reaction, expansion by fringe challengers, and new entry. We then use a game theory framework to analyze the actions and competitive reactions that market leaders use to achieve competitive advantage. A critical concern for managers of firms in dominant positions is the antitrust statutes pertaining to monopolization and attempted monopolization. Accordingly, we examine in some detail how monopolization prohibitions have been interpreted and what types of behavior might attract suits by the Justice Department.

Market Position as a Resource

The resource-based view of the firm highlights tangible and intangible resources of the firm.[4]

However, a firm's market position, while clearly of a different nature from intangible resources, can also be an important asset. Market position is defined as a firm's market share, and its value is supported by IO and strategy research showing significant positive relationships between market share and profitability.[5] Moreover, large market share is rare, held by only one or a few firms in a given market, and difficult to copy. In addition, high market share is often a key objective of smaller firms. Consider as examples BMW's goal to "beat out Mercedes-Benz as the number one maker of premium cars in the world" and not to "accept the position of number two,"[6] Fox News's resolve to overtake CNN in cable news,[7] Nike's vow to take the lead in the athletic shoe market, DEC's determination to regain the number 2 position in the workstation market and then to be number 1, and Ford's goal to be number 1 and supplant GM in the auto industry for the first time since 1931.[8]

The value of incumbency and the range of strategies employed to deter other firms from gaining leadership positions are well documented.[9] The notion that market share is a resource is also supported by research on first-mover advantages and switching costs.[10] Firms with a strong customer base in a given period have a significant advantage in competing for customers in ensuing periods. Consumer inertia—selection of the same products as in the past from force of habit—is strong. For many products, however, more explicit switching costs are incurred in choosing a firm different from the one chosen in the past. For example, a consumer who opts to do his or her checking account business with a different bank must go through the trouble of making sure all checks have come in, closing the account with the original bank, and opening an account with a new bank. Switching costs strongly deter consumers from making such changes and clearly work to the advantage of firms with strong market positions. In other words, a firm with a strong market position for a product or service with high switching costs has a head start in subsequent periods over firms with fewer customers. Firms with high market share also frequently have economies of scale in manufacturing, marketing, and finance that can lead to cost advantages as described in chapter 7.

Additionally, in conjunction with their market position, market leaders often have a multidimensional array of resources, including reputation and experience. In general, a firm's reputation has important consequences in the marketplace. A firm can have a reputation as an aggressive instigator of rivalry or as an aggressive responder to rivals' efforts to make inroads into its customer base.[11] Alternatively, a firm can be largely passive, with a docile or live-and-let-live image. Reputation has been studied both in the management literature and with IO game theory models. A firm's reputation has been discovered to affect rivals' tendencies to imitate actions and the number and speed of responses to competitive actions.[12]

Reputation can be either an asset or a liability. It is an asset if it influences rivals' actions in a desirable way and a liability if it helps rivals predict or anticipate competitive moves or responses. Reputation is particularly relevant for market share leaders. Large firms tend to receive greater scrutiny than smaller firms, so other firms have knowledge about market share leaders.[13] Because of their enhanced visibility, large firms should ensure that their reputations are favorable. We will examine the role of reputation-enhancing actions in a game theory context later.

Kodak is a good example of a firm using its leadership reputation to influence rivals. Kodak's dominance in the photographic industry was derived from its leadership in film technology. From its first introduction of color film for amateur photographers, Kodak was able to outdistance every other film company in almost every aspect of photography. Kodak was the first to foresee potential for color slides and prints in the consumer market. In fact, not until 1954, when the Justice Department forced Kodak to sell film and processing separately, were competitors able to participate in the color photography products market. Over the 20-year period that Kodak garnered all of the film and processing profits of the color market, it was able to prevent the formation of independent photofinishing laboratories with its reputation as a fierce competitor.

Even after the Justice Department decree, Kodak was able to improve on its previous success by constantly forcing competitors to upgrade their quality. Most competitors simply did not have the research expertise to continue the fight. During the 1950s, Kodak effectively displaced all foreign and domestic competitors from the amateur photography market in the United States. In addition, it successfully defended itself from major competitors such as Bell & Howell and Du Pont. Du Pont described how its color film research program failed against Kodak's market dominance. Each time it was able to improve its film to meet Kodak's high quality, Kodak film would mysteriously become even better. In 1961, when Du Pont's film was finally ready for introduction to the amateur market, at a cost to tens of millions of dollars, Kodak responded to the action with Kodachrome II, a color slide film with much better quality than the original against which the Du Pont entry was targeted. Du Pont eventually withdrew its product from the market. Kodak's well-known reputation for taking on any foe has since caused other rivals to reevaluate plans. In 1976, most competitive color film products were sold at a slight premium over Kodak's prices. In fact, most of Kodak's competitors owed their existence to a small group of users who wanted to avoid the mass market image of Kodak.[14] Kodak has maintained its dominance in film sales, with close to 70 percent of the U.S. market in the 2000s, and leveraged that market position to take advantage of growth opportunities arising from globalization and digital imaging technology. Internationally, Kodak holds a strong presence in Europe and Japan and in emerging foreign markets like eastern Europe. In the digital arena, Kodak leads in photo-quality paper for inkjets with a 40 percent market share and holds a number 2 position behind Sony in the U.S. (and among the top three in the world) for digital camera sales.[15]

In chapter 1 we described the extreme competition between Ralston Purina and rivals in the pet food industry, and in chapters 5 and 7 we discussed Microsoft and eBay's dominance in the software and online auction industry, respectively. Each of these firms has developed a reputation in its industry as a very aggressive industry leader that fights at all costs to win. By aggressively engaging Quaker Oats with product imitations, a huge array of new products, amid significant price cutting, Ralston forced Quaker to exit the industry and built a reputation for combative behavior. That reputation signals its willingness to fight to all current rivals and potential entrants. Similarly, by hawkishly attacking Apple and IBM with low prices, aggressive marketing campaigns, and product updates, Microsoft developed a reputation for aggressive, belligerent behavior. Likewise, by leveraging its network effects of a large customer base and launching a series of preemptive moves such as marketing alliances and user feedbacks, eBay minimized the competitive threat of Amazon.com's entry into online auctions.

In addition to reputation, dominant firms often have an experience resource advantage. Specifically, as discussed in chapter 5, prior experience with manufacturing processes and other aspects of firm operations can give a firm a learning curve advantage over less experienced rivals. In this respect, the Ricardian cost advantages discussed in chapter 5 intersect with the market share advantage examined in this chapter.

Deterrent Actions to Exploit a Strong Market Position

We define deterrent actions and reactions as moves taken by dominant firms to deter rivals and defend market position.[16] A substantial literature in industrial organization economics considers the set of strategies a firm can employ to deter entry and prolong a strong market position. Deterrent moves include limit pricing, predatory pricing, product proliferation, aggressive/preemptive innovation, information manipulation, price leadership, learning curve effects, and similar tactics. Each is discussed in turn. We note that while dominant firms with resource advantages vis-à-vis their rivals can clearly pursue Ricardian advantages to further enhance market position, the focus here is on the more defensive deterrent actions designed to protect or slow the erosion of market share.

Limit Pricing

Limit pricing involves setting a lower price than would otherwise be most profitable to inhibit or slow the rate of new entry.[17] A firm with a strong market position could choose to exploit its market power by charging high prices and obtaining maximum short-term profit. However, over time the high prices and profit will attract entry and responses by competitors, which will erode the firm's market position. Alternatively, the firm could focus solely on inhibiting response by charging very low prices. It thus would retain its market leadership over a longer period, but obtain relatively small profit in each period. With limit-pricing action, a firm chooses the middle ground between those two options, charging a price lower than the one that would maximize short-term profit in an effort to inhibit entry but riot so low as to eliminate profit and entry completely. A firm engaging rivals with limit-pricing actions will generally lose market share over time in a gradual, almost calculated way but reap substantial excess profit while dominant. In other words, a dominant firm prices to maximize net present value of revenues in the long term and, in so doing, concedes market share to challengers over time. General Motors' use of a limit pricing strategy is an example.

General Motors first earned leadership through its wide range of model offerings and its yearly model modification. According to James Brian Quinn, who conducted an extensive study of GM's practices,

> GM had developed a complete spectrum of automobiles, consisting of five well-known lines. Each line had several models, occupied a specified price-quality niche, changed its styles annually, and competed not just with other manufacturers but also—at the margin—with other GM lines. This basic posture continued through the 1950s and well into the 1960s. Each line fulfilled a designated portion of GM's goal "to supply a car for every purse and every purpose."[18]

In many ways, GM has been the leader of the domestic auto industry. As of 1983, GM had nearly twice as many dealer outlets as Ford, its largest competitor since the 1940s. GM outspent its rivals on overall advertising in 1982, but spent the least per new car sold. GM is also the price leader, as it appears to lead or prevent price increases by Ford and Chrysler. During the period from 1947 to 1983, GM had the highest average profit rate, 19.5 percent.

Scholars examining the U.S. auto industry have concluded that GM apparently followed a limit-pricing strategy for years. It priced below short-term profit-maximizing levels but above competitive levels. Market share was gradually conceded to the Japanese.[19] However, had GM priced at higher levels to maximize short-term profit—that is, not pursued a limit-pricing strategy—its market position would have eroded much more rapidly, as its higher prices would have made entry even more attractive to other producers.

Predatory Pricing

One very aggressive form of limit pricing has been called predatory pricing. The term was popularized in the late nineteenth century to describe how firms use low prices to drive rivals out of business. The idea behind predatory pricing is that a firm lowers its price until it is below competitors' average cost, thereby forcing competitors to lower their prices below average cost and thus lose money. If rivals fail to cut their prices, they will lose all customers to the lower price player. If they do cut their prices, they will eventually go bankrupt because the prices will be lower than cost. After the competitors have been forced out of the market, the predatory firm raises its price, compensating itself for the money its lost while engaging in predatory pricing and thereafter earning higher profit.[20]

Predatory pricing theory developed with the famous Standard Oil Company case in which John D. Rockefeller was accused of cutting prices to drive competitors, such as Pure Oil Company, out of business. A more recent example involved Wal-Mart. In 1993, a state court in Arkansas ruled that the country's largest retailer was illegally engaging in predatory pricing by selling pharmacy products below its costs.[21] The Arkansas court ruled that Wal-Mart's pricing policies, as carried out in its discount stores, had the purpose "of injuring competitors and destroying competition" as defined in the Arkansas Unfair Trade Practices Act. The court awarded $289,407 in damages and enjoined Wal-Mart's stores from selling items below cost. The court ruled that Wal-Mart's competitors were hurt because below-cost pricing and the advertising of below-cost prices decreased their growth in sales and profit. The decision was later reversed, and Wal-Mart raised its prices.

Predatory pricing cases have also been brought in the airline industry. For example, Continental charged that American was setting prices "that would result in ruinous losses to weaken and destroy competitors."[22] In 1993, a Texas court rejected Continental's claims that American was trying to drive competitors out of business.

A special case of predatory pricing is addressed in the so-called anti-dumping laws. In the context of international trade, "dumping" occurs "when a foreign manufacturer sells a product in the U.S. at a lower price than is charged in the home market."[23] An example of this predatory pricing occurred in 1987 when the U.S. Department of Commerce ruled that "Japanese companies violated international trade laws by failing to increase their price to match the sharp rise in the value of the yen."[24] According to the Commerce Department, Japanese prices declined 23 percent from 1985 to 1987. The Commerce Department forced Japanese companies to raise their prices. In 1991 the Commerce Department charged the Japanese with dumping minivans in the U.S. market at prices 30 percent lower than those in their home market and imposed tariffs on Japanese products. Later in the chapter we discuss the relevant antitrust laws in detail. In short, if the dominant firm can establish that it is not pricing below cost, predatory pricing will generally be ruled "fair" and legal. As such, it can be a strong deterrent to fringe competitors.

Deterring Entry through Product Proliferation

Beyond limit and predatory pricing is a wider set of actions that deter rivals. Advertising and promoting a new product so intensively that strong brand loyalties deter entry and/or challenge by weaker firms[25] and investing in excess capacity to reduce attractiveness of challenge[26] are two examples. Interestingly, firms can also maintain a dominant position through excessive brand or product proliferation. An example of such behavior is found in the ready-to-eat cereal market.[27] The industry has been dominated collectively by four firms: Kellogg, General Mills, Kraft's Post, and Pepsi's Quaker Oats. In this instance, deterrent actions have been taken collectively, or in concert, by dominant oligopolists to protect their market positions. Over time the firms have strategically introduced a profusion of new products. From 1950 to 1972, the leading producers put more than 80 brands into general distribution. The goal has been to market enough different products to fill market niches, as well as available shelf space in supermarkets, and thus deter entry. That strategy has been largely successful in enabling the dominant firms to retain their strong position; however, it has been labeled an anticompetitive practice and was the subject of a Federal Trade Commission investigation in the 1970s.[28]

Defensive Innovation Actions

Firms in dominant positions can also engage in aggressive innovative activity. The lines between innovation to build a Ricardian advantage, as discussed in chapter 5, and innovation to protect a dominant market position are somewhat blurred. One distinguishing characteristic of the latter is preemptive patenting to secure persistence of dominant market position.[29] A dominant firm can maintain its market position by patenting new technologies before potential competitors, even if such patents are never used or licensed to others. Patents that are never used or licensed are called sleeping patents. This strategy was brought to light in a 1970s antitrust case in which SCM Corporation charged that Xerox Corporation was maintaining a "patent thicket" of sleeping patents to preempt rivals anti-competitively. Although the ruling held that Xerox had indeed successfully protected its market with a "patent thicket," it also held that SCM was not entitled to any damages because Xerox had lawfully acquired its patents, and its subsequent refusal to license was permitted under the patent laws.[30] More recent examples include industry leaders such as Intel, IBM, Motorola, and Sun Microsystems in the technology industries, which enjoy a competitive advantage over new entrants and smaller firms through patent rights from their existing portfolios and the use of cross-licensing agreements to exchange intellectual property with each other.[31]

Manipulation of Information to Deter Response

Manipulating information can be a key action to deter response. For example, firms with several divisions can obscure information about profitable product lines so as not to attract entry.[32] One firm that strategically manipulated information to keep competitors at bay is AT&T. Despite major changes in the telephone industry's competitive environment, AT&T remains dominant in the long-distance market. In 1990 it still had 70 percent of the market, down from about 90 percent in 1980. Its closest rival, MCI, had only 15 percent of the market. In addition, even though its market share has dropped, AT&T has grown in terms of volume, and while its prices have declined, its profit has remained high.[33]

When initially faced with competition from MCI and other nascent long-distance providers, AT&T retained its position by cutting prices and focusing on its advantages to limit the growth of its competitors. AT&T emphasized its reputation and longstanding customer relationships, raising customers' switching fears. It also capitalized on and promoted the historical advantages of its network. AT&T had a more extensive network, with lower construction costs, than its rivals. The fact that its long-distance service was less reliant on local telephone companies than that of the independent providers was another cost advantage. AT&T also had advantages in its 800 number and international services, which the independents were not immediately able to provide. The AT&T network was a result of decades of research, knowledge, and skills that continued to expand; competitors could never accumulate all that AT&T possessed. AT&T also had lower capital costs as its risk level was much lower than that of its competitors. Its profit could have easily covered any investment costs it incurred.[34]

A T & T responded quickly to market incursion with price discrimination, lowering prices where competition arose but holding prices high in other markets where it retained a monopoly. An integral part of this strategy was strategic manipulation of information.[35] In particular, A T & T was alleged to have strategically obfuscated and withheld cost information from the Federal Communications Commission (FCC) so that regulators could not determine whether prices in competitive markets were reasonable. Specifically, when the company met its new competitors with aggressive low prices, regulators tried to investigate whether those prices were justified on the basis of costs. The FCC investigation of costs dragged on for nearly two decades and was never resolved, but A T & T was accused of withholding the kind of cost data that might have caused its aggressive pricing to be prohibited in competitive markets. This and several other A T & T competitive tactics were deemed improper by the U.S. Department of Justice in its 1970s' antitrust suit. The suit ultimately led to a consent decree in 1982 and the breakup of the Bell System in 1984.[36]

Price Leadership

Dominant firms can exert price leadership in an industry. They can set prices so that a desired level of profit is achieved. Importantly, rivals do not undercut the leader's prices in an effort to gain market share, as any such aggressive pricing would provoke severe retaliation from the dominant firm. U.S. Steel provides an example of successful price leadership.

U.S. Steel was formed in 1901 through a merger of 10 large steel producers and finishers, and it held a large share of Minnesota iron ore reserves. At that time, it was the largest firm ever, and the first U.S. billion-dollar corporation. According to a study by Leonard Weiss, U.S. Steel controlled 44 percent of steel-ingot capacity and 66 percent of output in the early 1900s.[37] Its competitors each had approximately 5 percent of the market or less. Other large steel firms came into being, but, with the exception of the World War II period, U.S. Steel had the power to set prices until the 1960s. Even though U.S. Steel "set" domestic steel prices, it survived an antitrust case that lasted from 1911 to 1920.

U.S. Steel's strength in the first half of the century was enhanced by policies set by Judge Gary, the chairman of U.S. Steel for many years. Between 1907 and 1911, he established the "Gary dinners," at which policy was discussed by the leaders of all the steel industry firms. Although no written collusive agreement was made, firms generally followed the lead of U.S. Steel.

In general, price leadership occurs when prices are known and stable for a given period of time. Periodically, the dominant firm will take the lead in altering prices, for example, raising prices in conjunction with issuance of new models of a product. Other firms soon follow its lead, raising their prices by the same amount. If there is no formal agreement to raise prices in consort, such behavior is generally permissible under the antitrust laws.

Additional Deterring Actions

A variety of other actions that deter challengers are being employed by dominant firms. A recent survey reveals that excessive advertising and patent development are the most popular choices of dominant firms.[38] The survey also found, however, that firms had used other entry-deterring actions that had not been examined in detail, such as signing long-term contracts with key suppliers, having regulations designed that can be met only by the regulation proponent's product, reacting aggressively in rivals' test markets to invalidate their test information, keeping products secret, locking up raw material supplies, making early sales to critical buyers and opinion leaders, and announcing products long before they are ready. Managers should be aware of this wider range of actions but also need to he cautious of running afoul of antitrust laws. Microsoft is a dominant firm engaging in creative actions to retain its market position, and many of those actions have brought scrutiny from antitrust authorities.[39]

Deterrent Action, Reaction, and Competitive Advantage

As we have pointed out in preceding chapters, the effectiveness of a firm's actions depends crucially on the extent of competitive reaction. To the extent that a dominant firm can deter reaction, perhaps by intimidating rivals, the success of actions to maintain advantage can be enhanced.

Competitive rivalry between a dominant firm and weaker rival(s) can be examined by using a game theory framework. We begin with an example of an extensive game, shown in figure 8.2, that illustrates how the actions of firms in strong market positions yield advantage. Assume we have a dominant firm with high market share and a challenger. The challenger is a fringe player not currently threatening or competing with the dominant firm in any meaningful way. One posture the dominant firm could take can be characterized as "innocent behavior" (A_1). The challenger would then have two courses of action: remain a fringe player (R_1) or take on the dominant firm in a meaningful way (R_2). If the challenger stays on the fringe, the dominant firm gains a profit of \$100, the highest level of profit possible in the game. If a challenge takes place, the dominant firm can choose between a battle for market share (A_3) and a more passive sharing

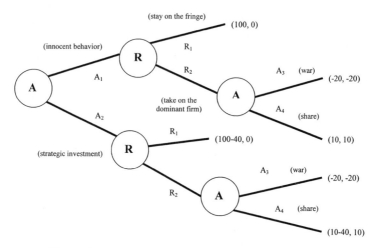

(stay on the fringe)
(100, 0)

(innocent behavior)

R

R_1

R_2

A_3 (war)
(-20, -20)

A_1

A

(take on the
dominant firm)

A

A_4

(share)

A_2

(10, 10)

R_1

(100-40, 0)

(strategic investment)

R

A_3 (war)
(-20, -20)

R_2

A

A_4 (share)

(10-40, 10)

Figure 8.2   Deterrent Action/Reaction and Advantage.

of the market with the challenger (A_4). Given entry, passive sharing will
yield higher profit than that attainable in the event of a battle, which in
fact will be negative.[40]

The threat of a market share battle may not be credible because the
challenger knows it is not the dominant firm's optimal response to a new
entrant. Two alternatives can be added to the game. First, if a sequence of
moves is possible between the dominant firm and the challenger or fringe
firm, losses from a battle in the first period (A_3) could be made up with
abnormal profit in the future if the dominant firm wins and deters future
challenges. The dominant firm gains a reputation for aggressive behavior
at a short-run cost of battle, and deters future action by fringe firms.

Rivalry in the artificial sweetener industry played out exactly that
way.[41] In the mid-1980s, NutraSweet held a dominant position in the low-
calorie artificial sweetener market. Such sweeteners are used primarily in
soft drinks, coffee, and tea. The firm's dominance was based on its ownership of worldwide patents for aspartame. However, the patents were due
to expire in Europe and Canada in 1987 and in the United States in 1992.
In 1985, the new Holland Sweetener Company started to prepare for entry
into the market after patent expiration. When HSC entered the European
market in 1987, NutraSweet had to decide between an aggressive and an
accommodating response. An aggressive response would establish NutraSweet's reputation as a fierce defender of its market share and deter
additional entrants in Europe. More important, such a response would
serve as a warning to anyone contemplating entry into the larger U.S.
market in 1992. Perhaps with the intention of establishing such an entry-
deterring reputation, NutraSweet did respond very aggressively to HSC's

entry, sharply reducing its prices and throwing HSC into a losing position. Over time, rivals, including HSC, sliced away at NutraSweet's dominant position to only half of the aspartame market in 2001.[42] Although the decline was inevitable, NutraSweet's aggressive response allowed it to maintain its dominant position longer than otherwise.

The Australian airline industry in the early 1990s was the scene of another aggressive response that appears to have successfully deterred subsequent challenges. As in the ready-to-eat cereal industry described previously, dominant firms took action in concert to protect their market positions from a new rival. Comprehensive regulation of prices and services in Australian interstate passenger aviation had been in place for more than 30 years. Under regulation, two major airlines dominated the domestic market, Australian Airlines (government owned) and Ansett Airlines (private sector). Entry from other airlines was largely excluded, and competition between the two incumbents was limited. However, in October 1990, government regulation of capacity, route entry, and fares under the Two Airline Policy was totally eliminated, and new domestic operators were allowed to enter trunk routes.[43]

Only one month after the formal start of deregulation, Compass Airlines presented a formidable challenge to the incumbents when it began operations. Compass followed a low-cost strategy, using large aircraft to serve the densest routes. It offered a one-class service and kept labor and overhead costs below those of the major airlines. According to the Australian Bureau of Transport and Communication Economics, Compass had a substantial cost advantage over the incumbents. Its total cost per available seat kilometer was estimated to be 8 cents, versus 14 cents for the incumbents. However, Compass also attempted to provide service quality comparable to or better than that of Ansett or Australian, with more leg room and in-flight video entertainment that was not offered by the incumbents. In its early months of operation, Compass expanded by adding more aircraft to its fleet. By the September 1991 quarter, Compass had gained 12 percent of the total aviation market and more than 20 percent of the markets in which it operated.

Compass tried to capitalize on its cost advantage by undercutting the incumbent airlines on price. However, both incumbents responded very aggressively to Compass, matching fares in round after round of fare cuts. All airlines were losing money during these intense price wars. Concern mounted about the financial condition of Compass. After a government rescue bid failed, Compass declared bankruptcy on December 20, 1991, and halted all service. In subsequent years, the two dominant airlines have faced few serious challenges. Their aggressive response to the new entrant, although causing a clear short-term loss to both firms in 1991, appears to have successfully sent a message to other would-be challengers.

As we discuss in more detail in the following section, dominant firms employing such actions need to be aware of possible antitrust problems. The

Compass collapse prompted several government inquiries. The Australian Trade Practices Commission began a study of the Compass collapse, with particular attention to possible anticompetitive practices of the incumbents.

Returning to the game theory model, we see in figure 8.2 that a second alternative is for the dominant firm to engage in strategic behavior prior to challenger entry. Specifically, the dominant firm can make specific and irrevocable investments to prepare for war, such as investing in additional capacity (A_2). The expenditure does not affect profit if war takes place but does reduce the profit of sharing with the challenger by an amount equal to $40. Recall that profit is $10 with passive sharing of the market and $-$20 in the event of warfare. However, if a sufficiently large strategic expenditure is made, warfare becomes the most profitable option in the face of entry. In our example, A's profit from sharing the market in the face of entry ($10) minus the strategic investment in additional capacity ($40) exceeds the payoff from warfare in the face of entry $(-$20), so it is credible for the incumbent to engage in war. The optimal strategy for the challenger is to not engage the dominant rival once such a commitment has been made. The model shows that a dominant firm can deter response by establishing credibility, or a commitment to fight, which can critically influence a rival's behavior.

A strategic form of the game can also be used to illustrate how actions of a dominant firm lead to advantage. We assume the dominant firm has substantial resource advantages, including deeper pockets, and can take a competitive action such as a price cut. If the challenger matches the cut, its revenues will not cover costs and it will soon go out of business and exit. If the challenger fails to match the cut, it will lose substantial market share and make negative profit, which will also result in an exit from the market. The game theory details of this example follow.

Two firms, Goliath and David, each can use two pricing strategies, high or low prices, which lead to the following payoffs.

		David's Pricing Strategy	
		High	Low
Goliath's Pricing Strategy	High	III, III	57, 122
	Low	122, 57	95, 95

In previous periods, both firms charged high prices and both made positive profit, although the dominant firm's profit was substantially higher. Goliath, the dominant firm, is contemplating lowering prices in the next period. If David does not follow the price cut, it will lose virtually all of its customers and receive negative profit (−$20). If David does lower its price, both firms will lose money in the short term. However, because it has deep pockets, Goliath will survive the price war, whereas David will have to exit. The ensuing period of no competition will allow the dominant firm to achieve a higher payoff. The dominant firm is clearly in command of the situation, controlling the rivalry in the marketplace. As discussed in the following section, the main concern for the firm dropping prices may well be fear of a Department of Justice investigation of monopolization practices.

Managerial Implications: A Note of Caution about Antitrust Laws

Our research on the deterrent actions of dominant firms has shown how such firms keep challengers at bay and how they cede their positions of power. Managers should be aware of the arsenal of actions available to defend a dominant position. Recall from chapter 1 that we have studied dominant and challenger firms across 41 different industries. Through that work, we found that dominant firms avoid being dethroned by challengers by responding quickly to challengers' actions and by taking a broad line of competitive actions (for example, not focusing just on limit pricing).We also found that dominant firms are often dethroned when they have limited resources for competitive action. Moreover, we observed that challengers make inroads into the leadership positions of dominant firms when those firms become complacent, either not engaging challengers or responding slowly to challengers' actions.[44] Firms clearly can benefit from employing a wide range of the actions detailed in this chapter. However, managers of dominant firms must be aware of the proscription of monopolization in the antitrust laws.[45]

The Sherman Act, section 2, states that it is illegal to monopolize or attempt to monopolize an industry. Similar proscriptions apply in most other countries as part of what is commonly known as "competition policy."[45] In this section we first review the public policy economist's perspective on monopoly and discuss the motivation for section 2 of the Sherman Act. Then we detail the administration of section 2 over time, noting with examples the actions that may run a dominant firm afoul of antitrust laws. Finally, we discuss implications for managers.[46]

Monopoly: The Economist's Perspective

The structure-conduct-performance model has been very influential with economists and antitrust policy makers, as discussed in more detail in

Chapter 2. The model posits a causal linkage between the structure of an industry, the conduct of the firms within that industry, and the performance of the industry. In other words, structure will determine firm conduct, which in turn will determine performance.

Within the structure-conduct-performance paradigm, monopoly stands at the extreme negative pole from the point of view of the public-policy-oriented economist. Such economists believe that under conditions of monopoly, prices will be high amid output constrained, resulting in excessive costs to consumers. Of course, monopoly may be as attractive to business as it is unattractive to consumers or the public interest. Some companies may be highly motivated to attain, and retain, market power that reduces the level of competition for their products or services. The preceding sections and chapters describe ways for firms to defend a dominant position. However, managers must be cognizant of the antitrust implications. The antitrust laws and their administration through actual cases are discussed next.

The Sherman Act Proscription of Monopoly

The notion that monopolies work counter to the public interest has led to longstanding legal proscriptions of monopoly. Section 2 of the Sherman Act prohibits monopolization, attempts to monopolize, and conspiracy to monopolize: "Every person who shall monopolize, or attempt to monopolize, or combine or conspire with any person or persons, to monopolize any part of the trade or commerce among the several states, or with foreign nations, shall be deemed guilty of a misdemeanor." The meaning and interpretation of Sherman section 2 are best clarified through a review of several important cases brought under that section.

Standard Oil (1911). In the mid-1860s, Rockefeller entered the oil refinery business. By 1880, Standard Oil had built a market share exceeding 85 percent and maintained that dominant position into the 1900s. The Justice Department brought an antitrust suit against Standard Oil, alleging that it had illegally monopolized the oil industry. Ultimately the case was decided by the Supreme Court, which ruled not only that Standard Oil had established a monopoly but also that the actions were "of such a character as to give rise to the inference or presumption that they had been entered into or done with the intent to do wrong to the general public."[47] Standard Oil was found guilty of bad intent because of "acts and dealings wholly inconsistent with . . . the development of business power by usual methods, but which necessarily involved the intent to drive others from the field and exclude them from their right to trade."[48] Those acts included predatory price cutting, control of transportation of oil (through both ownership of oil pipelines and advantageous rail rates obtained with market leverage), and other unfair practices. As a remedy to its illegal monopolization, Standard Oil was dissolved into several smaller firms.

Alcoa (1945).   Aluminum Company of America (Alcoa) had a longstanding dominant position in aluminum, dating back to initial ownership of patents that legally eliminated direct competition. In the 1940s, Alcoa held 90 percent of the market for virgin aluminum ingots sold in the United States. Although by other market definitions (for example, secondary aluminum) Alcoa had a smaller share, the courts opted for the narrowest market definition. The company's conduct had shown evidence of preemptive expansion of capacity:

> There were at least one or two abortive attempts to enter the industry, but Alcoa effectively anticipated and forestalled all competition. . . . Nothing compelled it to keep doubling and redoubling its capacity before others entered the field. It insists that it never excluded competitors; but we can think of no more effective exclusion than to embrace each new opportunity as it opened.[49]

Thus, Alcoa was found guilty of monopolization. The remedy was for Alcoa to subsidize entry by its rivals Reynolds and Kaiser Aluminum through sale of its war plants at low prices.

IBM (1982).   As is well known, IBM was a dominant firm in the emerging computer industry in the 1950s and 1960s. In 1969, the Department of Justice filed suit against IBM, charging it with monopolizing the general computer market. The government contended that IBM held a market share of 70 percent and had engaged in improper tactics, such as bundling systems of components, to exclude rivals that sold just one component. IBM was also accused of predatory pricing when facing competition. The argument was that IBM charged higher prices when it did not face competition.

The trial began in 1975 and dragged on for six years without resolution. An early action of the Reagan administration was to dismiss the suit against IBM, thus signaling a significant change in antitrust enforcement.

AT&T (1982).   AT&T was granted a public utility monopoly in the early 1900s, largely based on the rationale of scale economies. In other words, AT&T was considered a "natural monopoly," in that production costs would be significantly lower with one producer than they would be if more than one firm were present. Accordingly, A T & T's monopoly in telephone service was sanctioned by the government, with regulators controlling the levels of prices and profit to a great degree. In 1974, however, the Department of Justice filed a monopolization suit against A T & T. The emergence of microwave technology had enabled new firms to enter the long-distance business; the most aggressive of these was MCI A T & T reacted to this entry by lowering prices where it faced such competition. A T & T was charged with improperly using its control of local service to disadvantage its nascent long-distance rivals, erecting barriers to entry in potentially competitive markets.

When faced with the antitrust suit, A T & T defended its actions and argued that its status as a regulated firm shielded it from such suits. The government argued that regulation was imperfect and only partially effective, giving A T & T some freedom, and that the antitrust laws should hold. More specifically, A T & T's alleged monopolistic, anticompetitive conduct included refusal to buy telephone equipment that was not manufactured internally A T & T was charged with raising competitors' costs by unnecessarily requiring protective devices when non-Bell equipment was used and by requiring long-distance rivals to use very cumbersome long-distance telephone numbers. Abuse of regulatory process was charged, the argument being that A T & T strategically withheld information from regulators and designed accounting systems that were impenetrable to regulators. That point was important in establishing why regulation was only partially effective and why the antitrust laws applied. Finally, A T & T was accused of predatory pricing, or "pricing without regard to costs," in that prices varied greatly in response to the degree of competition for particular products and services.[50]

Like that of IBM, A T & T's trial went on for seven years with no end in sight. Finally, the Reagan administration reached a settlement with A T & T that resulted in the breakup of the Bell System, with divestiture of the local telephone companies into seven independent regional Bell operating companies. The decree barred A T & T from some old markets but allowed it to enter some new markets such as computer equipment.

Microsoft (2000). For several years in the early 1990s, Microsoft Corporation was under investigation by the U.S. Department of Justice and the Federal Trade Commission for monopolization of segments of the computer software industry. Microsoft's MS-DOS and Windows operating systems controlled about 85 percent of the market. The company had engaged in several controversial tactics, including pricing aggressively, targeting specific rivals with anticompetitive actions, hiding certain pieces of code that could hamper the performance of rivals' products, and announcing future products years in advance, the so-called vaporware, to dampen enthusiasm for competitors' alternatives.[51]

In July 1994, Microsoft settled the four-year antitrust investigation by agreeing to some changes in the way it offered volume discounts to hardware manufacturers that bundled Microsoft products. At issue was Microsoft's practice of giving volume discounts when manufacturers paid a royalty fee for each machine produced, whether or not Microsoft operating software had been installed. That was an effective way of keeping manufacturers from using other firms' operating software, because the manufacturers were unlikely to pay royalties to two software firms. Microsoft agreed to halt the practice under terms of the settlement, but the Justice Department and the European Commission retained the right to reopen their investigations.

Other allegations have been made by competitors about "vaporware," or Microsoft's practice of announcing new products years in advance. In addition, Microsoft has allegedly hidden certain codes in its operating software that cause its competitors' application software to perform less well than that developed by Microsoft.[52] Finally, in 1990 Microsoft was accused of deliberately misleading competitors and IBM by publicly supporting a new operating system (OS/2) while actually only working on a new Microsoft application, Windows 95. Overall, the current Justice Department investigation and the settlement with Microsoft sent a cautionary signal to dominant firms that antitrust enforcement policy is becoming more aggressive, particularly in monopolization cases, than it was during the Reagan administration.

In 1998 the U.S. Department of Justice, along with 20 states and the District of Columbia, charged Microsoft with maintaining a monopoly in PC operating software and attempting to monopolize web browser software. In 2000, the courts agreed with the charges and ordered the breakup of Microsoft into two separate companies. Microsoft appealed and lost the monopoly maintenance claim but reversed the liability awards and breakup of Microsoft. Eventually, Microsoft settled the case with the Justice Department and several of the states by agreeing to self-impose a series of restrictions on its business practices, for example, to disclose more of its operating software code to enable rival applications to operate with Windows, and not to retaliate against computer sellers who use competing software.[53]

Implications for Managers

Managers contemplating defending their firm's strong market position with deterrent actions need to be keenly aware of the antitrust laws on monopoly and how those laws have been interpreted. As noted in a leading business law text:

> The maxim "Ignorance of the law is no excuse" certainly holds true in this area of restraints of trade and monopolies. Reliance on legal counsel

in this "sophisticated" realm is, of course, important. Yet, it is no substitute for a solid understanding of those activities that may cause antitrust problems to the firm.[54]

A recent scan of the business press suggests continuing allegations and investigations of antitrust violations by dominant firms. For example, in the mid-1990s, Toys "R" Us, the leading U.S. toy retailer at the time, was investigated by the FTC for antitrust violations. Toys "R" Us had to reduce prices as it was facing increasing competition from discounters such as Wal-Mart. The competitive pressure increased as warehouse clubs such as Costco began to sell more toys. Fearing a greater threat to its market share and profits from the warehouse clubs, Toys "R" Us responded by pressuring toy manufacturers to deny popular toys or to sell them at less favorable prices to warehouse clubs. Thus, the FTC sued Toys "R" Us for abusing market power and ordered it to stop engaging in anticompetitive practices.[55]

Around the same time, the Department of Justice scrutinized the snack food giant Frito-Lay and the brewer Anheuser-Busch, which held around 50 and 45 percent of the U.S. market, respectively, for possible anticompetitive practices. The retail practices being investigated reportedly included using their dominant positions to purchase shelf space in grocery stores and reward distributors and retailers who favored their products to improperly lock out competitors.[56]

Such antitrust scrutiny can reach organizations other than private businesses. For example, the U.S. Postal Service has recently been sued under antitrust laws for illegally restricting competition. Flamingo Industries, an Illinois-based maker of mail sacks, has claimed that the U.S. Postal Service has violated five antitrust laws and attempted to reduce competition in the mail-sack manufacturing industry by shifting its purchases to less expensive manufacturers in Mexico.[57]

Violation of antitrust laws can result in significant damage to reputation, large fines, and even jail sentences for managers. In addition, Justice Department investigations and court actions related to monopolization can be very expensive for firms, even if no culpability is found in the end. Moreover, section 4 of the Clayton Act allows for private antitrust suits. Any party possibly damaged by anticompetitive action can bring suit in federal court. If successful, the plaintiffs can recover treble damages, or three times the estimated harm from the anticompetitive actions. Such suits can be an effective competitive weapon for rivals of dominant firms, as well as a potentially serious pitfall for market leaders.

An example of such action can be found in the railroad industry's efforts to maintain its dominant position in coal transportation in the face of potential competition from coal slurry pipelines. Coal is the most important commodity for railroads in terms of both volume and revenue. In the 1970s, a nationwide network of coal slurry pipelines was proposed. Coal slurry, pulverized coal mixed with water, can be forced through a pipeline as a technologically feasible coal transportation alternative to rail. Railroads fought to preserve their market dominance in coal transport in several ways, including lobbying efforts at the state and federal levels to deny the power of eminent domain for construction of coal slurry pipelines. When it appeared that one such pipeline (ETSI) would receive eminent domain permission in all the relevant states, the railroads aggressively targeted key coal shippers—electric utilities—and signed them to preemptive long-term contracts at favorable rates. ETSI finally abandoned its plans but promptly filed an antitrust suit against the railroads for monopolization of coal transport. An initial court decision found the railroads guilty. In the end, settling the case cost the railroads hundreds of millions of dollars.[58]

To avoid potential suits from rivals, managers must understand certain specifics of the antitrust laws, especially how the monopolization statutes are enforced. Although a monopoly is defined by economists as a firm with 100 percent of the market, the standard threshold used in early cases was 75 to 80 percent. The argument was that a firm with such a commanding market share is actually a monopoly and able to wield the type of market power that results in undesirable consequences. In recent cases, more than market share has been used to determine whether a monopoly is held, but, according to antitrust experts, "the 75 to 80 percent guideline is, nevertheless, still a reliable shorthand indicator."[59]

Managers, then, need to be aware of how markets are likely to he defined so as to assess their standing in relation to this threshold. It may be wise to keep rivals "in the game" so as not to surpass the 75 to 80 percent threshold of monopoly, given the uncertainty as to whether competitive behavior will be judged as improperly monopolizing or attempting to monopolize an industry. In our game theory example, a company may want to refrain from actions that knock out its competitor. Even if short-term profit is increased, the ultimate payoff may be an expensive antitrust suit. It has been argued that Intel has been "allowing" Advanced Micro Devices, which has been its only significant rival over the years, in the market for microprocessor chips just to avoid the ire of the Justice Department.

Although economists ascribe a set of evils to monopoly regardless of how it is acquired and retained, the law is clear that monopoly in and of itself is not illegal. The classic statement of this point comes from the 1966 Grinnell case:

> The offense of monopoly under section 2 of the Sherman Act has two
> elements: (1) the possession of monopoly power in the relevant market

and (2) the willful acquisition or maintenance of that power as distinguished from growth or development as a consequence of a superior product, business acumen, or historic accident.[60]

Managers should be aware that hard, honest competition per se will not be judged illegal; in practice, however, the allowed versus proscribed behavior is not always easily discerned. We can provide some generalizations about what behavior would be likely to result in monopolization problems.

The prohibited territory consists of two areas, attempted monopolization and monopolization. For the former, the presumed intent of competitive action is of critical import. In some cases direct evidence of intent can be found in specific documents obtained through a discovery process. A plan to "conquer" the opposition or to "do whatever it takes" to develop a dominant market share could be used as proof of intent to monopolize.[61] A specific written plan is not essential as proof; circumstantial evidence can suffice. In this instance, the overall pattern of business activities is examined. A critical question is whether the activities have a sound business purpose other than to harm a competitor.

Let us consider two examples of alleged predatory pricing. Suppose a firm with a 50 to 60 percent market share sharply drops its price below cost, and in so doing loses large sums of money in the short term. Also assume that the firm's price cuts put enormous pressure on smaller rivals, driving them out of business. Such price cuts could well be seen as an illegal attempt to monopolize, as there could be no gain or benefit for the firm if competition were not eliminated in the process. Conversely, suppose an airline with the leading market share in its market matches the low fares of an upstart rival. In so doing, the dominant firm prices below its costs and loses money. The upstart firm, once the fares are matched, cannot generate sufficient revenues to cover costs and ultimately exits the market. In both of these examples, predatory pricing may be alleged. However, instigating a price war from a dominant position is very different from matching the low fares of an upstart. In the first case, the dominant firm sets out to harm a rival; in the second, the dominant firm is merely defending itself.

Attempt to monopolize involves *seeking* or *attaining* monopoly by *improper* means. Monopolization involves proactive attempts to hurt rivals to *protect* a monopoly. Again, fair, normal competition is allowed, and many of the actions described in this chapter can be effective deterrents to rivals. Introducing new products, advertising, and innovating are generally seen as normal business practices. However, a firm must be wary of any practices that smack of excluding or exceptionally disadvantaging a rival. Cutting off a rival from a key source of supply, for example, could be questionable, as could efforts to raise a rival's costs. Using a dominant market position to leverage share in another market, as AT&T's extension of monopoly into equipment and use of its local monopoly to improperly impede long-distance rivals, can also be problematic.

Summary

In this chapter we discuss actions by firms to take advantage of strong market positions. We use the term "deterrent actions" in this context but reiterate that we do not mean to suggest that such tactics are improper. Indeed, we discuss relevant antitrust laws in some detail so that a firm's managers can properly assess the legality of potential actions they might take to defend the firm's strong market position.

Chapter 9

WINNING THE PEACE

Taking "Co-optive" Actions in the Absence of Resource Advantage

---

C hristie's International and Sotheby's Holdings have long dominated the art auction industry, evenly sharing 95 percent of the $4 billion per year global market in 2002. The two firms profited by charging sellers and buyers a fee for auctioning art and other exclusive items. They essentially had no competitors and were very similar in key resources and competitive strength. It was well known among industry observers that both firms cooperated, for example, scheduling alternating auctions so more buyers and sellers could attend and charging sellers and buyers the same fees. For over two centuries, Christie's and Sotheby's had competed and cooperated without much scrutiny. However, in 1997 the U.S. Justice Department began to investigate the two industry leaders on charges of price fixing. To illustrate, both firms on two occasions had implemented the same changes to the fee structure for sellers and buyers within two months of each other over the last few years. But even with this evidence, the investigation had not advanced very far until 2000, when Christie's announced that it would begin to cooperate with the criminal antitrust investigation. Christie's decision was motivated by U.S. antitrust law, which provided leniency to the first party from criminal prosecution who cooperated. Weeks after the decision to cooperate, Christie's lowered its fee, which was matched by Sotheby's a few months later. Although Christie's has avoided criminal charges, both firms eventually settled and agreed to pay several hundred million dollars in fines from the civil charges.[1]

Kellogg and General Mills have also long dominated the breakfast cereal industry, evenly sharing 65 percent of the $7 billion market in 2002.[2] As in the case of the art auction industry, many industry observers over the years have argued that the two industry leaders, along with major rivals (i.e., Kraft's Post and Pepsi's Quaker Oats), cooperated or at least exhibited restrained competition, for example, by limiting in-pack premiums (e.g., toys and gifts) and trade dealing (e.g., retailer promotions and discounts) and by keeping prices well above competitive levels. While competing on other aspects such as advertising and new product introductions, these co-optive actions among industry players have occasionally led to antitrust investigations, but without any action being taken against the industry.[3]

Lead-based antiknock compounds have long been used in the refining of gasoline to prevent engine "knock." The best way to prevent knock is to use lead-based compounds to raise the octane level of gasoline. In the 1970s, the four domestic producers of lead antiknock compounds (and their market shares) were Du Pont (38.4 percent), Ethyl (33.5 percent), PPG (16.2 percent), and Nalco (11.8 percent). They had few foreign competitors and were also at relative parity in key resources and competitive strength. Beginning in 1973, changes in U.S. government regulations significantly reduced demand for the lead-based compounds. New cars were required to have catalytic converters, with which unleaded gasoline must be used. In addition, the amount of lead that could be used in "leaded" gasoline was significantly curtailed. Subsequently, the demand for these lead-based compounds dropped significantly. The sharp cuts in industry demand, with large fixed and sunk costs, resulted in considerable excess capacity. Such circumstances would normally generate substantial price cutting and intense price competition between the firms in the industry. However, the four firms successfully and legally engaged in cooperative activities that largely eliminated price competition and maintained prices at relatively high levels. The activities included quoting prices on a uniform delivered price basis, announcing price changes well in advance of the effective date, and including in contracts with customers the right for the customer to receive any discounts extended to other customers.[4]

The foregoing industry examples illustrate that firms can reduce competition through co-optive actions, although certain co-optive actions may infringe on antitrust laws. In preceding chapters we considered relative firm resources, competitive actions, and advantage—how to take actions that delay rivals' responses. In this chapter, we examine firm actions and reactions in markets where both resources and competitive strength are relatively equal among firms. In such situations, co-optive actions may well be in the best interest of all firms in the industry. Table 9.1 is a comparison of entrepreneurial, Ricardian, deterrent, and co-optive actions.

The field of strategic management relies heavily on the metaphor of war to explain competitive interaction among rivals.[5] The metaphor is so widespread that it is rarely questioned. For example, a large literature on generic strategies identifies the specific fundamental strategies that will be superior to others.[6] It can even be said that the common thread in strategy literature is an emphasis on competition or warfare, and the notion that a

Table 9.1 Key Distinctions among Entrepreneurial, Ricardian, Deterrent, and Co-optive Actions

Category	Entrepreneurial Actions	Ricardian Actions	Deterrent Actions	Co-optive Actions
Goal	Avoid rivals	Engage rivals	Deter rivals	Reduce Rivalry
Source	Opportunity based	Resource based	Market based	Driven by lack of advantage; resource and market share parity
Intent	Spontaneous, based on opportunities created from disequilibrium	Deliberate outcome of plan to exploit resources	Deliberate outcome of plan to defend resource platform	Deliberate outcome to exploit joint behavior
Criteria for evaluation	No guidance on conformance; newness	Conform to criterion of economic efficiency or maximization	Conform to the criterion of long-term profit maximization, but not economic efficiency	Conform to criterion of joint profit maximization, but not economic efficiency
Credit	Credit goes to discoverer	Credit goes to owner of resource	Avoid credit	Avoid credit
Outcome	Unpredictable	Predictable	Predictable	Unstable

firm must outcompete its rivals if it wants to be successful or even survive. Several interrelated propositions are incorporated in the warfare metaphor, and one of the most important of these is the backbone of the preceding chapters: *when one firm in an industry makes a highly visible competitive move, other firms will respond to it or at least consider responding to it to defend or advance their own positions.*

This chapter considers a very different and alternative perspective on achieving strong financial performance, the idea that a firm may well achieve maximum profit by undertaking cooperative, not competitive, moves. More specifically, when no one firm in an industry has a decisive resource advantage over the others, firms acting collectively to *limit* rivalry can achieve higher profit for all than would be possible if rivalry were intense. Figure 9.1 shows the relationship among resources, action and reaction, and advantage as it pertains to this chapter.

The field of IO economics, which differs from strategic management in its greater focus on the industry level of analysis and emphasis on society's

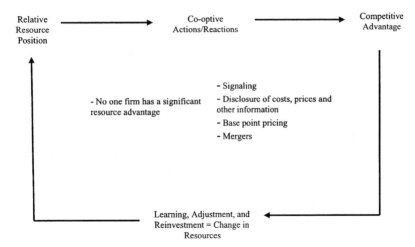

Figure 9.1 Co-optive Actions and Competitive Advantage.

rather than an individual firm's welfare, has historically highlighted the tendency of oligopolistic industries to move toward coordination over time. A central question in IO is whether a small number of firms dominating an industry will recognize their mutual interdependence and collude in some presumably legal way to achieve above-normal profit. Firms in such industries, although they may be partial to the war metaphor, realize that they may kill each other if they follow the metaphor to its logical conclusion. In particular, price wars, in which prices are repeatedly slashed in response to price reductions by competitors, are clearly to be avoided in the best interests of all firms' profit. Avoiding such intense rivalry will enable all firms to "win the peace."

Co-optive actions are defined as actions that reduce or attempt to reduce rivalry. Our focus here is situations in which a firm has no clear resource advantage over rivals, is not attempting to achieve one, and pursues co-optive actions to reduce competition. We do not include cooperative actions such as joint ventures and other horizontal or vertical linkages whose purpose is to combine resources to compete more effectively against other rivals. Only cooperative actions that are designed to reduce rivalry overall are considered.

In chapter 1, we described the forces that have intensified the degree of competition in many industries, such as the increased number of new firms entering the marketplace. One may be led to conclude that co-optive actions—efforts to moderate or contain rivalry between competitors—are no longer feasible or desirable in today's environment.[7] In actuality we believe such actions are still being pursued in many instances and, in the aggregate, may even be on the rise. The forces that are raising the level of competition in many markets are the same forces that may drive firms to seek reduction of competitive intensity. One indicator of the current level of co-optive activity is data from the Department of Justice (DOJ) Antitrust Division's investigations of restraint-of-trade activity. DOJ investigations into potentially illegal cooperative activity indicate that such activity has not disappeared. The number of investigations initiated under the Sherman Act, section 1, Restraint of Trade, had increased considerably from 71 in 1990 to 136 in 1994 but declined in recent years to 80 in 2001.[8] These data also underscore the importance of a clear understanding of antitrust statutes. Like firms that take deterrent actions, firms engaging in co-optive actions need to be careful not to cross the line into illegal collusion under the Sherman Act. Antitrust considerations are covered in more detail at the end of the chapter.

In the following section, we discuss factors that affect the intensity of rivalry, noting common barriers to cooperation and actions that can decrease rivalry. Next, we examine specific co-optive actions in some detail. We then use game theory to illustrate the links between co-optive actions, responses, and competitive advantage. Finally, we examine the critical issue of antitrust considerations in pursuing co-optive actions.

Factors Affecting Intensity of Rivalry

Firms in an industry where no one firm has a significant resource advantage will often do better if they maximize their collective interests instead of pursuing actions to defeat each other. More specifically, firms can compete on selected dimensions such as advertising, product characteristics, and innovation but refrain from competing vigorously on price. Such limited competition on nonprice variables can ensure comfortable levels of profit for industry participants. We define refraining from aggressive competitive moves, especially on price, as *mutual forbearance.* It is most common in oligopolistic industries, with a small number of firms, each very aware of the other's characteristics and competitive moves. Hence, unlike the scenario in chapter 6, the possibility of exploiting blind spots and uncertainty is limited. Unlike the situation in chapter 7, no one firm has a critical relative resource advantage, so none can "win the war" with a knockout punch.

Industries in which mutual forbearance is appropriate are typically ones in which technology is well settled and significant technological advances are unlikely. Firms in such industries have comparable technology and costs. Innovation is "around the edges." The few changes in technology that do occur generate only modest advantages and are unlikely to constitute "creative destruction." Also commonplace is a product or service with little potential for brand identification or product differentiation advantages, a "commodity." Customers are largely indifferent as to which firm they select when prices are comparable. Accordingly, any price differential among competitive offerings will often be the key factor in product selection. Unlike the situation in chapter 8, no one firm has a decisive market share advantage and a commensurate ability to pursue aggressive deterrent actions.

In this resource setting, the best course may well be co-optive actions, or working toward collectively "winning the peace." When a firm without a clear resource advantage attempts to compete aggressively on price, the result is most likely to be a bitter price war in which all participants end up losers. One example is the U.S. airline industry. Destructive competition and low profit levels have been the industry norm since deregulation. Another example of a price war between oligopolists occurred in the breakfast cereal industry, which traditionally has exhibited restrained competition. Post began the warfare with 20 percent price cuts on all cereals in April 1996. In early June, Kellogg responded with price cuts averaging 19 percent on selected cereals. Ten days later, General Mills followed suit with substantial price reductions. Concerns were expressed in the trade press about negative impacts on profit, with early indications including a 4 percent drop in the price of Kellogg's stock.[9] A third example of an industry affected by a price war comes from the technology sector. Dell Inc., which is known for its direct, low-cost business model, has become the industry leader in personal computers by initiating price cuts, and has now begun to undercut rivals in servers, data-storage equipment, and printers, three of its newest businesses. Rivals, such as Hewlett-Packard in personal computers and Sun Microsytems in servers, have responded by pushing prices even lower.[10]

Several key factors facilitate mutual forbearance and cooperation: small number of competitors, strong and stable industry demand and homogeneity of firms, and multimarket contact. We discuss each of them in turn and illustrate them with examples.

Small Number of Competitors

Coordination is greatly facilitated when there are few competitors, ideally two. As more firms compete in a market, rivalry becomes more intense, and the chances are greater that any one maverick firm can set off a fierce competitive skirmish. In addition, coordination or tacit collusion becomes more difficult because the firms are likely to have different notions about what price levels will maximize profit. As more firms are added, the number of two-way communication channels, through which coordination must occur, increases exponentially.[11] For example, with two firms there is only one communication channel, with three firms there are two, with four firms there are six, and with five firms there are ten. The presence of five firms rather than two means that 10 times as many communication channels must be maintained. A breakdown in any one of them could destroy coordination efforts for the entire industry.[12] Therefore, as the number of competitors in an industry increases, the intensity of rivalry will also tend to increase, and achieving mutual forbearance will become more difficult.

In the example of the lead antiknock compound market, we can see that the number of firms provided an atmosphere conducive to mutual forbearance. There were only four domestic producers, with two dominating the industry. And the industry's entry barriers were strong. From 1964, when the last of the four current producers entered, through the 1970s, there were no new entrants or any reasonably close substitutes for the product. The stable industry atmosphere, with a relatively small number of participants, facilitated mutual forbearance.

Another example of how the number of competitors affects intensity of rivalry is provided by our action-based study of the U.S. airline industry. The degree of rivalry was measured by counting the average number of actions and responses for each year for each firm in the industry. When the average number of actions and reactions a firm undertakes is high, industry rivalry will be high; when the number is low, rivalry will be lower and it is reasonable to conclude that implicit coordination is greater. We found that the degree of rivalry for each year was closely related to the number of competitors in the industry for that year. With fewer competitors, rivalry declined; with more competitors, rivalry increased.

A final example of how the number of competitors affects rivalry comes from our action-based study in the brewing, long-distance telecommunications, and personal computer industries.[13] Examining a sample of new product introductions and responses from 1975 through 1990, we found that rivalry was stronger when the number of competitors was higher. Specifically, response time shortened and threats became greater as the number of competitors increased.

Although coordination of actions may be easier in a concentrated industry, some scholars have argued that it can also be achieved through a fragmented industry or in industries where no firm has a significant market share and can strongly influence outcomes. Such industries are characterized by a large number of small to medium-sized firms. For such firms, signaling as a mechanism for collective action is not a reasonable alternative because information exchange and recognition of interdependence are difficult to achieve. Moreover, because the firms are small, private ownership will delay the development of a central authority to regulate industry members or enforce compliance with agreements. For those reasons, most researchers have argued that collective action will be limited in fragmented industries. Marc Dollinger has argued, however, that pair-wise interorganizational agreements can be achieved in fragmented industries and can spread from firm to firm over time so that an entire industry may achieve collective action.[14] The argument is that as repetitions of pair-wise agreements occur over large enough number of industry participants, those organizations will become loosely linked so as to enhance interorganizational communication. Pair-wise agreements can take the form of direct joint purchase, marketing, research, and training agreements with competitors or with suppliers and buyers. The agreements can also be indirect through membership in trade associations and use of industry-wide standard costing or price lists. They might include membership in chambers of commerce and executive round-tables, or interlocking boards of directors. When such actions or agreements spread through an industry, a collective cooperative industry atmosphere may emerge. Such pair-wise cooperation is most likely when the rewards of cooperation outweigh the payoffs of noncooperation and when the current level of rivalry is only moderate. When rivalry is high, there will be no trust for pair-wise cooperation, and when rivalry is low, there will be no motivation.

One example of pair-wise coordination occurred in the off-road vehicle aftermarket, an industry composed of many small firms. The lack of industry standards and a poor safety record industry-wide led firms to team up to solve those problems. After a couple of initial meetings, the participants formed and sponsored an industry association that would work to set product safety standards and standard price lists.

Firms in such fragmented industries can also enlist government regulation to assist them in achieving the cooperation described by Dollinger. Such action was taken in the U.S. motor carrier industry prior to recent deregulation. The motor carrier industry is highly fragmented because of a general lack of scale economies and consists of many hundreds of firms. In the absence of cooperation, such a structure may well lead to intense competition between rivals. However, for decades the firms in this industry were able to cooperate by forming "rate bureaus" whereby carriers agreed on common prices across given markets. That practice was endorsed and enforced by government regulation, beginning with the Motor Carrier Act of 1935. The value of achieving such cooperation in a fragmented industry is confirmed by examining the status of the motor carrier industry since the regulations were removed in 1980. Cooperation is no longer allowed, and the industry is characterized by intense rivalry, generally low profitability, and bankruptcies averaging more than 1,000 a year.[15]

Strong and Stable Industry Demand

Growing industry demand fosters a "live and let live" attitude on the part of firms. In general, demand growth encourages stability as each firm can increase in size without rocking the boat.[16] However, a decrease in demand, or even in the growth rate, can lead to competitive warfare. Related to industry demand is the degree of capacity utilization in the industry. Firms producing near full capacity have little incentive to increase output by lowering prices. In contrast, firms faced with excess capacity and idle resources may be tempted to lower prices in an effort to increase volume. Consequently, when capacity cannot easily be reduced, a drop in industry demand is particularly likely to cause an increase in rivalry. Under such conditions, mutual forbearance can be very difficult to achieve.

The environment in the lead antiknock compound market in the 1970s resulted in substantial excess capacity and strong motivation to cut prices, but the firms successfully countered the temptation. In the airline industry, however, excess capacity resulted in price warfare. Airlines want to have high scheduled flight frequency on every important route to differentiate their product,[17] and try to fly their aircraft as much as possible to defray their high fixed costs. Once flights are scheduled and committed, capacity in the form of available seats is a perishable good. The marginal cost of filling an otherwise empty seat is very low. Because demand fluctuates, even across different days of the week, months of the year, and times of day, excess capacity is common. The airlines tend to drive down prices to garner at least some revenue from otherwise empty seats. The end result, however, is intense rivalry, low average prices, and losses for most participants in the industry.

Homogeneity of Firms

Firms that have similar cost structures will find it easier to agree on price and maximize joint industry profit than ones that do not. Widely varying costs among firms generally result in strong rivalry. In addition, if firms are similar on other dimensions, such as size, corporate culture, or length of time in the industry, coordination will be easier and rivalry will be less intense. In particular, the extent to which products are standardized can play an important role.

If product differentiation is significant, so that each firm's product differs markedly from that of other firms, coordination is difficult.[18] For example, a firm that incurs significant costs to produce a very high-quality product would seek a relatively high prevailing price, whereas a firm that makes a low-cost, low-quality product would perhaps push for a lower industry price. This observation is consistent with studies of strategic group influences on rivalry,[19] which suggest that rivalry is more intense between than within strategic groups. It follows that if distinctions between strategic groups are not pronounced, the industry as a whole will be better able to coordinate actions for the benefit of all. Hence, if firms in an industry are relatively similar in cost position, degree of product differentiation, size, and the like, we would expect less rivalry.

In the lead antiknock compound market, the two largest firms had similar production costs, the technology used was well established, and the product was relatively simple. In addition, the product was fungible, a commodity, and the opportunity for product differentiation was limited. Evidence supporting the argument that increasing heterogeneity in an industry will result in increased rivalry was found in a recent study of firms' conduct in the U.S. computer software industry. Rivalry was less intense when competing firms' cost structures were more similar.[20]

Multimarket Contact

When firms compete in multiple related markets, each firm has the opportunity of acting and reacting in more than one market. This high degree of contact can facilitate cooperation and reduce rivalry. A firm is much less likely to compete aggressively against a rival in a given market if it knows the rival can retaliate in many other markets. An example of extensive multimarket contact is provided by the leading U.S. western railroads. Burlington Northern–Sante Fe became a dominant railroad in the West after the merger of those two companies. In response, the two other leading western railroads, Union Pacific and Southern Pacific, announced their own merger. The resultant two mega-railroads would compete in virtually every market west of the Mississippi, with no other railroad providing competition in most markets. This extensive multimarket contact has raised concerns that competition between the two railroads would be minimal because of the degree of overlap.[21]

Next, we detail specific co-optive actions that are particularly useful when conditions do not encourage mutual forbearance (i.e., when there are a larger number of competitors, slack demand and excess capacity, or heterogeneity among industry rivals).[22]

Co-optive Actions

Signaling Advance Information on Price Changes

To coordinate actions successfully across an industry, firms need to be very aware of the actions of others and sensitive to their strategies. An important co-optive action is market signaling—alerting rivals to changes in prices and other competitive moves to lessen the possibility of an outbreak of warfare.[23]

According to Michael Porter, "a market signal is any action by a competitor that provides a direct or indirect indication of its intentions, motives, goals, or internal situation."[24] Market signals can be truthful indicators of intentions or mere posturing; information or disinformation can be provided, as fits the situation. Signals can achieve a variety of objectives and can take a variety of forms, such as announcements of actions after they have occurred, discussions of moves with major customers with the expectation that the news will circulate throughout the industry, initiation of regulatory or legal actions such as private antitrust suits, prior announcement of moves, and explanations of one's moves.

Our focus is on signaling as an instrument for creating a cooperative atmosphere within an industry. Market signals can greatly facilitate the establishment of industry norms on pricing, discounting, advertising, and other dimensions of competition. Clear understanding of those norms can aid firms in acting within the established boundaries of what is considered "fair" competition within an industry, and avoiding actions that are seen as bellicose and provocative. Prior announcement of moves and explanations of one's moves are particularly important forms of signaling. A firm can announce a move in advance and carefully explain the move in public forums to minimize the likelihood that the action will provoke rivals to respond sharply. For example, if a firm intends to reduce prices, it can announce that fact in advance with a careful justification, for example, lower costs. A price reduction could also be explained in terms of limited duration or market coverage. For example, an auto dealership might announce an upcoming price reduction for certain models and for a specific time period. That approach is particularly important when a firm does not want a move to be interpreted as an aggressive "knockout punch" and wants to avoid retaliation by a rival. Interestingly, this situation contrasts with that described in chapter 6, where a firm might cut prices to signal aggressiveness, announcing an intention to maintain low prices for a long period of time, in an effort to eliminate or deter rivals.

A variety of media can be used to signal competitors, including company promotional materials, annual reports, press announcements, and the Internet. In addition, firms can specifically train employees and salespeople to signal. In some cases, intermediate contacts such as banks, law firms, and investment houses send the signal.

A common agenda for firms using signaling is to send a clear message that the firm will be cooperative so long as rivals are cooperative, but will respond aggressively should another firm initiate an aggressive competitive action. That strategy has been described as "tit-for-tat." A firm can send a message that it is pursuing a tit-for-tat strategy by initially cooperating but responding aggressively in the next period should provocation occur. This choice is common and effective in game theory experimental simulations, where participants play a repeated prisoner's dilemma game such as that described in chapter 2. Specifically, a player chooses a co-optive strategy in the first period, and maintains that strategy in subsequent periods so long as the other player also chooses a co-optive strategy. Should the opponent select an aggressive strategy however, the player will respond by switching to the aggressive strategy in the next period. If a player is sure the opponent is committed to a tit-for-tat strategy, cooperation becomes the best alternative; commitment to a tit-for-tat strategy thus becomes an effective mechanism for avoiding the negative combative solution of the prisoner's dilemma.

In actual competitive interaction, however, it can be difficult for a firm to make clear to a rival through actual moves and responses that it is committed to a tit-for-tat strategy. Over time in a dynamic industry environment, a wide range of actions, reactions, and changed circumstance can make the firm's actual intent ambiguous. In such cases, signaling becomes of paramount importance. A firm can announce that it will respond aggressively to aggressive actions, but otherwise not rock the boat, in effect announcing a tit-for-tat strategy. A common example is an announcement to match any price discounting by rivals, as in the words: "We will not be undersold!" That statement does not mean "we will *lower* prices aggressively"; it merely means "we will *match* prices aggressively."

The lead antiknock compound market provides another example of the role of co-optive signaling. Recall that there was little chance for a resource-based competitive advantage in that industry. However, the strong decline in demand and presence of excess capacity in the face of significant fixed costs created strong pressures for price cuts. Moreover, sales were made in large volumes to the major oil companies. There were opportunities and strong temptations for secret discounts. Oil companies could bargain hard for discounts and provide large volumes of business in return. That leverage, combined with reduced sales and large excess capacity, was a very strong inducement for the firms to cut prices to fill their own excess capacity. There was a clear need for firms to engage in cooperative activity and to take specific actions to develop mutual forbearance in the absence of encouraging industry conditions.

The key co-optive action pursued successfully in that industry was advance notice of price changes. All firms in the industry gave at least 30 days' notice of price increases. For example, if PPG were initiating a price increase on September 1, it would notify customers and rivals of the change no later than August 1, and typically in the latter part of July. Uncertainty about whether rivals would follow would be eliminated before the price increase actually went into effect. Even if a rival did not follow until early August, prices would be out of sync for only a few days.

Disclosure of Prices and Other Competitive Information

Full disclosure of prices can eliminate the temptation for secret price cutting and create an open atmosphere in which cooperation can be maintained. In the lead antiknock compound market, all of the firms regularly issued press notices about price changes. That practice provided full information from price leaders about competitive moves and accurate and timely information about the degree to which rivals followed. Although other information sources, such as customers, could also be used to discover rivals' moves, they are not always timely and accurate and hence involve a degree of uncertainty. Co-optive actions to eliminate such uncertainty will facilitate coordination.

Trade associations and industry groups can disseminate price and cost data to industry participants and thus reduce industry uncertainty. The Tag Manufacturers Institute is an example of an industry association that provides extensive price information in an effort to enforce uniformity and perhaps stifle rivalry.[25] Its members are makers of standardized tags and tag devices that are attached to merchandise at retail outlets. The industry is oligopolistic, with a small number of firms supplying most of the product. A standard industry practice, implemented through the industry's trade association, is publication of standardized price lists issued to sales personnel, distributors, and customers.

Base Point Pricing

One difficulty in coordinating prices and refraining from price warfare is that disparate transportation costs complicate the sale of industrial goods.[26] A co-optive action designed to cope with that problem is commonly known as base point pricing, whereby all companies incorporate transportation costs into their prices. It enables companies to settle on a common and stable price industry-wide.[27]

An example can be drawn from the early days of the U.S. steel industry, which maintained a common system known as "Pittsburgh plus." Steel was sold at a delivered price equal to a base price plus the railroad freight rate from Pittsburgh to the point of delivery. That delivered price was charged even if the actual origin was not Pittsburgh and the actual freight costs to the destination were substantially different.

A similar co-optive strategy was followed in the lead antiknock compound industry. The four producers in that industry had six plants, and the customer's plants were located throughout the country. Transportation costs varied from sale to sale, so even if product prices were identical, delivered prices would vary when transport costs were added. The pricing differential provided incentives to compete. In other words, the firm with the lowest transport price would garner the business if all firms had the same FOB or product price. Others would then be tempted to cut prices, absorbing higher transport costs. Retaliation could lead to price warfare. The firms therefore quoted prices inclusive of transportation, regardless of the customer's location, so that the effective list price was the same for all customers throughout the United States. Thus, coordination and matching of prices was greatly facilitated.

Co-optive Actions, Response, and Competitive Advantage

A simple game theoretic formulation can be used to highlight the relationship between co-optive actions, response, and competitive advantage. Assume there are only two firms, each with a choice of a high or low price. The following payoffs to each firm are a function of the prices each of them charge.

		Firm B's Price	
		High	Low
Firm A's Price	High	111, 111	57, 122
	Low	122, 57	95, 95

If both firm A and firm B charge a high price, their payoffs will be identical (111, 111), assuming everything else is equal. Similarly, if each firm charges a low price, their payoffs will be identical (95, 95) but lower than in the first instance simply because of the price asked. However, if one firm sets a low price and the other sets a high price, the firm with the low price will have a higher payoff because of increased sales (122, 57). The payoff (95, 95) is the Nash equilibrium to this game, or the best each firm can do given the action of the other. It can also be seen as a conservative, "cut your losses" type of solution, or more formally a "maximin."

The challenge for both firms is to achieve the superior payoffs that are a function of the less intense competitive rivalry, that is, for both to set the higher price. This example illustrates that the individual pricing strategy each firm pursues is not nearly as important as coordinating prices to achieve the optimal outcome for both firms.

The game theory model can be used to examine the competitive moves of Kodak and Polaroid in the instant photography industry between

January 14, 1976, and November 23, 1977.[28] Using the game theoretic formulation just described, we see that fighting led to low profit for both Kodak and Polaroid as one firm was in a fighting mode while the other sought detente. An unstable situation resulted. Only detente on the part of both Kodak and Polaroid led to moderate profit. The message of this example seems to be that fighting hurts both firms and that detente is preferable.

The U.S. airline industry is a good example of a context in which no one firm can win the war against any other and co-optive actions may well be the best approach. It illustrates the difficulties of pursuing mutual forbearance in such a context and the consequences of unsuccessful cooperation. Airlines have been engaged in destructive competition since the industry was deregulated in 1978, and it intensified in the 1990s to 2000s. Cumulative losses in the U.S. airline industry have been in the billions of dollars since 1990 to $18 billion during the two years from 2001 to 2002.[29] The industry has had a number of airlines fold (e.g., Eastern, Pan Am) or be acquired (e.g., TWA) and undergo Chapter 11 (e.g., US Airways, United, Hawaiian) or verge-of-bankruptcy proceedings (e.g., American, Delta).

In the early 1990s and early 2000s, the recessions, along with the terrorist actions on September 11, 2001, and a spike in fuel prices during the wars in Kuwait, Iraq, and Afghanistan, contributed to the financial woes of the industry during those periods. However, those challenges in the external industry environment do not fully explain the poor performance. As we described in chapter 3, at the core, airlines are subject to forces that result in very fierce competition,[30] including industry demand that is highly inelastic, large overhead costs, capacity that is difficult or costly to reduce, and a tendency for very deep price cuts.[31]

Other factors make mutual forbearance difficult. There are relatively few ways to differentiate the product of airline service. Flight frequency can be increased, frequent flyer programs offered, or inflight comforts increased, but such differences are minimal in comparison with the brand identification and loyalty, or actual product differences, of other products. Hence the airlines compete on price because they cannot compete on other dimensions. The degree of multimarket contact is high, as firms compete with each other across many origin-destination pairs. Evidence shows that such contact intensifies competition when demand is slack and facilitates collusion in good times.[32] By the standards of many industries, the number of firms in each market is small, but competition increases as the number of firms increases. In addition, maverick firms such as Southwest Airlines and JetBlue that are very different from the others in cost structure play a very important role in stimulating competition. Finally, many firms bankrupt under chapter 11 remain in business. Evidence suggests that such firms are instrumental in increasing rivalry and initiating price wars.[33] Overall, the U.S. airline industry provides an example of the critical link between excessive rivalry and low profitability, and the challenge of designing co-optive actions to address that problem. While not necessarily the primary purpose of such actions, alliances and code-sharing arrangements among airlines might be one potential mechanism to reduce the level of rivalry.

A second game theory example illustrates more specifically the importance of response in formulating payoffs to moves.[34] Assume two identical gas stations A and B are selling private brand gasoline with no rivals around for miles. Each charges a price of $1.00/gallon, a competitive price at which there is no excess profit. Each holds 50 percent of the market. Station A is considering a move of raising its price to $1.25/gallon, which has been calculated as the joint profit maximizing price should station B follow with an identical price increase. The price raise will be profitable for A if B matches, but will be very unprofitable should B maintain the price of $1.00/gallon, as all of A's customers will presumably switch to B. Figure 9.2 describes the game and associated payoffs.

It appears risky for A to raise its price without a formal assurance or agreement that B will also raise its price. Of course, that type of formal agreement is illegal under the antitrust laws. However, if A increases its price it will learn very quickly whether B will follow with a commensurate price increase. If B does not follow, A can, and presumably will, immediately lower its price back to the $1.00/gallon level. That possibility affects the payoffs for B and in turn its optimal strategy. By keeping the price at $1.00, B will have a brief period of large market share but then will return to a normal level of profit. If B follows the increase, the prospects are good that both stations will be able to maintain the high prices and excessive profit. Alternatively, A could signal by announcing that in 30 days it will raise prices to $1.25. If B were to make a similar announcement, A could avoid having to take a risky action. Should B not announce similar intentions, A would have time to cancel its price increase before the implementation date.[35]

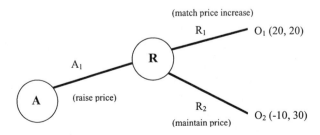

Figure 9.2   Response Will Determine Payoff to Co-optive Moves.

Here the key to the firms' ability to cooperate is the openness of prices and the ability to quickly and at low cost switch prices first up and then, if need be, back down. The same type of feeling out of a rival, testing the waters to see whether a rival will concur in a price increase, can be done in an even more sophisticated and ingenious way in the airline industry with modern computer reservation systems.[36] For example, in the summer of 1989 United announced $20 increases on many fares in and out of Chicago, to take effect in September. American Airlines, United's biggest competitor in that market, immediately announced that it would match the increases in September. If American had failed to match the increases, United could have returned to the original prices before the September effective date. Such signaling has also been used in advancing the expiration dates of discount fares, another method of raising fares. For example, both Northwest Airlines and Midway Airlines were offering bargain fares on the route from Chicago to Grand Rapids, Michigan, until July 31. Continental and American had the same low fares but moved their expiration date up to July 17. Northwest and Midway subsequently moved their expiration dates up to within a few days of July 17. Presumably, if the latter two airlines had continued their low fares until the end of July, Continental and American could have reinstated their discounts until the end of July.

In addition to being used to elevate prices above competitive levels, co-optive actions can be taken to end costly price wars. Again, the ability to signal clearly, as with computer reservation systems(CRSs), can be useful.[37] Suppose carrier A tries to boost business with lower ticket prices and enters reduced fares into the CRS for some future date. Carrier B might not only match the lower fares for the same markets but also lower fares in other markets served by carrier A, or might go beyond a simple match to an even lower fare in the affected markets. Carrier B could even attach special codes to its new fares to be sure the message is clear. Carrier A would feel the threat and cancel its reduction, returning fares to the more cooperative level. As all of these actions take place as signaling of future fares, no actual fares may ever change.

One factor that may enhance cooperation in an industry is dominance by one firm. That firm can serve as a leader and intimidate others into cooperating. For example, if carrier B is a dominant firm, it will serve many more markets than carrier A. It can lower prices all over to intimidate A and persuade A not to reduce prices. Many observers believe co-optive pricing in the U.S. auto industry was prompted for many years by GM's market leadership. Such bullying can be more difficult to achieve if the rival is a new entrant. New entrants are often renegade firms that need to rock the boat to build market share. They have no interest in maintaining the status quo, which by definition would give them no place in the industry.

Managerial Implications
and Antitrust Considerations

The war metaphor, although clearly critical in explaining firm behavior in today's competitive environment, should be supplemented by one emphasizing coordination among firms, especially in certain kinds of industries or market segments. Any action taken has implications beyond that firm's costs and revenues; it also affects the degree of competitor response and industry rivalry. For example, a price cut might be expected to increase market share and possibly revenue in the short run, but if it brings about a protracted price war, such an action may well be unwise.

Several factors influence the degree to which coordination can be achieved in an industry: the number of competitors, the state of industry demand, and homogeneity of costs, as well as others such as the background of top executives within the industry. Although coordination may be desirable for incumbent firms in a given industry, it may well be impossible to achieve because of those and related factors. A firm considering entry into or exit from an industry therefore should be aware of factors affecting intensity of rivalry, as future profit may well hang in the balance.

Formal collusion, such as overt agreements to fix prices at certain levels or divide markets, has been illegal in the United States since passage of the 1890 Sherman Act.[38] Nonetheless, such activity continues to be uncovered and prosecuted by the Antitrust Division of the Department of Justice. The DOJ initiated 94 restraint-of-trade investigations in 2002. Of particular salience to individual managers is the fact that restraint of trade is a felony violation, and jail sentences are becoming more common. In 2002, of the 23 criminal cases filed for violation of restraint-of-trade laws, the Justice Department won all, including several pending cases. In addition, corporations received fines of more than $93 million in 2002 for antitrust violations overall.[39]

The observation that firms engage in such conduct in spite of the antitrust laws underscores the role coordination can play in enhancing firm performance. Sometimes executives are found to be in blatant violation of antitrust laws, as happened in the U.S. electric utilities industry in the 1950s. The informal agreements about the distribution of market share that were maintained for decades in that industry were viewed as very rational by some executives, and they went to great lengths to bolster and sustain them. For instance, meetings among executives of several electric utility firms were held in major American cities during the 1940s and 1950s to establish pricing agreements. The sites for the meetings were chosen to coincide with various phases of the moon to confuse Justice Department investigators who were seeking to prove that the firms were colluding. Indeed, many years elapsed before investigators established the relationship between the cycles of the moon and the scheduling of the meetings. Several executives were fined, and some were sent to jail for their price-fixing actions.

Another example illustrates how easy it is for executives caught up in competitive battles to consider engaging in illegal behavior. In 1982, a fierce competitive battle was raging between American Airlines and Braniff International on several routes served from the Dallas/Fort Worth Airport. As the airline industry has little opportunity for product differentiation and leading firms in the industry are homogeneous in terms of resources, price was the main competitive weapon. Robert Crandall, the president of American Airlines, placed a phone call to Howard Putnam, the chairman of Braniff, to suggest a more cooperative approach between the two firms:

Crandall: I think it's dumb as hell for crissakes, all right, to sit here and pound the [expletive] out of each other and neither of us making a [expletive] dime.

Putnam: But...I can't just sit here and allow you to bury us without giving our best effort....Do you have a suggestion for me?

Crandall: Yes, I have a suggestion for you. Raise your [expletive] fares 20 percent. I'll raise mine the next morning....You'll make more money, and I will, too.

Putnam: We can't talk about pricing.

Crandall: Oh [expletive], Howard, we can talk about any [expletive] thing we want to talk about.[40]

The suggested pricing behavior, if implemented, would clearly have been illegal. In fact, Putnam taped the conversation and turned the tape over to the Justice Department.

Another price-fixing case showed the president of Pepsi-Cola Bottling Company agreeing with a Coca-Cola bottler to halt discounts to retailers. That action resulted in a fine and jail term for the guilty managers. In another case, Southland and Borden were found to have rigged bids for dairy products sold to Florida school milk programs.[41]

Overt price fixing was alleged recently in the baby food industry.[42] In 1993, several grocery concerns filed a class-action lawsuit against the three largest baby food companies: Gerber Products, H. J. Heinz, and Ralston Purina. The complaints alleged that the three companies had secretly agreed to "fix, raise, maintain and stabilize" prices of baby food since at least 1975. The companies have denied the charges, but fighting such charges clearly entails major legal expenses. The companies eventually settled out of court for $128 million within the year.[43]

Price-fixing suits have also been brought in recent years against companies in diverse industries, from art auctions (illustrated in the beginning of the chapter) to vitamin manufacturing to Wall Street houses trading on the Nasdaq stock exchange. Large settlements have been the predominant outcome in those cases.[44] One particular Justice Department investigation of price fixing in food products has received substantial attention in part because of the role of an internal whistle-blower. Archer Daniels Midland and at least three other U.S. milling companies were under investigation for possibly fixing the price of corn products.[45] The impetus for the investigation was conversations taped secretly over a three-year period by an FBI informant, an Archer Daniels Midland executive. The company eventually agreed to settle with the government for $100 million.[46]

Such overt agreements to restrict competition are clearly illegal, presumably relatively uncommon, and not to be encouraged, but antitrust precedents allow for a range of less overt "tacit" coordination and "conscious parallelism" activity. For example, firms may charge the same prices and change prices together over time, and as long as there is no overt agreement to do so such activity will not generally be judged illegal.[47] In addition, all firms in an industry can maintain high prices in relation to costs, thereby earning handsome profit; again, in the absence of a formal agreement, such activity is not illegal.

Market signaling is an important co-optive action but can constitute a "gray area" in terms of restraint of trade under the Sherman Act.[48] Given the clearly per se illegality and potential felony jail sentences associated with overt price fixing, price signaling is perhaps a much more common device for cooperation. The boundary between legal and illegal price signaling is difficult to define. Certainly much of what might be considered signaling is appropriate and, to consumers, beneficial transmission of information about prices and products. However, antitrust activists have charged that signaling is frequently harmful to the competitive process and should be closely monitored by the Department of Justice.

> To the antitrust regulators, price signaling is merely a modern variant of the collusive activities of 100 years ago. The current practice benefits suppliers and hurts customers. According to this view, price signaling is an immoral, unethical, and even criminal activity that parades under euphemisms such as "industry cooperation" and "competitive marketing strategy."[49]

A recent example from the airline industry illustrates both the range of possible coordination activities and the care firms must take not to run afoul of the antitrust laws.[50] In particular, this example directs attention to the role of cooperative signaling and the care that must be taken not to cross the line to illegal activity when engaging in it. As we discussed previously, airlines use their computer reservation systems to signal and provide information on price changes. However, nine major domestic carriers have been charged with price fixing because of actions taken through such systems. More specifically, critics claim that airlines use CRSs to improperly signal their pricing actions, better coordinate pricing, and alert rivals of intended retaliatory action in response to price cuts. A recent *Wall Street Journal* article discussed this behavior in the context of potential antitrust violations:

> Airlines have used future fare reductions to pressure rivals to back off pricing actions they don't favor. The airlines have done this by filing fare cuts with a future effective date in a rival's hub market. The price cuts would be withdrawn if the rival carrier withdrew its own pricing action.[51]

The article went on to state that two firms, TransWorld Airlines and Northwest Airlines, had agreed to alter certain of those practices as part of a proposed settlement to remove them from the price-fixing lawsuit.

Although our primary focus has been on applicability of U.S. antitrust laws, proscription of collusion is common throughout the world. In most countries, such laws are known as competition policies. Canada, for example, has passed a Competition Act for the purpose of maintaining and encouraging competition in that country. The European Economic Community (EEC) also has established a competition policy and associated enforcement mechanism to promote free enterprise throughout its member countries.[52] Like the U.S. laws, EEC policy strictly forbids any agreement between companies that has the "object or effect the fixing of prices of products or services."[53] Tacit collusion is also addressed by the outlawing of anticompetitive "concerted practices." A concerted practice has been defined as a "form of coordination between undertakings which, without having reached the stage where an agreement properly so-called has been concluded, knowingly substitutes practical cooperation between them for the risks of competition."[54] In one recent case, competitors were found in violation of this provision through parallel pricing practices. Prices of numerous products were repeatedly raised by identical percentages at about the same time, in different markets, accompanied by similar wording of instructions to subsidiaries to carry out the price increases.

Managers therefore must be fully aware of the antitrust laws and take all possible steps to avoid antitrust violations. Any activities that might be construed as violations, especially discussions with competitors or with buyers about their future prices, should receive particular attention. Employees should be encouraged to inform managers whenever there is any potential for antitrust violation, and to seek the advice of corporate counsel on those matters. All companies should develop codes of conduct and disseminate them to their employees. The following statement is an excerpt from the Antitrust and Competition section of Dun & Bradstreet Corporation's Policy of Business Conduct:

> Dun & Bradstreet will not tolerate any business transaction or activity that violates the letter or spirit of the antitrust and competition laws of any country that apply to the Company's business. . . . Follow these general guidelines: Report facts, be concise and objective, and indicate where information came from to establish that there is no cooperation with competitors. . . . Do not refer to "industry policies," "industry price" or similar expressions that imply a common course of action exists even though it does not. Do not use language that would suggest a false intent to harm competitors, such as, "This new program will 'destroy' the competition" or "establish a dominant position." . . . Consult with the Legal Department about when communications with a lawyer can be "privileged."[55]

In addition to carefully avoiding violation of antitrust laws, managers should conduct themselves in a highly ethical way when considering co-optive actions. Clearly, it is impossible to discuss in detail how to act ethically in a complex array of business situations. However, one source on the matter has provided a set of useful questions to aid in exploring ethical ramifications of business decisions:

1. Have I thought about whether the action I may take is right or wrong?
2. Will I be proud to tell of my action to my family? To my employer? To the news media?
3. Am I willing for everyone to act as I am thinking of acting?
4. Will my decision cause harm to others or to the environment?
5. Will my actions violate the law?[56]

Summary

This chapter supports the contention that, when no resource advantage is present, coordination with competitors to avoid wars may well be related to increased profit for all of the firms involved. Emphasizing only the war or competitive metaphor may be not only misleading but also misguided. Our research suggests that under such conditions firms would do better to avoid war if at all possible. Cooperation may not be possible in all cases but should be explored if a firm wants to survive and prosper when competitive alternatives are unavailable, with careful attention to applicable competition policies.

Chapter 10

USING THE ACTION MODEL

Predicting the Behavior of Rivals

L et us consider the future outlook of the hotel and specialty coffee industries. In the hotel industry, the growth in supply of hotel rooms has exceeded the demand for rooms coming on line, mainly because of a slower economy. As a result, occupancy and room rates have been pushed downward. The new industry conditions have encouraged many companies, such as Cendant Corporation and Intercontinental Group (Holiday Inn), to cut properties. For example, Cendant has terminated more than 340 properties, comprising more than 30,000 guestrooms, and Holiday Inn (part of Intercontinental) has terminated more than 200 agreements.[1] The increased supply of rooms in prior years, however, still raises concern about overcapacity and increased rivalry.

Also undergoing significant change is the retail specialty coffee industry, which began rapid growth in the early 1980s. The trend started in the Pacific Northwest and quickly spread across North America. As a consequence of that growth, many firms entered the industry, raising the level of rivalry. Starbucks and Second Cup are two such firms; their markets increasingly overlap as both try to boost market share and profit. For example, Starbucks went from a small northwestern firm with 11 stores in 1987 to the national leader with more than 5,900 stores by 2002.[2]

This chapter offers additional insights on how our action model can be used in practice. In particular, imagine you are at the head of Cendant in the hotel industry or Starbucks in the specialty coffee industry. How can you use the material presented in this book to take actions that maximize your firm's competitive advantage? More specifically, how should you engage rivals such as Holiday Inn in the hotel industry or Second Cup in the coffee industry? Drawing from all the material in prior chapters, we answer those questions by proposing an analysis of internal and external resource positions, and a related competitor analysis. More specifically, we first examine how a focal firm, such as Cendant or Starbucks, can analyze its relative internal resources and external market position to aid in formulating the most appropriate actions: entrepreneurial, Ricardian, deterrent, or co-optive. Second, we introduce a competitor analysis model and show how it can be used to predict the most likely future competitive actions and reactions of rivals. Such prediction is critical to the effective implementation of a firm's competitive action. The relationship between those two analyses and our action model is portrayed in figure 10.1.

Recall that the action model focuses on the *relative* internal resource and external market positions (firm-specific resources and market position) of firms. Although a manager may attempt to relate those positions of his or her firm to industry averages or to a set of specific competitors, the analyses should generally be conducted on a pair-wise basis, between a focal firm and a single direct competitor. As Chen argues, competitor analysis is best carried out as an intraindustry comparison derived from the study of the relationships between pairs of firms. Moreover, any asymmetry between firms can be assessed only by looking from the point of view of a focal firm. Thus, the focus of the analysis is not on understanding groups of firms or individual competitors in isolation but on assessing the competitive tension between firms and thus the potential of these two firms for engaging in rivalrous behavior. Only through this kind of micro analysis can the subtlety and nuances of competition and rivalry be revealed.[3] Therefore, relative resource and competitor analyses are most appropriately conducted for the focal firm and every one of its primary competitors.

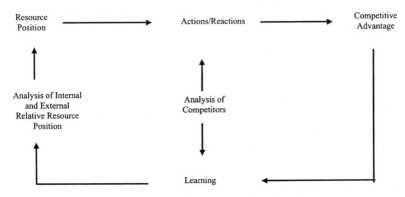

Figure 10.1 Analyzing Resources and Competitors.

Analyzing Internal Resources
and External Market Position

Throughout this chapter, we use two industries, the hotel and specialty coffee industries, to develop example analyses. Assume that Cendant is the focal firm in the hotel industry and that Starbucks is the focal firm in the specialty coffee industry. The beginning point in carrying out the relative resource and external market position assessments is the identification of a competitor for pair-wise analysis. We define competitors as firms that are vying with the focal firm for the same *customers* in the same *markets*. Of course, primary attention should be given to key competitors, ones with the greatest degree of customer and market overlap.

In the hotel industry, we consider the rivalry between Cendant and Intercontinental Hotels Group. The Cendant brands include AmeriHost, Days Inn, Super & Motel, Travelodge, Ramada, Howard Johnson, Knights Inn, Villager, and Wingate Inn.[4] Intercontinental Hotels Group includes Intercontinental Hotels, Holiday Inns (and Express), Crowne Plaza, and Staybridge Suites.[5] Intercontinental is one of Cendant's primary rivals, especially in the United States, where both companies seek midscale and economy customers in many of the same locations. In the specialty coffee industry, we highlight the rivalry between Starbucks Coffee and Second Cup. Starbucks has recently established locations that compete directly with Second Cup in many Canadian markets.

Once the principal competitors have been defined, the next step is to analyze each rival's key resources in relation to those of the focal firm. Recall from Chapter 4 that we defined resources as all information, knowledge, capabilities, organizational processes, and tangible assets controlled by a firm that enable the firm to undertake competitive action. Recall also that we recommended that resources be evaluated by comparing the value chain of the focal firm and its rival(s). We showed that by breaking the firm down in terms of the discrete resource activities it performs to deliver the product or service, such as the key functions of the organization, one can better understand key sources of advantage and therefore likely actions. Although firms in the same industry often have similar resources, subtle differences in configuration of resources among competitors can be a source of different competitive actions. We first examine the relative resource positions of Intercontinental Group and Cendant, the focal firm.

Cendant and Intercontinental Group

Marketing expertise and the brand equity of its name are perhaps Intercontinental and Holiday Inn's greatest resources. Over the years, Holiday Inn has developed an outstanding reputation for quality and value. For example, Holiday Inn has been ranked as one of the 100 most-recognized brands in the world.[6] Holiday Inn appears to be exploiting that resource advantage by attempting to transfer its brand image to segments other than midprice and economy, for example, with the introduction of Holiday Express. Cendant, in contrast, operates with many different brands. Certain brands controlled by Cendant, such as Days Inn, have strong awareness, but they are not nearly as well known as Holiday Inn.

Holiday Inn also has greater financial resources and access to capital. It is part of Intercontinental, which in 2002 had $5.4 billion in capital reserves. Holiday Inn, as a business unit, maintained $60 million in operating cash flow in 2002 and earned more than $387 million.[7] In contrast, Cendant reported $126 million in cash and noncash equivalents in 2002, and a debt-to-equity ratio of more than 280 percent. Moreover, Cendant earned only 64 percent of Intercontinental Group's income, or $247 million.[8]

Another resource advantage of Holiday Inn and Intercontinental is its reservation and online system, which are considered one of the best in the industry. Customers can call from anywhere in the world to reserve a room, or they may access a wide variety of services through the internet. Rival companies, such as Cendant, have spent many millions of dollars trying to develop comparable reservation systems, but all fall short of Holiday Inn's systems. Figure 10.2 provides a summary of the *relevant* resource comparison between Cendant and Intercontinental group.

Although Intercontinental Group has significant internal resource advantages over Cendant, Cendant has a slightly stronger external resource position, measured in terms of market share, than Intercontinental Group. Holiday Inn has a 16.2 percent market share, and Cendant has a 17.5 percent share, the highest in the industry. Figure 10.3 depicts the relative market and resource positions of the two firms, with Cendant shown at an overall relative resource disadvantage.

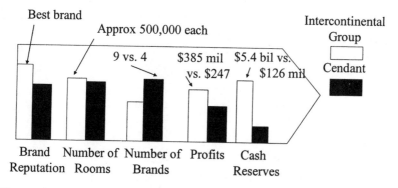

Figure 10.2 Relative Resource Comparison: Value Chain of Cendant and Intercontinental Group.

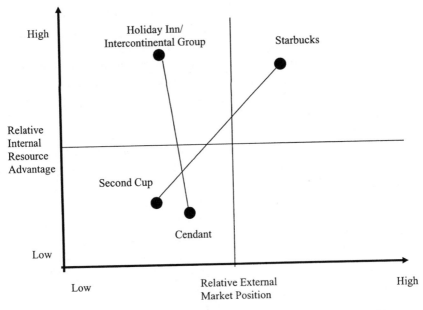

Figure 10.3   Summary Description of Internal and External Resource Positions.

Starbucks and Second Cup

Starbucks, our focal firm, is the retail specialty coffee industry leader with more than 5,900 locations as of 2002. Second Cup has more than 390 locations in Canada.[9] In 1996, Starbucks entered the Canadian market, challenging Second Cup in locations such as British Columbia, Ontario, Quebec, Nova Scotia, New Brunswick, and Prince Edward Island. In response, through acquisition, Second Cup has challenged Starbucks in Arizona, Texas, and California. From 1996 until recently, Second Cup and Starbucks competed for customers in many of the same markets and are potential competitors in many other markets.

In terms of products, Starbucks offers 30 coffee blends and a line of Starbucks brand machines and bean grinders, coffee accessories, and gift packs. Second Cup has a limited product line, generally coffee and food items. It also has specialized coffee days and offers a small selection of coffee mugs and a few other accessories.

In terms of facilities, both Second Cup and Starbucks have many types of locations, including street-front stores, shopping mall stores, and kiosks in airports, arenas, and other high-traffic areas. Starbucks has a significant resource advantage in that it built a 370,000-square-foot distribution and roasting facility in York, Pennsylvania, in addition to its facilities in the state of Washington. These facilities enable Starbucks to have greater control of costs and to monitor coffee bean quality more carefully. Second

Cup does not have such facilities and relies on contracts for preroasted beans from Kraft.

Second Cup, prior to 2000, did not conduct formal advertising. Most promotion was done on a store-by-store basis. No national radio or TV advertising was used, as it was deemed too expensive. In contrast, Starbucks spent $28 million on advertising in 2001 as part of store operating expenses. Focused advertising has strongly established the Starbucks brand name throughout the world.

Starbucks and Second Cup are both financially strong. However, Starbucks has an advantage in terms of its size and ability to finance growth and endure tough competition. Although Second Cup's sales exceeded $108 million U.S. for the year of 2001,[10] they were still less than 4 percent of Starbucks' for the same period.[11] Second Cup has a relatively small amount of long-term debt, 14 percent, but Starbucks has even less long-term debt, 0.2 percent. Second Cup has a $4 million credit line, and Starbucks has a $30 million credit line. Starbucks' cash and cash equivalents, which exceed $252 million, are nearly 15 times greater than Second Cup's, and Starbucks' $181 million in earnings is almost 64 times Second Cup's earnings.

Starbucks seems to be able to move faster than Second Cup in seizing market opportunities and implementing change. Second Cup relies on a franchising system to expand, whereas Starbucks plans to grow to more than 25,000 stores through direct ownership and joint ventures. Because of the nature of the franchise system, Second Cup stores are designed individually, which may slow location openings. In addition, implementation of company-wide changes may be slow if some franchisees resist. Second Cup's managers and board of directors are homogenous and primarily composed of insiders, whereas Starbucks' managers are more diverse, drawn from major marketing powers such as Pepsi, Honda, and Hallmark. Indeed, Second Cup has demonstrated little ability to move fast. Starbucks first showed its interest in Canada when it entered the market in 1987, but it did not enter Toronto until nine years later and Second Cup should have been ready. Instead, Second Cup has been slow to respond to Starbucks' moves, which are consistently innovative and creative. New products, new product lines, and strategic alliances are standard Starbucks actions. Figure 10.4 provides a qualitative summary of the preceding relative resource analysis.

In terms of relative market position, Starbucks has more than 5,900 locations in the United States and Canada, nearly 15 times as many as Second Cup. Market share is difficult to assess in the very fragmented specialty coffee industry; however, given that Starbucks is the industry leader and Second Cup earns less than 4 percent of the revenue earned by Starbucks, we can reasonably conclude that Starbucks' overall market share is at least 26 times that of Second Cup. Therefore, we conclude that Starbucks has a significant advantage over Second Cup in both internal resources and

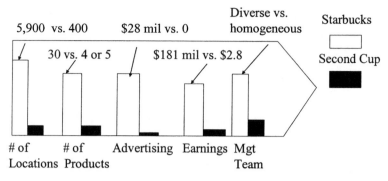

Figure 10.4   Value Chain of Starbucks and Second Cup.

external market position. Figure 10.4 depicts the relative resource positions of Starbucks and Second Cup. We will return to hotel and specialty coffee competitors analyses, but first we broaden the framework.

Analyzing Competitors and Predicting Future Competitive Actions

The purpose of competitor analysis is to develop a profile of the likely actions and reactions of rivals. We are concerned with the actions a particular rival will take and the way the rival will react to the focal firm's actions. Although we note that the analysis of relative resource position provides insight about how a focal firm will move against a particular rival, a more comprehensive understanding of that rival is necessary to predict its future competitive behavior. Our model of competitor analysis has three dimensions: competitor beliefs, competitor intent, and past competitive actions and reactions. By analyzing what a competitor believes about the focal firm and the broader industry, what the competitor intends to achieve in the industry, and the way the competitor has acted and reacted in the past, one can develop a profile of the competitor's likely future actions and reactions. Figure 10.5 portrays the basic competitor analysis model.

Competitor Beliefs

In the perennial gale of competition, there will be a variety of beliefs about the future direction of industry evolution, about which competitors are most and least dangerous, and about alternative ways to compete. As we noted in chapter 4, few organizational events are totally unique. Managers consequently process information about specific events through their existing knowledge systems. In chapter 6, we refer to those knowledge

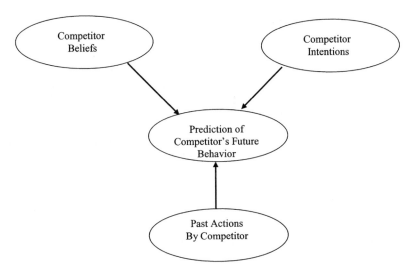

Figure 10.5 Analysis of Competitors.

systems as "schemas." Recall that managerial schemas provide viewpoints about how competitors will behave and how the business environment operates. Schemas are cognitive systems of beliefs, theories, and propositions that individuals develop over time on the basis of their own experiences. They help us to categorize events efficiently and evaluate their importance. In discussing how managers acquire business-related schemas, Gary Hamel and C. K. Prahalad note:

> Managers acquire their frames of reference (schemas) invisibly from business school and other educational experiences, from peers, consultants and the business press, and, above all, from their own career experiences. But invisible as the frames themselves may be, their consequences are visible at every turn in how a company's senior managers understand what it means to be "strategic," in their choice of competitive stratagems, in their relationships with subordinates. In this sense, managerial frames (schemas), perhaps more than anything else, bound a company's approach to competitive warfare and thus determine competitive outcomes.[12]

Action choices are guided by what a rival decision-maker thinks about the industry, competitors, and the best way to compete. Therefore, an understanding of rival managers' belief structures can provide important insights about likely future behavior.

Beliefs about the Industry. Ever-changing technology, globalization, and deregulation leave predictions about industry evolution and structure open to judgment and speculation. Even so, decision-makers must make organizational commitments for the unknown future, and therefore must make educated guesses about industry evolution. We have shown how Coke's belief that the U.S. soft drink industry had matured in the early 1970s moved Coke's attention toward global markets. That incorrect belief about the evolution of the soft drink industry enabled Pepsi to make inroads at Coke's expense. Industry beliefs consist of expectations about industry growth rate, capacity expansions, competitive entry and exit, extent of rivalry, extent of future buyer and supplier power, and the role of substitutes. Those beliefs often vary among managers of different companies, particularly in industries with high change rates.

Beliefs about Competitors.   Just as firms may be uncertain about the future evolution of an industry, they may be uncertain or incorrect in their beliefs about which competitors are the most dangerous. During the late 1960s and early l970s, Coke managers were not allowed to mention Pepsi in the boardroom. Coke did not believe Pepsi was a worthy competitor. Caterpillar, the world leader in earth-moving equipment, long defined its competition in terms of U.S. firms, such as John Deere and International Harvester, totally ignoring the Japanese firm Komatsu. At the time, Japanese firms did not have a reputation for high-quality products, but Komatsu subsequently became a major player in the earth-moving equipment world market.

Beliefs about the Firm Itself.   A firm can also be incorrect, or have faulty beliefs, about its own competencies and abilities. For example, a firm can believe it is the industry leader in technology, even when there is evidence that it is not. Similarly, the firm may fail to recognize that its marketing techniques are no longer effective or may attempt to exploit a competency it no longer has. Jay Gaibraith and Robert Kazanjian introduced the idea of "center of gravity" to describe how firms develop competencies over time in certain areas of the organization, and how those competency centers become centers of gravity that drive future firm behaviors.[13] Firms consequently view themselves in terms of what has worked well in the past. Of course, changing environments can make those viewpoints inaccurate, but they can provide insights to rivals' future behavior nonetheless.

Competitive Intent

In addition to considering rivals' beliefs about industry, competitors, and themselves, firms need to analyze rivals' intentions and goals. Intent is not as difficult to determine as one might think, as firms often make public statements about their intentions. Some examples are Komatsu's goal to "encircle Caterpillar," Canon's attempt to "beat Xerox," and Toyota's objective to become "a second Ford, a leader in automotive innovation."[14]

Michael Porter notes that knowledge of a rival's goals indicates whether or not the rival is satisfied with its current position and what it is attempting to achieve.[15] For example, a rival attempting to increase sales may react aggressively to an action that threatens sales growth, and a rival attempting to maximize profit is likely to respond to actions that could adversely affect its profit.

Porter has argued that the diagnosis of goals should be conducted at multiple levels of analysis—at the corporate level, the business level, and the functional level.[16] In considering corporate goals, a firm should examine the role of the rival's business unit in the overall corporate plan. Is it to supply cash flow? Do the corporate managers see the rival as tomorrow's star? How important is the rival firm to the corporate portfolio? Answers to these questions may provide insight about how the corporate level will direct the rival to behave toward its competitor.

It is also important to consider the rival's goals at the business unit level. Has the firm established financial goals? Are they specific and measurable? Are managers within the firm held accountable for meeting those goals? Is the firm's compensation package linked with the achievement of goals? Many firms have sales, cost, and profit goals for each year. What the rival firm is emphasizing, whether it be sales, cost control, profit, or even all three, will provide important clues to its future competitive behavior. For example, a firm attempting to maximize sales will probably react to a competitor's low-pricing action, as it could undermine achievement of the firm's sales goal.

In considering functional areas, a firm should examine what the rival's goals are for new product development, R & D, marketing, and manufacturing. Is the firm attempting to introduce new products at a faster rate? What are its R & D goals? How many new markets is the firm attempting to enter? Does the rival plan to add capacity in the near future? What capacity goals does the rival have?

In the absence of public statements about intentions, it may be possible to infer intentions from the composition of management. For example, a CEO with a marketing background may emphasize sales growth and the marketing function, whereas a top management team composed mostly of engineers may emphasize new products, patents, and technology. A firm led by a team of finance and legal managers may pursue cost-cutting measures and emphasize stockholder value.

Past Competitive Action

We have stressed throughout this book that organizations are creatures of their past. Successful actions will be repeated; effective past actions will be emphasized in the future. For example, firms that have used pricing actions effectively to achieve organizational goals are likely to continue using pricing actions in the future. Firms that have developed their market position through strong product promotion actions will tend to use such moves in the future. A company with poor performance may reintroduce actions that were effective in the past. Therefore, a study of past actions and reactions can provide important information about possible future actions. We now return to our industry examples by examining the competitive beliefs, intentions, and past actions of our focal firms' rivals, Intercontinental Group (Holiday Inn) and Second Cup.

Cendant and Intercontinental Group

Recall that Cendant is the focal firm and Intercontinental Group (Holiday Inn) is the rival. First, Cendant must consider Intercontinental Groups' *beliefs*. An analysis of annual reports and other published material on Intercontinental and Holiday Inn reveals that the company sees itself as an industry *leader*, able to compete successfully in all market segments. The company realizes it has certain weaknesses, such as inconsistent quality, but it has initiated programs to overcome them. Importantly, Holiday Inn's managers believe its brand name is perceived as representing high value across all customer segments. The company therefore does not see segmentation in the industry as problematic because it believes its brand image can be used to exploit multiple segments. In particular, the company appears to believe that the business traveler segment of the industry is the most profitable and has created many programs to cater to it.

Judging from Intercontineneetal Group's competitive behavior, we can reasonably conclude that it is very aware of its competition. Examination of rival actions followed by Holiday Inn's reactions confirms that inference. For example, when Cendant announced its new internal rating program in March 1994, Holiday Inn responded with its own program within six months. When Marriott announced a frequent flyer program, Holiday Inn announced an equivalent program within seven months. Finally, when Cendant launched a new upscale product, Plaza Hotels, Holiday launched its own new brand, Crowne Plaza Hotels, within the year. Moreover, as Cendant increased efforts to improve overall quality by using inspection teams, Holiday Inn increased the staff in the same area and started a campaign highlighting its blue-ribbon hotels in its own consumer directory, thus directing customers to these topnotch locations through its toll-free reservation center.

Holiday Inn appears *intent* on increasing its market share. In particular, it seems to be very sensitive to price cuts, promotions, and discounts instituted by rivals. For example, in June 1994 Holiday Inn was the industry leader in announcing a "weekend giveaway" in a clear attempt to draw customers from rival firms. That goal is also exemplified by its pricing and promotional campaigns designed to draw new customers from rivals.

Holiday Inn is attempting to increase its international presence. For example, after the acquisition of Holiday Inn by Six Continent PLC., the corporate newsletter noted a "new global orientation to the company and a new global focus to the brand."[17] However, Holiday Inn has not ignored local markets; for example, it recently introduced a new brand, Holiday Inn Garden Court, that is positioned to address the needs of local markets. Most recently, under guidance of Intercontinental Group, Holiday Inn opened Holiday Express, and Express by Holiday Inn, presumably in an attempt to capitalize on its brand recognition.

Holiday Inn appears to be a risk-taker, acting in innovative ways, such as being one of the first hotels to offer online reservation service. Efforts to capitalize on its brand equity by entering new market segments must also be considered innovative. Those moves required large amounts of capital and a strong marketing push, and subsequently engaged rivals entrenched in the targeted segments. Most of the risky moves were made prior to Holiday Inn's acquisition by Six Continents Group, now Intercontinental Group. Yet the new parent company also appears to be a risk-taker, even in its acquisition of Holiday Inn.

Holiday Inn recently hired a new executive vice president away from Pepsico, a firm well known for creative marketing. The fact that Holiday Inn's management team is relatively young (the average age is 51) supports their risk-taking propensity. In addition, the team has several years of hotel operating experience.

Holiday Inn has taken *past aggressive strategic actions*. In the fall of 1994, the firm began new branding actions by introducing hotels that would compete in all segments—economy, midpriced, business, and luxury. The new brands are Holiday Inn Express in the economy segment, Holiday Inn and Holiday Inn Garden Court in the midprice segment, Holiday Inn Select in the business segment, and Crowne Plaza Hotels and SunSpree Resorts in the luxury segment. Prior to those initiatives, the company had maintained a single brand. Holiday Inn has become particularly aggressive in the business segment, where it has acted to offer in-room fax machines and additional work space.

The company is also acting internationally, with hotel openings in 100 countries and territories as of 2003. In addition, Holiday Inn has instituted several quality control moves that it hopes will ensure consistent quality standards across all operations. Finally, the company placed its service on the Internet in 1995, enabling customers to make reservations, check room availability, and receive general information.

Holiday Inn takes major actions, such as marketing campaigns and promotions, every nine months on average. The frequency of such actions varies sharply, however, as a function of rivals' actions, which the company quickly imitates. On average, Holiday Inn has responded to Cendant's past actions in less than six months.

From the analysis of Holiday Inn's beliefs, intentions, and past actions, Cendant should expect Holiday Inn to react promptly to any aggressive or threatening actions, and especially to actions that target key segments, particularly the business segment. Its aggressive, risk-taking managers and history of innovative actions are factors to which Cendant must pay attention. Recent globalization efforts may divert some management attention from the domestic market, but Intercontinental Group's experience as a global player supports Holiday Inn's international moves. Cendant should be cognizant of Holiday Inn's actions to exploit its brand and its efforts to improve quality.

Starbucks and Second Cup

Recall that Starbucks is the focal firm attempting to predict the behavior of Second Cup. With regard to Second Cup's beliefs about itself, the firm may well be of the opinion that it has just begun to realize its potential. Second Cup is currently the leading coffee retailer in Canada. Publicly, the company acts as though its leadership will not be challenged. Alton McEwen, the president of Second Cup, commented after Starbucks announced its 1996 Toronto opening: "We are confident that Second Cup will continue to dominate. We believe that this will heighten awareness of specialty coffee and stimulate growth for all specialty coffee retailers. This is very good news for Second Cup."[18] In 2002, McEwen similarly commented: "The foundation is in place to achieve meaningful, reliable growth in earning over the next three years."[19] Why Second Cup feels so secure in its position is unclear, although such comments may well be only a public stance. The company seems concerned about competition because it has recently sought alliance partners and has stated in a second quarter report that it is stretched. In terms of positioning, Second Cup sees itself as an upscale retailer.

In beliefs about the industry and competitors, Second Cup managers think the industry will continue to grow and that competition will intensify because of low entry barriers. Perhaps those beliefs are driving its acquisitions and strategic alliances. Second Cup *intends* to grow and improve its market share. For example, it opened 18 new stores in Canada. Moreover, with the Gloria Jean chain, Second Cup had the intended goal of opening 40 new shops each year in the United States.

Second Cup's managers are relatively homogeneous but recently have made some attempt to diversify. For example, they brought in Gregg Landauer, whose background is in food service and chain restaurants, to head the Coffee Plantation chain, and a new executive vice president who has retailing experience with Thrifty Car Rental. The fact that three of the six Second Cup board members are from inside the organization and two of the other three are retired executives suggests a fairly conservative, risk-averse management team.

Importantly, Second Cup has recently begun to tie top managers' compensation to increased shareholder value. The shareholder value goal also suggests that the organization will be risk averse, which may conflict with its acquisitions of the Gloria Jean and Coffee Plantation chains and its goal to open 40 new stores per year. The organization does not appear to emphasize innovation.

In terms of *past strategic actions*, Second Cup undertook more competitive actions in 1995 than in its previous 19 years combined. Its acquisition of the Gloria Jean chain in the United States doubled its size. Moreover, it acted to develop alliances, including moves to join with Canadian Airlines and Borders Books in Canada. The company uses two forms of distribution, direct sales and mail order. However, it had not conducted formal advertising, relying instead on in-store promotions such as a "coffee of the month." Most recently, Second Cup began to imitate many of Starbucks' product actions. It introduced True Cool drinks, a line of iced beverages, and The Chiller, a frozen cappuccino drink. Both products are imitations of Starbucks' brands. Indeed, Second Cup's acquisitions appear to be in direct response to Starbucks' entry into Canada. Moreover, in 2001, Second Cup started its first formal advertising campaign: "Second Cup. First thing."[20] Finally, it announced a number of social responsibility programs, which are very similar to early efforts by Starbucks.

The competitive profile of Second Cup is one of contradictions. The firm emphasizes growth but also desires shareholder value; these, at least in the short term, may conflict. Recent efforts to sell Gloria Jean reflect moves toward contraction. The firm publicly expresses no fear of competition but recognizes that competition is on the rise. The firm claims leadership and no fear of Starbucks but is joining with other firms in vertical alliances. Second Cup also imitates Starbucks' new products and follows Starbucks' customer alliance strategy. Finally, the company is bringing in new managers in recognition that additional skills are needed. The competitive consequences of having the new managers are difficult to predict, but the current management incentive system emphasizes shareholder wealth.

Implications: Using the Relative Resources, Market Position, and Competitor Analyses

Cendant. Let us recall that Cendant and Intercontinental have about equal market shares but that Cendant is at a distinct internal resource disadvantage in relation to Holiday Inn (see fig. 10.3). In other words, based on the relative resource analysis, Cendant does not have a resource advantage from which it can effectively engage Intercontinental Group, except perhaps with its broad assortment of brands. In chapter 6 we argued that firms with a distinct internal resource disadvantage should try to avoid direct confrontation with rivals. For Cendant such an effort would be especially important in building brand reputation, pricing, computer reservations, and finance, which are Intercontinental's strong areas.

From the competitor analysis we learned that Intercontinental is an aggressive risk-taker, seeking market share in all segments. Its brand name is its most significant asset, and it seeks to capitalize on it in all segments. Holiday Inn, as part of Intercontinental, reacts to all visible moves by Cendant within six months. Global moves have increased Holiday Inn's scope of operations.

At a minimum, the analyses suggest that Cendant should not seek to engage Holiday Inn with Ricardian actions or attempt to fend off Holiday Inn with deterrent actions. To do so would probably provoke a significant reaction by resource-rich Intercontinental. To compete effectively with Holiday Inn, Cendant's best option, at least until it can enhance its relative internal resource position, is to seek customers in segments and locations in which Holiday Inn is not interested, such as the supereconomy and economy business segments of the industry. Cendant should expect, however, that Holiday Inn might respond to those moves because it attempts to be strong in all segments. Cendant should also consider being innovative in creating new segments and moving into international markets in which Holiday Inn does not have a presence. In current markets where Cendant competes directly with Holiday Inn, Cendant should move to exploit its multiple brands and quality, as quality is one of Holiday Inn's weak spots, but should not be overly aggressive in doing so.

The analyses suggest that in the longer term, Cendant must seek to improve its relative internal resource position. Therefore, it should be investing in and working on its brand reputation, reservation systems, financial position, and response capability. Only by improving its relative internal resource position will Cendant be able to engage Intercontinental Group directly or deter its threatening moves. Finally, Cendant's recent diversification moves indicate that it may be moving away from head-to-head competition with Holiday Inn. Recent acquisitions such as the Century 21 Real Estate Corporation and the extended-stay Villager Lodge chain may be appropriate alternatives to aggressively engaging Intercontinental. Figure 10.6 portrays the action plan for Cendant.

Starbucks. Recall that Starbucks has distinct internal and external resource advantages over Second Cup, that is, Starbucks has multiple resource advantage to effectively engage Second Cup. Furthermore, the

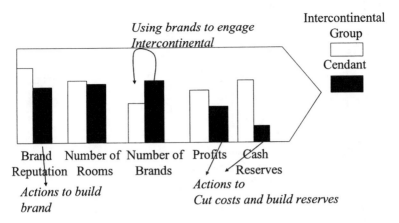

Figure 10.6   Value Chain of Cendant and Intercontinental Group: Action Plan.

competitor analysis suggests that Second Cup is confused in its beliefs, intentions, and actions, and that its competitive actions tend to imitate those of Starbucks. Many contradictions are revealed in the competitor analysis; for example, Second Cup managers believe that the company is a market leader, despite information to the contrary.

Starbucks must decide whether Second Cup is a threat to its long-term superiority. Should Starbucks engage Second Cup directly with Ricardian actions, or does it need a fringe competitor like Second Cup? Should Starbucks defend against Second Cup with deterrent actions?

Adding a mix of Ricardian and deterrent actions to Starbucks' current emphasis on innovative actions is probably most appropriate. Starbucks may want to engage Second Cup directly with Ricardian pricing actions in Canada, where Second Cup is relatively stronger. Fierce rivalry there would arguably hurt Second Cup more than Starbucks, provided that Starbucks' overall strength in advertising, costs and earnings, and number of products would enable it to weather the competitive skirmishes better than Second Cup. In addition, such actions would serve as an important signal for Second Cup to back off in U.S. markets and would frustrate Second Cup's shareholder value goal overall. In the United States, where Second Cup has begun to back away, Starbucks may want to deter Second Cup by carrying out preemptive new product introductions or preemptive advertising that will raise Second Cup's costs of competing.

While undertaking those actions, Starbucks should closely monitor Second Cup's resource position. If its resource position improves, Starbucks may want to combine Ricardian and deterrent actions more aggressively. Throughout, Starbucks will have to be mindful of U.S. antitrust laws and

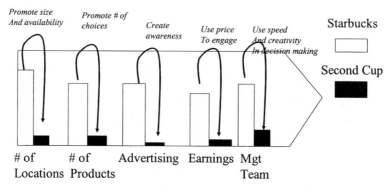

Figure 10.7   Value Chain of Starbucks and Second Cup: Action Plan.

comparable Canadian competition policy. Figure 10.7 portrays Starbucks' possible action plan.

Gathering Information on Competitors.

The pair-wise analysis of internal and external resource positions and the competitor analysis require gathering a large amount of competitor information. Information must be collected about each rival's internal and external resources, as well as their managers' intentions, beliefs, and past competitive actions and reactions. If rival firms are public, an assessment of their tangible resources, expenses, and intentions can be conducted through annual and 10K reports. The financial resources of private firms can be examined by reading reports by Dun & Bradstreet or other credit agencies. Focal firms should also search for any recent business press articles or brokerage reports that mention competitive actions and developments within rival firms. The Internet has increasingly become a useful source of company information. The appendices at the end of this chapter provide more details about information sources. Appendix 1 lists industry analysis information guides, while appendix 2 lists sources of company information. Interviewing customers, suppliers, or past employees of rival terms can be an excellent way to get a good approximation of a firm's key intangible resources, beliefs, and intentions.

The analyses presented in this chapter were conducted primarily with publicly available information. Firms in an industry are likely to have much more immediate and better knowledge about one another, which would clearly make the analyses even easier to carry out. However, players within an industry are not always the best judges of a competitor's resources, intentions, and actions, in that they may have similar inaccurate schemas or may have inappropriate competitor beliefs of their own. Therefore, information derived from in-depth experience should be validated with a study of public data. For the most part, the kind of information collected for the examples presented in this chapter is readily available.

Summary

This chapter explains how focal firm managers can examine rivals through internal and external relative resource analysis and competitor analysis. Using those two different but related analyses, we examine the hotel and specialty coffee industries. In doing so, we ground our model of "strategy as action" in real firm behaviors and show how it can enable a focal firm to base its actions on its relative internal resource position and the expected actions of a competitor.

APPENDIX I: Sample Sources of Industry Information

Reference Sources

Encyclopedia of American Industries   Provides information on industries and those involved arranged by SIC codes.

F & S Index of Corporations and Industries   Provides hard-to-find industry information, including over 700 trade journals.

Moody's Industry Review   Information on companies as well as industry averages arranged by industry groups.

U.S. Industrial Outlook   Information of changes in supply and demand, market prices, employment and capital expenditures for many industries with projections.

Service Industries USA   Statistical information by SIC codes for the service industry.

Standard & Poor's Industry Survey   Includes both narrative and statistics describing the current situation, recent developments, and prospects for many industries.

Value Line Industry Review   Provides current trends, economic conditions and forecasts, and quantitative perspectives for a multitude of industries.

Value Line Investment Survey   Provides industry analysis for over 95 industries.

Internet Sources

www.census.gov/epcd/www/naics.html
   Search on industry keywords to find yearly North American Industry Classification System (NAICS) codes.

www.osha.gov/oshstats/sicser.html
   Search on industry keywords to find yearly Standard Industrial Classification System (SIC) codes.

stats.bls.gov/iag/iaghome.htm
   Contains industries at a glance, which profiles nine industry divisions based on SIC code system.

Library Databases

ABI/Inform   In-depth coverage of business conditions, trends, corporate strategies and tactics, management techniques, competitive and product information, and a wide variety of other topics.

Business and Company Resource Center   Includes more than 300 full text business journals, more than 300,000 company profiles, investment reports, Thomson Financial content, Investext Select reports, and indexing and abstracting for more than 1,000 titles.

Factiva   Provides articles from more than 4,000 Reuters and Dow Jones publications worldwide and more than 900 non-English sources.

Hoovers Online   Provides financial information, comparing top competitors, industries, and markets.

Infotrac/Business Index ASAP   Provides articles from more than 460 business and management journals, trade/industry publications, and national business magazines.

LexisNexis   Provides access to a wide range of news, business, government, legal, and reference information.

Standard and Poor's Market Insight   Provides financial information for more than 130 industries and 200 industry composites.

APPENDIX 2: Sample Sources of Company Information

Reference Sources

America's Corporate Families: The Billion Dollar Directory   Provides brief data such as sales, number of employees, and officers' names on U.S parent companies and their subsidiaries and divisions.

Dun and Bradstreet Million Dollar Directory   Provides information such as sales, number of employees, type of ownership, and principal executives and biographies in approximately 1.6 million U.S. and Canadian leading public and private businesses

International Directory of Company Histories   Provides information on the historical development of large companies.

Moody's Investor Service   Provides comprehensive index to over 21,000 corporations, including company histories, mergers and acquisitions, subsidiaries, products, principal plants and properties, officers, number of employees and stockholders, and financial information.

Standard & Poor's Corporation Records   Provides corporate background, products, lines of businesses, subsidiaries, and financial data.

Standard & Poor's Stock Reports   Provides stock reports for companies traded on the U.S stock exchanges.

Value Line Investment Survey   Provides stock and company research for over 1700 companies.

Ward's Business Directory of U.S. Private and Public Companies   Provides company data such as company rank by sales and employee size with each industry and approximate market share.

Internet Sources

www.sec.gov/edgar.shtml
> Registration statements and periodic reports such as 10K, 101, and other documents filed by companies to the Securities and Exchange Commission for investors.

www.corporateinformation.com
> Provides research reports including analysis of sales trends, R & D expenditures, and financial data of publicly traded companies.

www.finance.yahoo.com
> Provides stock and company research.

Library Databases

ABI/Inform   In-depth coverage of business conditions, trends, corporate strategies and tactics, management techniques, competitive and product information, and a wide variety of other topics.

Business and Company Resource Center   Includes more than 300 full text business journals, more than 300,000 company profiles, investment reports, Thomson Financial content, Investext Select reports, and indexing and abstracting for more than 1,000 titles.

Factiva   Provides articles from more than 4,000 Reuters and Dow Jones publications worldwide and more than 900 non-English sources.

Hoovers Online   Provides financial information, comparing top competitors, industries, and markets.

Infotrac/Business Index ASAP   Provides articles from more than 460 business and management journals, trade/industry publications, and national business magazines.

LexisNexis   Provides access to a wide range of news, business, government, legal, and reference information.

Standard & Poor's Market Insight   Provides access to company histories, stock reports and extensive reports from Compustat for a large number of U.S. and global companies.

Chapter 11

STRATEGY AS ACTION

Integration and Evolution of Resource Positions

O ur starting point was the notion that today's business environment has become dramatically more competitive and will become even more so in the future. Chapter 2 contained a review of the prominent economic approaches to understanding competition and competitive advantage, and chapters 3 and 4 presented frameworks to understanding a firm's relative market and resource position.

Chapter 5 introduced the action model of advantage, which extends the action-based approach and integrates elements of a firm's relative market and resource positions. At its core, the model posits that relative internal and external resources determine actions and reactions, which in turn determine competitive advantage. Figure 11.1, the action model of advantage, highlights those relationships. Firm resources are defined as all information, knowledge, capabilities, organizational processes, and tangible assets controlled by a firm that enable the firm to undertake competitive action. Resources are heterogeneous across firms, and a key determinant of a firm's actions is its comparative resource position in relation to that of rivals at a given point in time. Competitive actions and reactions are the crux of the model. A competitive action is a specific and observable competitive move, such as a new product introduction, advertising campaign, or price cut, initiated by a firm to build, exploit, or defend its relative competitive position. Reactions are rivals' responses to such actions, which can be fast or slow and imitative or nonimitative.

Four combinations of internal and external relative resource positions, along with the corresponding actions appropriate for each position, were developed in the subsequent four chapters. Chapter 6 explored the situation in which a firm has a very limited resource advantage or perhaps none. In other words, the firm cannot beat its rivals with lower production

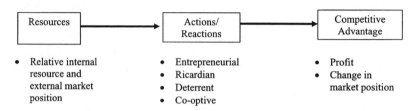

Resources	Actions/ Reactions	Competitive Advantage
• Relative internal resource and external market position	• Entrepreneurial • Ricardian • Deterrent • Co-optive	• Profit • Change in market position

Figure 11.1   Action-Based Model of Competitive Advantage.

costs or superior product quality, and has an insignificant market position. Firms in that situation must rely solely on the knowledge and skills of managers as a resource to achieve advantage. Such firms must exploit blind spots and competitive uncertainty by formulating and implementing entrepreneurial actions. Entrepreneurial actions include introduction of new products or services, product or service improvements or efficiency enhancements, geographic or segment transfer, and response to supply shortage. Chapter 6 explored such actions in detail, with a focus on introduction of new and improved products and services. Game theory models were used to illustrate how blind spots and competitive uncertainty lead to delays in response and subsequent competitive advantage.

In chapter 7, we turned to the situation in which the firm has a superior internal resource advantage, an example being a farmer with land significantly more fertile than that of rivals. Such firms can engage rivals head-on with Ricardian actions. An example of a Ricardian action is to set low prices in anticipation of a price war, winnable because of a cost advantage derived from large-scale plant and equipment. Another Ricardian action would be to set a premium price based on product differentiation, such as superior product quality. Game theory models were developed to show how rivals cannot respond effectively in the face of such superior resources, and advantage is achieved in conjunction with delays in response.

Chapter 8 described the situation in which a firm has a discernible external resource advantage derived from market leadership. Firms with that resource position undertake deterrent actions to achieve advantage. Such actions include limit pricing, product proliferation, aggressive and preemptive innovation, information manipulation, and exploitation of reputation effects to achieve advantage. When pursuing such actions, a firm must be cognizant of the proscription in the United States and most other industrialized countries against monopolizing or attempting to monopolize an industry. At the end of the chapter we provided an overview of the relevant U.S. antitrust laws, along with case examples.

In chapter 9, we examined the situation in which resources and competitive strength are relatively equal among firms and, because of product maturity and stability, there is little opportunity to exploit competitive uncertainty or blind spots. In such a case, the appropriate actions may be co-optive ones designed to reduce rivalry in the industry. The firm attempts to "win the peace" collectively with other firms in the industry, recognizing that aggressive forays will only lead to warfare with losses for all. Co-optive actions include signaling advance information on price changes, disclosure of prices and other competitive information, and base point pricing. As with deterrent actions, a critical constraint to pursuit of co-optive actions is the antitrust laws, which we discuss at the end of chapter 9.[1]

We put the action model into practice in chapter 10 by presenting two forms of analysis—an assessment of relative resource position and competitor analysis—that managers can use to help formulate and implement effective action. The analyses were illustrated by examining firm resources and competitors in the hotel and specialty coffee industries.

In the remainder of this chapter, we explore linkages across the four resource situations as we examine a more dynamic or longitudinal version of the action model of advantage. We consider firms that can choose between entrepreneurial and Ricardian actions, then explore how firms with strong market position can combine deterrent actions with entrepreneurial and Ricardian actions. Finally, we examine cooperative actions that may have a primary effect of building a resource position, as opposed to reducing rivalry.

Putting the Pieces Together: Linkages across Resource Positions

In preceding chapters, we examined each of the four resource positions as distinct and discrete, with firms in one and only one of the categories. In reality, the distinctions are often blurred. There are important intersections across the positions. For example, a firm may simultaneously hold multiple resource advantages, as described in chapters 6 through 8. In other words, a firm may have superior management skills in perceiving uncertainty and blind spots but may also have superior relative internal and external resources and a dominant market position.

Combining Entrepreneurial and Ricardian Actions

Conceptually, many firms should be able to take both entrepreneurial and Ricardian actions, or combinations thereof, but we do not observe many firms exploiting such options. R. R. Nelson and S. G. Winter offer a possible explanation in their "evolutionary theory." They note that "organizations remember by doing";[2] firms learn by taking action and judging the effectiveness of the actions. Successful actions, ones that delay response and generate profit, are reinforced and routinized into an organization's action repertoire. Unsuccessful action leads to further action experimentation.[3]

Importantly, the firm that is successful in taking entrepreneurial actions may continue to undertake such actions even when its resource position has changed and would allow for Ricardian actions. Similarly, a firm that is successful in taking Ricardian actions may continue to take such actions even though its performance could be enhanced by implementing entrepreneurial actions.

Another extension of the action model of advantage considers how a firm progresses from one stage to another over time. For example, one could begin with a small startup firm in which, by definition, organizational resources are primarily the managerial skills of the entrepreneur. Actions, predominantly entrepreneurial, are then taken over time that lead to advantage but may also lead to a stronger resource position and the ability to undertake Ricardian actions.

Figure 11.2 is a revision of the action model of organizational evolution presented in chapter 5, with additional detail to portray the process steps in development. The firm that has learned only to take entrepreneurial action and has invested to improve its relative resource position must be motivated to learn how to implement Ricardian actions to exploit its new position. Such learning may require a fundamental change in the organization, what has been called "the transition to professional management."

As the firm evolves from being one with limited resources to being one with relative resource advantages, attention will shift from entrepreneurial discovery and entrepreneurial action to the exploitation of specific resources with Ricardian actions. The transition will require new learning and therefore different management capabilities, perhaps a shift in emphasis from entrepreneurial discovery to professional management. In any case, managers must design Ricardian actions based on the specific resource advantages held by the firm. By exploiting specific resources with Ricardian actions, the firm can impede rivals' responses and improve its relative competitive position, perhaps to the point of industry leadership.

Figure 11.3 depicts a firm that can choose between entrepreneurial and Ricardian actions. The firm has evolved from the limited resource phase and now is in a position to exploit factor of production advantages. However, such a firm must be careful in its selection of actions and cognizant of the potential reaction of competitors. An example of a firm that faced difficulties in evolving from entrepreneurial actions to Ricardian actions is People Express airline.[4]

People Express began in the 1980s after deregulation of the U.S. airline industry in 1978. Led by Donald Burr as CEO, People Express undertook

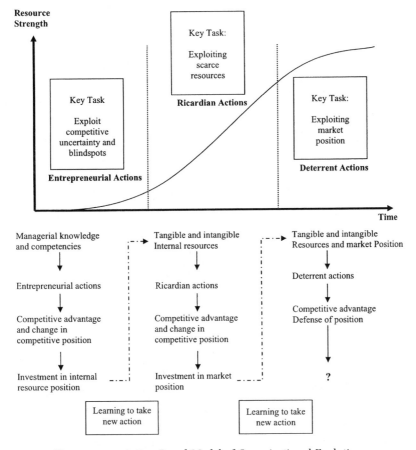

Figure 11.2 Action-Based Model of Organizational Evolution.

several entrepreneurial actions to exploit industry blind spots, such as establishing a hub-and-spoke operation centered in a little-used freight terminal at the Newark, New Jersey airport (action A_1 in fig. 11.3). Burr also introduced many innovative management practices to the airline industry, and created a lean, decentralized organizational structure featuring extensive worker participation. The airline grew rapidly and was very successful in the early 1980s. As its traffic and revenues grew, People Express established a substantial cost advantage over its industry rivals.

In attempting to exploit that resource advantage, however, People Express expanded too rapidly, taking on industry giants such as American and United with an acquisition of Denver-based Frontier Airlines (A_2). The competitive reaction of the industry leaders was swift and hard-hitting, including initiation of frequent flyer programs, significantly discounted fares in markets where People Express competed, and countervailing cost reductions. By the mid-1980s, People Express had fallen as fast as it had

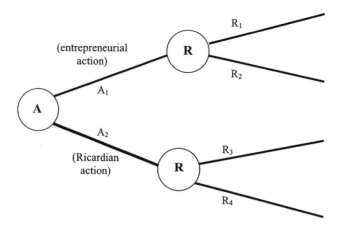

Figure 11.3 Some Firms Can Undertake Both Entrepreneurial and Ricardian Actions. This model should be viewed as one stage of a repeated game, so that over time a firm can combine entrepreneurial and Ricardian actions. Responses are as discussed in preceding chapters.

risen and, on the brink of bankruptcy, was acquired by Texas Air/Continental Airlines.

Industry experts generally agreed that the upstart had erred in not picking specific venues in which to exploit its cost advantages and not anticipating the strong reactions of rivals. In addition, the organizational structure of the company did not adapt well to growth and more complex management challenges. Perhaps People Express would be around today if it had taken a more appropriate combination of entrepreneurial and Ricardian actions.

Combining Deterrent Actions
with Other Action Types

Returning to the action model of organizational evolution depicted in figure 11.2, we note that most firms aspire to achieve resource advantages and exploit them to become dominant in the markets in which they operate. Becoming the market leader may necessitate another shift in orientation for the firm, perhaps away from exploitation of specific resource advantages with Ricardian actions to defense of market position with deterrent actions. Again, the transition may require new management competencies. The task for a firm in this stage is to exploit resources not only to expand the business but also to defend its market leadership against attack. As discussed in chapter 8, deterrent actions in defense of position might include limiting output, acting with predatory pricing, buying out competitors, and securing sources of scarce material. The desire to ensure a

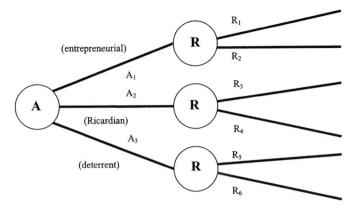

Figure 11.4   Entrepreneurial, Ricardian, or Deterrent Actions: Choosing the Right Mix.

satisfactory return on prior investments in resources may also make the firm more defensive.

Figure 11.4 depicts the options facing such a firm in choosing the right mix of entrepreneurial, Ricardian, and deterrent actions. Indeed, a critical issue for firms in a dominant market position, in addition to defending the resource of market leadership, is how to build and exploit other resource advantages. A firm that becomes too preoccupied with defensive strategies may well lose the sharp edge that enabled it to achieve the superior market position in the first place. An example is General Motors, long dominant in the American marketplace and perhaps, over time, overly preoccupied with defending its position against weaker U.S. rivals. Eventually GM lost its competitive edge and became vulnerable to incursions by foreign rivals that offered automobiles with both lower prices and higher quality.

In fact, maintaining dominance of an industry for a prolonged period is a difficult task. Several studies have shown that over a long period of time, the majority of industry leaders are dethroned.[5] One of the more recent studies found firms dropping out of the *Fortune* 100 at a rate of 2.9 firms per year from 1977 to 1987, which was substantially higher than the rate in the 1958–77 period, perhaps because of the ever-increasing competitiveness of the economy.[6] Dominance can be prolonged or extended if the dominant firm takes advantage of favorable structural factors in the market. High barriers to entry have been related empirically to greater stability of market shares; firms can erect and increase entry barriers by a variety of actions such as those discussed in chapter 8. Market share stability has also been found to be related to stability of technology, intensity, of advertising, high levels of capital intensity, and a high degree of vertical integration.

Recent research has explored more directly the role of actions and reactions by the dominant firm and its challenger in the dethronement of the dominant firm.[7] Data for the study consisted of leader/challenger matched pairs in 41 different industries for the period 1987–93. The diverse set of firms included General Mills/Kellogg, Levi/VE, Exxon/Mobil, Nike/Reebok, Maytag/Whirlpool, Boeing/McDonnell Douglas, Hasbro/Mattel, American Airlines/United, Federal Express/UPS, Home Depot/Lowe's, Kelly/Manpower, and Circuit City/Tandy. Two measures of market share position were examined: persistence of market share leadership or dethronement of market share leader and the net erosion or increase in the market share gap between the market share leader and the challenger. The findings support the notion that remaining competitively active will enhance a leadership position and forestall dethronement. In particular, market share leaders that execute a greater number and broader range of actions against challengers have less market share erosion and are less likely to be dethroned. In addition, market share leaders that respond faster than rivals to competitive actions by challengers have less market share erosion and dethronement.

In sum, market leaders should complement deterrent actions with Ricardian and entrepreneurial actions. However, carrying out alternative types of action may be difficult for large, dominant firms. In American industry, for example, firms have been criticized for getting away from what they do well. C. K. Prahalad and Gary Hamel castigate U.S. firms for emphasizing portfolio management (e.g., the harvest defensive strategy) instead of exploiting key resources.[8] In fact, the emphasis on total quality, reengineering, and core competencies of the organization highlights the need for firms to exploit their unique resource advantages. The value of those techniques is that they center attention on the competitive advantage or resources of the firm in relation to those of other firms. Our addition to these perspectives is the notion that unique resources must lead to Ricardian actions.

Large, dominant firms have also been criticized for their lack of entrepreneurship.[9] Unlike an entrepreneur, corporate managers who create something new seldom have a personal stake in the creation. As a consequence, there is increased attention to create ownership incentives for corporate managers that may make them more entrepreneurial or innovative.

One large firm that has been able to maintain innovation and an entrepreneurial spirit is Minnesota Mining and Manufacturing (3M). In 1992, 3M offered "60,000 products in 23 major businesses, based on more than 100 basic technologies, with operations in 55 countries employing 89,000 people."[10] In 1997, it employed 6,500 scientists, engineers, and technicians worldwide, spent over $1 billion on R&D, and earned over $15 billion in annual revenues.[11] In the mid-1990s, the company established a new objective of generating 30 percent of annual revenues from products that had not existed four years earlier.[12] The main strength of 3M is in-novation is that "technical staff are allowed to spend 15 percent of their time "bootlegging"—working on pet projects in the hope that they will come up with profitable innovation. The aim is for 3M to constantly re-invent itself."[13] Because the focus is on innovation, 3M's organizational structure must allow for such freedom. At 3M, each major business area is distinct and has different levels (global, regional, and local) of authority. In addition, cross-functional teams have been created to enhance communi-cation and innovativeness.

Large corporations have attempted to be more aggressive by down-sizing, acquiring small firms, developing new venture startup units, cre-ating spontaneous entrepreneurial teams, and promoting new business incubator centers. Yet making large firms more aggressive remains a dif-ficult problem, and many large firms need to develop more capabilities for entrepreneurial actions. Understanding and promoting entrepreneurial discovery as presented in chapter 6 could be the first step.

Cooperating to Enhance Resources and Competitiveness

Another example of a linkage across resource positions and action types can be derived from a broader assessment of cooperative actions than that provided in chapter 9. In that chapter, we considered only co-operative actions designed to reduce or eliminate rivalry. However, there are other types of cooperative actions whose primary purpose is ostensibly to enhance resources and position a firm more effectively against rivals. Figure 11.5 depicts a firm's choices of cooperative actions that enhance competitiveness.

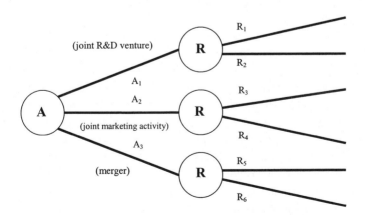

Figure 11.5 Cooperative Actions to Enhance Resource Position.

One such action is merger or consolidation of two or more firms. Merger activity has increased markedly in the past two decades. For instance, the dollar value of mergers increased from approximately $0.5 trillion to $2.4 trillion, while the number of mergers increased from about 11,000 to 26,000 from 1990 to 1998.[14] The merger wave included such recent transactions as the $150 billion marriage of AOL and Time Warner in the media industry,[15] the $53 billion marriage between Pfizer and Pharmacia in the pharmaceutical industry,[16] and Hewlett-Packard's $19 billion acquisition of Compaq in the technology industry.[17]

Perhaps the primary motive for merger to enhance the resource position is the prospect of scale economies in the consolidated firm. Expanding the scale of an operation can result in production cost savings, whether the firms' products are identical or complementary. Marketing economies also can result from consolidating companies with extensive product lines. Mergers can enhance efficiency when poorly managed companies are acquired by firms with stronger leadership. In fact, even the threat of takeover can discipline corporate managers and promote efficiency. Vertical integration can reduce transaction costs such as those from contracting between upstream/downstream firms.

Of course, the motive for, or the effect of, mergers may also be to reduce competition. In the United States, mergers that "may substantially lessen competition or tend to create a monopoly" are illegal according to section 7 of the Clayton Act. Merger enforcement is provided by the Federal Trade Commission and the Antitrust Division of the Department of Justice. Both agencies have issued detailed guidelines about their approach to evaluation of mergers, with particular focus on mergers between direct competitors.[18] Interestingly, the EEC has no particular laws on mergers in its competition policies; attempted prohibition of mergers has proceeded mainly under the provision covering abuse of dominant position, as discussed in chapter 6. Merger policy is therefore generally more permissive in Europe than in the United States.[19]

In practice, merging firms generally argue that they will achieve significant efficiency gains from their merger and that their ability to compete effectively will be greatly enhanced. Opponents of a given merger are typically skeptical of the motives and effects. A recent example is the merger of the Union Pacific and Southern Pacific railroads, which was approved by the U.S. Surface Transportation Board. The merger applicants argued that their consolidation will result in major cost savings, such as from elimination of duplicative rail lines, and will enable them to compete more effectively with their primary rival, Burlington Northern–Sante Fe (BN). Prior to the consolidation, BN was the largest rail carrier in the United States, with annual revenues of $7.66 billion. With annual revenues of $9.14 billion, a combined Union Pacific–Southern Pacific will replace BN as number 1. Opponents of the merger have argued that rail competition will be reduced substantially. The Department of Justice Antitrust Division opposed the merger and argued that it would cost rail customers on the order of $800 million as a result of higher prices.[20]

Many other types of cooperative activities can enhance resources and competitiveness. For example, firms can engage in strategic alliances whereby two firms cooperate to compete more effectively against mutual rivals. Firms can cooperate through technical training agreements, patent licensing, franchising, management or marketing service agreements, trade association activities, and consumer education efforts and by developing markets through activities such as industry shows or trade fairs.[21] Such cooperative actions are increasingly part of the changing landscape of competition, particularly in the global marketplace.

An important dimension for classifying such cooperative activities is vertical versus horizontal. Vertical alliances involve firms that are in an upstream/downstream relationship, whereas horizontal alliances involve two or more firms that compete in the same industry. Vertical alliances have become increasingly common in the international airline industry, particularly in the form of marketing alliances, code sharing, and scheduling coordination.[22] That movement has been driven by the increasingly competitive environment of global airlines, as regulations restricting entry and fare competition have been liberalized in many international markets. Alliances were motivated primarily by the need to reduce costs and achieve greater scale economies in response to intensifying competition. For example, Delta, Continental, and Northwest launched a marketing alliance in mid-2003 that involved cooperation in frequent flyer programs, code-sharing arrangements to ease booking and passenger transfer between airlines, and sharing of lounge club programs.[23] Similar airline alliances, some including exchange of equity shares, have been formed among carriers across borders, resulting in three major alliance networks: "Skyteam," which includes Delta, KLM, and Air France, among others; "Oneworld," which includes American, British Airways, and Cathay Pacific, among others; and "Star Alliance," which includes United, Lufthansa, and Air Canda, among others.[24]

Firms can also cooperate to strengthen their ability to compete through joint research and production ventures. One such example is Sematech, a horizontal cooperative action. Sematech is a joint venture of a group of more than 40 companies in the semiconductor industry, including Hewlett-Packard, Advanced Micro Devices, IBM, General Electric, Intel, Digital Equipment, Motorola, and Texas Instruments. Sematech is funded jointly by the member companies and the U.S. government to promote technological advancement that will enable U.S. companies to compete successfully with strong foreign rivals. In its first five years, Sematech spent about

$500 million.[25] Prior to Sematech's formation in 1988, the market share of U.S. chip makers had steadily declined in the 1980s, reaching a low of 40 percent in 1988. Sematech has mainly been judged a success. It is widely credited with helping boost U.S. chip makers' market share. For example, in 1993 it succeeded in producing computer chips half the size of the then state-of-the-art industry product.[26] Sematech disseminates such advances to member firms, which carry out design and marketing individually. Although Sematech was originally formed to help U.S. firms compete against foreign rivals, it has recently extended its membership to foreign firms— Samsung Electronics and LG Semiconductor of Korea in 1996 and Siemens of Germany and Taiwan Semiconductor Manufacturing, for example, in 1998—because of the increasing research costs, capital investments, and complexity and short life span of the technology.[27]

Another example of cooperation to strengthen resources and facilitate competition with strong foreign (in this case, U.S.) companies is Airbus. The aircraft industry has long been dominated by American firms, in particular Boeing and McDonnell Douglas. In the early 1970s, U.S. firms held a 90-plus percent share of the worldwide market. In 1971 several European countries, led primarily by Germany, Britain, and France, created the Airbus consortium. The consortium received substantial government funding, estimated to be in excess of $26 billion by 1993. Airbus was very successful in developing aircraft rivaling Boeing's, had achieved a market share approaching 30 percent by the 1990s,[28] and overtook Boeing, which has been recently placing greater focus on its defense contracting businesses, by winning more orders in 2002.[29] Collective action may be the only feasible way to challenge a dominant international rival such as Boeing in the aircraft manufacturing industry. The Airbus consortium recently reorganized to become a single company, known as Airbus Integrated Company, in 2000.[30]

These types of cooperative actions raise interesting and important questions for government policy-makers, especially in the area of antitrust. The resolution of these issues is of critical importance to firms that want either to engage in or prevent such alliances. The current antitrust laws and their interpretation are in a state of flux.[31] The law has been largely supportive of joint research efforts, provided that production and marketing are done independently. The National Cooperative Research Act of 1984 states that joint R&D activities, not extending to subsequent production or marketing and not involving exchanges of information between companies unrelated to the joint R&D, will not be viewed as per se illegal. In other words, such actions will not be judged in the same light as collusive price-fixing arrangements. As discussed in chapter 9, certain actions are per se illegal, or illegal on their face, regardless of their intentions and effects.

For joint R&D alliances, a so-called rule of reason approach is used, with analysis of competitive effects in relevant markets of the specific joint activity. Importantly, factors such as the government's encouragement, support, or approval of the venture would be included in evaluation of potential competitive effects of the venture. The act states clearly that technological advances are critical to the promotion and expansion of the national economy and that antitrust laws should promote, not inhibit, such activity.[32] For example, under this standard, joint activities such as Sematech have been exempted from antitrust scrutiny.

An important motivation for passage of the National Cooperative Research Act was the belief that Japanese firms are strong global competitors in part because such cooperation is commonplace in Japan. To enhance efficiency and global competitiveness in key industries, public policy-makers wanted to put U.S. firms on an equal footing. The act was designed to "encourage commercial entities to enter into and secure the benefits of joint R&D activities in order to increase industrial innovation, productivity and the economic competitiveness of the United States."[33]

Many writers have argued for a looser interpretation and permissive approach under the antitrust laws, particularly where a strategic high-tech industry is at issue and alliances can strengthen U.S. firms in competition with foreign rivals.[34] Others, however, have recommended more vigorous antitrust enforcement and imposition of constraints to restrict, limit, or condition such alliances. For example, there is particular concern about production joint ventures, whereby competitors combine forces in the production of a product, process, or service. A substantial literature on the subject details the concerns and the public policy debate over application of competition policy to such ventures.[35]

The major concern raised by production joint ventures (PJVs) is that coordination on one aspect of production will reduce the rivalry of firms. For example, Donald Stockdale argued in a review of PJVs that, in comparison with research joint ventures, PJV "offer fewer social benefits and pose greater social costs."[36] Firms that are partners in provision of infrastructure will have reduced incentives to attract business from each other, because the contribution to shared infrastructure costs from the rival that loses business will be correspondingly reduced. Stockdale also argues that PJVs increase the likelihood of tacit or explicit collusion in other product markets. Discussions and coordination on aspects of shared infrastructure costs would facilitate collusion on costs, and prices, throughout the system. Rivals would lose their independence, and their tendency to "go at each other's throats" would diminish. Such effects are not mere speculation. They have been demonstrated across several industries: "Econometric analyses of a large sample of U.S. joint ventures in a number of industries further suggests that where participants are horizontal competitors, a potential for market-power augmentation exists."[37]

Finally, Stockdale notes:

> Anticompetitive effects [of production joint ventures] are more likely where the relevant market is concentrated and exhibits entry barriers and where the participants collectively account for a significant portion of the market. This suggests that production consortia involving a majority of the firms in an industry pose a special antitrust risk.[38]

Joint production ventures have been common between U.S. and foreign auto manufacturers, such as the GM/Toyota alliance in Fremont, California. However, because particular joint ventures do not include a majority of firms in the auto industry, they do not pose the major antitrust concerns alluded to by Stockdale.

Government policy is of paramount importance for firms attempting to build and exploit many types of resource advantages, or block rivals from so doing. In our opinion, continued evolution of antitrust laws is critical for protection and promotion of competition, but they must not inhibit innovation. The importance of innovation has increased, and will continue to increase, as the expansion of the global marketplace causes rivalry to intensify. Many innovations can benefit both upstream and downstream industries within a country, and such innovations in strategic industries can provide an engine of growth for the entire economy. Increasingly, large sums of capital are needed for successful innovation, sums that may be beyond the reach of companies without R & D consortia.

Michael Porter, however, after an exhaustive study of why industries achieve competitive advantage in certain countries, has argued that ensuring strong domestic rivalry is important for the success of domestic companies and entire economies.[39] Rivalry itself will stimulate and foster innovation. Policies should not reduce rivalry by allowing cartels or mergers between dominant rivals. Policies of consolidating national rivals in an effort to compete better internationally have largely been shown to fail, an example being the consolidation of British Leyland, ICI, and Alfred Herbett in the British automobile industry. Any government restriction of competition by maintaining a state monopoly, fixing prices, or controlling entry works against innovation. Firms become unduly protective and defensive, directing their attention to regulatory agencies and lobbying efforts rather than developing new products and becoming stronger competitors. Deregulation, allowing competition in U.S. industries such as transportation and telecommunication, has spurred remarkable gains in productivity and efficiency in recent years. As discussed by Porter, protecting a dominant local firm will rarely result in lasting international competitive advantage.

Moreover, policy-makers must closely scrutinize other cooperative activities such as joint production activities and exclusionary vertical cooperation. Trade policies should aim at opening markets and promoting competition. Intervention or restriction of foreign investment should be rare, used only when rivalry is threatened or restrictions are needed as a lever to open access to foreign markets. New business development must be encouraged.

An important dimension of competitive activity in many industries is the legal, regulatory, and policy interface. The public and private antitrust activity in computer software, the immense efforts to shape policy for entry and competition in long-distance and local telephone markets, the efforts to exempt horizontal joint ventures from antitrust laws, and the battles for imposition or relaxation of trade barriers across many industries provide examples. Indeed, the intrusion of HSC into NutraSweet's dominant market position, as discussed in chapter 8, was marked by numerous legal and regulatory skirmishes. HSC first went to court in a successful effort to force NutraSweet to back off from long-term contracts with Coke and Pepsi under European antitrust laws. When NutraSweet responded to HSC's European entry with aggressive lowering of prices, HSC filed dumping charges under international trade agreements and was successful in forcing NutraSweet to raise its prices.

Strategy as Action: A Final Note

The dynamic version of our action model of advantage, which views the interaction of firms' resource positions and actions over time, is a powerful and appropriate way in which to analyze competition and understand advantage. It will become even more germane as rivalry and change in the global economy intensify and static approaches become less effective. It provides a powerful tool for managers and a fertile agenda for future research in competitive strategy.

However, we emphasize that the methods and models discussed in this book are not limited in their applicability to industries where the competitive environment is turbulent. The model can be applied across industries with varying levels of rivalry and dynamism. Some industries have not yet undergone the same degree of revolutionary change as the ones affected by import competition, technological advances, and deregulation, as outlined in chapter 1. Nonetheless, the action-based approach is appropriate for relatively stable as well as dynamic industries and for markets where a single firm has been dominant for decades as well as settings in which change is occurring rapidly.

Similarly, we note that our approach is a synthesis of and logical progression from previous approaches to competitive advantage. We are not arguing that today's environment has made such approaches obsolete but only that an action-based approach is particularly apt today. We see value in grounding our model in previous approaches to competitive advantage, such as the Porter Five-Forces model and the resource-based view. Throughout this book, we have applied and integrated many ideas from IO economics, the resource-based perspective, and the Schumpeterian approach to competitive advantage. We do not want our work to be viewed as a "theory du jour," sandwiched between yesterday's and tomorrow's fad. Our goal is simply to "stand on the foundation built by giants" to add another building block for a better understanding of competitive advantage and business success.

NOTES

Chapter 1

1. I. Leveson, 1991, *American challenges: Business and government in the world of the 1990s* (NewYork: Praeger); H. Browne and B. Sims, 1993, *Runaway America: US. jobs and factories on tile move* (Albuquerque: Resource Center Press); P. C. Peterson, 1993, *Facing up: How to rescue the economy from crushing debt and restore the American dream* (New York: Simon and Schuster); J. Naisbitt and P. Auburdene, 1990, *Megatrends 2000* (New York: Morrow); R. D'Aveni, 1994, *Hypercompetition: Managing the dynamics of strategic maneuvering* (New York: Free Press); G. Hamel, 2000, *Leading the revolution* (Boston: Harvard Business School Press).

2. A recent study challenges the notion of hypercompetition, as it found no decline but an increase in industry and firm performance from the late 1980s to mid-1990s relative to the late 1970s and early 1980s. See G. McNamara, P. M. Vaaler, and C. Devers, 2003, Same as it ever was: The search for evidence of increasing hypercompetition, *Strategic Management Journal* 24: 261–278. However, high performance does not necessarily preclude the notion of hyper-competition, as other studies have found that rivalrous actions can increase firm and industry performance. See L. G. Thomas, 1996, The two faces of competition: Dynamic resourcefulness and the hypercompetitive shift, *Organization Science* 7: 221–242, and G. Young, K. G. Smith, and C. M. Grimm, 1996, "Austrian" and industrial organization perspectives on firm-level competitive activity and performance, *Organization Science* 7: 243–254.

3. R. Lee, 2000, The five-year wireless boom, *Wireless Week*, September 25; P. J. Howe, 2003, Firms can no longer count on explosive growth in subscriber bases, *Boston Globe*, January 6.

4. D. Mermiga, 2003, Rivalry to grow between stations, cable systems, *Electronic Media*, January 6; C. Boyd, 2002, Broadcasters prepare for local radio to go digital, *Orlando Sentinel*, September 29.

5. J. Doebele, 2003, Ends and means: As Korea globalizes, the chaebol is streamlining itself and its products, *Forbes*, February 3; H. A. Bolande, 2003, Handsets from China driving down prices, *Wall Street Journal*, January 30; Anonymous, Samsung pressure gives Motorola insomnia, 2003, *Total Telecom*, January 3.

6. J. Collis and T. Stuart, 1991, Cat fight in the pet food industry (A), case no. 9-391-189 (Boston: Harvard Business School).

7. Interestingly, the acquisition of Gaines by the industry outsider Anderson Clayton three years previously posed no threat to Ralston. However, the bid by Quaker Oats, an insider and direct competitor of Ralston, was an entirely different matter.

8. E. Bryon, 2003, Computer forensics sleuths help find fraud, *Wall Street Journal*, March 18; A. Serwer, 2001, P & G comes clean on spying operation, *Fortune*, August 30; Anonymous, 2000, Corporate warfare: Oracle hired detective firm to snoop on Microsoft, *Atlanta Journal and Constitution*, June 28.

9. A. Toffler, 1990, *Powershift: Knowledge, wealth and violence at the edge of the twenty-first century* (New York: Bantam Books), 155.

10. J. Schumpeter, 1976, *Capitalism, socialism, and democracy* (London: Allen and Irwin).

11. C. M. Christensen, 1997, *The innovator's dilemma: When new technologies cause great firms to fail* (Boston: Harvard Business School Press).

12. K. C. Smith, C. Grimm, and M. Gannon, 1992, *The dynamics of competitive strategy* (Newbury Park, CA: Sage).

13. G. Young, K. G. Smith, and C. Grimm, 1996, "Austrian" and industrial organization perspectives on firm-level competitive activity and performance, *Organization Science* 7: 243–254.

14. W. Ferrier, 1995, *Creative destruction: An action-based study of industry leaders and challengers* (Ph.D. diss., University of Maryland, College Park).

15. A. Schomberg, C. Grimm, and K. G. Smith, 1994, Avoiding new product warfare: The role of industry structure, in P. Shrivastava, A. Huff, and J. Dutton (eds.), *Advances in strategic management* (Greenwich, CT: JAI Press), 145–174.

16. H. Lee, K. G. Smith, C. M. Grimm, and A. Schomberg, 2000, Timing, order, and durability of new product advantages with imitation, *Strategic Management Journal* 21: 23–30.

17. R. Agarwal and M. Gort, 2001, First mover advantage and speed of competitive entry, 1887–1986, *Journal of Law and Economics* 44: 162–178.

18. Anonymous, 2000, Industrial robots today are nothing like their '70s counterparts, *Red Herring*, August 1.

19. D. Welch, 2003, Rick Wagoner's game plan, *Business Week*, February 10; T. H. Willis and A. F. Jurkus, 2001, Product Development: An essential igredient of time-based competition, *Review of Business*, March 22.

20. G. Edmondson, C. Palmeri, B. Grow, and C. Tierney, 2003, BMW like clockwork, *Business Week*, June 9.

21. D. Glennon, 2002, Shorten your cycles, *Telephony*, November 18.

22. C. Edwards, I. Moon, and P. Engardio, 2003, The Samsung way, *Business Week*, June 16.

23. J. Williams, 1992, How sustainable is your competitive advantage? *California Management Review* 34(3): 29–51.

24. C. Fishman, 2003, Which price is right? *Fast Company*, March 1.

25. C. Edwards, I. Moon, and P. Engardio, 2003, The Samsung way, *Business Week*, June 16.

26. R. D'Aveni, 1994, *Hypercompetition: Managing the dynamics of strategic maneuvering* (New York: Free Press).

27. A. R. Rao, M. E. Bergen, and S. Davis, 2000, How to fight a price war, *Harvard Business Review* 78(2): 107–116.

28. Ibid.

29. B. Berkowitz, 2002, Sony out to claim victory as game giants battle, *Reuter News*, May 22.

30. C. Morris, 2002, Coming soon: Video game price cuts, How soon? How much? And what about the next generation? *http:/money.cnn.com*, December 15.

31. B. Brewin, 2002, Dell takes a swipe at IBM, HP with new blade servers, *Computerworld*, December 2.

32. S. Prestegard, 2001, Competition and health care, *Marketplace Magazine*, June 19; J. Vande Water, 2001, Laser eye surgery discounters have turned the industry on its ear, *St. Louis Post-Dispatch*, January 15.

33. L. Johannes, 2000, Cost of laser-eye surgery likely to drop, *Wall Street Journal*, February 24.

34. C. Edwards, I. Moon, and P. Engardio, 2003, The Samsung way, *Business Week*, June 16.

35. G. Edmondson, C. Palmeri, B. Grow, and C. Tierney, 2003, BMW like clockwork, *Business Week*, June 9.

36. R. Martin, 2001, Can Kodak find its focus? *Industry Standard*, July 5.

37. K. Rebello, 1992, Microsoft: Bill Gates' baby is on top of the world, *Business Week*, February 23.

38. I. Morrison and G. Schmid, 1994, *Future tense* (New York: Morrow); W. Brock and R. Hormats, 1990, *The global economy* (New York: Norton).

39. For example, the Japanese have a longstanding practice of cooperating within Japanese markets while competing for market share against foreign competitors. Japanese markets have also generally been more difficult for foreign entry. Europeans have a within-country cooperative norm and a more gentlemanly view of how to compete. Within the new European market, however, the norms of competitive behavior have yet to be established. American businesses have traditionally been prohibited from cooperating with one another by antitrust laws, and the American markets vary greatly in terms of the level of competition. American markets have traditionally been relatively open to foreign competitors because of the American belief that competition is healthy for both American business and the American consumer.

40. I. Morrison and C. Schmid, 1994, *Future tense* (New York: Morrow); I. Leveson, 1991, *American challenges: Business and government in the world of the 1990s* (NewYork: Praeger).

41. G. Dennis and J. Goodrich, 1990, *Privatization and deregulation in global perspective* (Westport, CT: Quorum Books).

42. Ibid.

43. I. Morrison and G. Schmid, 1994, *Future tense* (New York: Morrow).

44. I. Leveson, 1991, *American challenges* (New York: Praeger).

45. R. A. Bettis and M. A. Hitt, 1995, The new competitive landscape, *Strategic Management Journal*, special issue, 16: 7–20.

46. Ibid.

47. J. P. Clark and M. C. Flemmings, 1986, Advanced materials and the economy, *Scientific American*, October, 50–57.

48. S. Kotha, 1995, Mass customization: Implementing the emerging paradigm for competitive advantage, *Strategic Management Journal* 16: 21–42.

49. R. Sanchez, 1995, Strategic flexibility in product competition, *Strategic Management Journal* 16: 135–160.

50. R. A. Bettis and M. A. Hitt, 1995, The new competitive landscape, *Strategic Management Journal*, special issue, 16: 7–20.

51. R. D'Aveni, 1994, *Hypercompetition: Managing the dynamics of strategic maneuvering* (New York: Free Press).

52. G. Hamel and C. K. Prahalad, 1989, Strategic intent, *Harvard Business Review* 67(3): 63–76.

53. M. Porter, 1994, Toward a dynamic theory of strategy, in R. Rumelt, D. Schendel, and D. Teece (eds.), *Fundamental issues in strategy* (Boston: Harvard Business School Press), 423–462.

54. M. E. Porter and J. W. Rivkin, 2000, Industry transformation, article no. 9-70-008 (Boston: Harvard Business School).

55. D. Miller, 1990, *The Icarus paradox: How excellent organizations can bring about their own downfall* (New York: Harper Business); J. Schumpeter, 1934, *A theory of economic development* (Cambridge, MA: Harvard University Press); F. A. Hayek, 1948, *Individualism and economic order* (Chicago: University of Chicago Press).

56. Through interviews the researchers were able to identify meaningful ways of measuring actions and responses. In addition, the interviews were helpful in gathering background data on each firm and for soliciting the support of each firm for the second phase of the study.

57. R. Jauch, R. R. Osborn, and J. N. Martin, 1980, Structured content analysis of cases: A complementary method for organizational research. *Academy of Management Review* 5: 517–526.

Chapter 2

1. L. Pepall, D. Richards, and G. Norman, 2002, *Industrial organization* (Cincinnati: South-western), 62.

2. M. R. Baye, 1996, *Managerial economics and business strategy* (Chicago: Irwin).

3. E. H. Chamberlin, 1933, *The theory of monopolistic competition* (Cambridge, MA), 56.

4. M. R. Baye, 1996, *Managerial economics and business strategy* (Chicago: Irwin).

5. F. M. Scherer and D. Ross, 1990, *Industrial market structure and economic performance* (Boston: Houghton Mifflin), ch. 10.

6. W. Baumol, J. Panzer and R. Willig, 1982, *Contestable markets and the theory of industry structure* (New York: Harcourt Brace Jovanovich).

7. D. Waldman and E. Jensen, 2002, *Industrial organization* (Boston: Addison Wesley), ch. 7.

8. For example, in the basic Cournot duopoly model, two firms maximize profit by setting optimal output quantities, assuming the quantity produced by the rival will be fixed. An extension of the model to more than two firms produces the result that profit declines as the number of firms increases. Porter later drew on this insight to highlight the importance of interfirm rivalry; as the number of firms increases, so does the level of rivalry. See M. Porter, 1980, *Competitive strategy: Techniques for analyzing industries and competitors* (New York: Free Press).

9. R. Amit, I. Domowitz, and C. Fershtman, 1988, Thinking one step ahead: The use of conjectures in competitor analysis, *Strategic Management Journal* 9(5): 431–442.

10. R. Schmalensee, 1988, Industrial economics: An overview, *Economic Journal* 98: 643.

11. G. J. Stigler, 1968, *The organization of industry* (Homewood, IL: Richard I. Irwin), 1.

12. Mason's paradigm dominated the field of IO, in particular the emerging Harvard school, which used as a primary method the industry study or "detailed empirical analysis of an individual industry in the framework of the structure-conduct-performance paradigm." See D. Blackwell, 1984, Industrial organization and its schools of thought, *Survey of Business*, summer: 5–9. The field thus emerged as an empirical field, drawing on extant models of competition, oligopoly, and monopoly for theoretical grounding. A strong emphasis of the field was public policy prescription, determining government policies such as antitrust, regulation/deregulation, and nationalization/privatization to facilitate the best possible performance of individual markets.

13. F. M. Scherer and D. Ross, 1990, *Industrial market structure and economic performance*, 3rd ed. (Boston: Houghton Muffin).

14. Bain also advanced the field methodologically by formulating empirically testable hypotheses and using statistical tools to subject hypotheses to formal testing. Over time, the use of cross-sectional data with formal statistical tools, primarily regression, replaced the Mason-type industry study as the dominant method in IO.

15. D. Blackwell, 1984, Industrial organization and its schools of thought, *Survey of Business*, summer: 5–9.

16. See, for example, N. R. Collins and L. E. Preston, 1969, Price-cost margins and industry structure, *Review of Economics and Statistics* 51: 271–286.

17. F. M. Scherer and D. Ross, 1990, *Industrial market structure and economic performance*, 3rd ed. (Boston: Houghton Muffin), chs. 7–8; D. Rosenbaum and L. Manns, 1992, Cooperation vs. rivalry, working paper.

18. R. E. Caves and M. E. Porter, 1977, From entry barriers to mobility barriers: Conjectural decisions and contrived deterrence to new competition, *Quarterly Journal of Economics* 91: 241–261; M. Porter, 1979, The structure

within industries and companies' performance, *Review of Economics and Statistics*, 61: 214–227.

19. N. Collins and L. E. Preston, 1969, Price-cost margins and industry structure, *Review of Economics and Statistics* 51: 271–286; B. Gale, 1971, The existence and direction of causality in cross-section analysis of hypotheses: A paper in research strategy, *Proceedings, Business and Economic Statistics Section, American Statistical Association*, 314–319; W. G. Shepherd, 1972, The elements of market structure, *Review of Economics and Statistics* 54: 25–37.

20. D. Ravenscraft, 1983, Structure-profit relationships at the line of business and industry level, *Review of Economics and Statistics* 65: 22–31.

21. M. Porter, 1981, The contributions of industrial organization to strategy management, *Academy of Management Review* 6: 609–620.

22. In addition, consistent with the firm-specific IO literature relating strategy to performance, Porter argued that selecting the proper generic strategy is also critical in achieving competitive advantage.

23. M. Porter, 1980, *Competitive strategy: Techniques for analyzing industries and competitors* (New York: Free Press).

24. However, a careful reader of Porter's book would note an extensive discussion on how to predict structural change. Public policy concerns about consumer welfare also are a basis for criticism of IO ideas as applied to strategy and competitive advantage. That is, the cardinal goal of most IO research, understanding the forces that produce perfect competition, is reversed in strategy research, which seeks to curb the competitive forces so as to produce monopoly power and therefore threatens consumer welfare. Rumelt contended that the market power perspective as derived from IO involves "colluding behind strategically erected entry barriers in order to make money" (R. Rumelt, 1988, Competitive marketing strategy, panel discussion, ORSA/TIMS Marketing Science Conference, Seattle).

25. R. Nelson, 1976, Goldschmid, Mann, and Weston's industrial concentration: The new learning. *Bell Journal of Economics* 7: 729–732.

26. K. G. Smith, C. M. Grimm, and M. J. Gannon, 1992, *Dynamics of competitive strategy* (Newbury Park, CA: Sage).

27. Kreps (1990) laid out the basic notions of noncooperative game theory. See D. M. Kreps, 1990, *Game theory and economic modeling* (Oxford: Oxford University Press). In cooperative game theory, the emphasis is on groups or coalitions and what type of outcome the coalition can achieve. In noncooperative game theory, the focus is on individual participants such as countries or firms.

28. This example follows a similar one given by Oster, which also provides a good introduction to extensive form game theory. See S. M. Oster, 1990, *Modern competitive analysis* (Oxford: Oxford University Press).

29. J. Barney, 1986, Types of competition and the theory of strategy: Toward an integrative framework, *Academy of Management Review* 11: 791–800; R. D'Aveni, 1994, *Hypercompetition: Managing the dynamics of strategic maneuvering* (New York: Free Press); R. Jacobsen, 1992, The "Austrian" school of strategy, *Academy of Management Review* 17: 782–807; K. G. Smith, C. M. Grimm, and M. J. Gannon, *Dynamics of competitive strategy*.

30. M. Rothbard, 1973, Praxeology as the method of economics, in N. Natanson (ed.), *Phenomenology and the social services* 2 vols. (Evanston, IL: Northwestern University Press), 311–339.

31. This is counter to the predominant IO structure-conduct-performance viewpoint. See F. M. Scherer, 1992, Schumpeter and plausible capitalism, *Journal of Economic Literature* 30: 1416–1433.

32. J. Schumpeter, 1942, *Capitalism, socialism, and democracy* (NewYork: Harper), 106.

33. W L. Baldwin and J. I. Scott, 1987, *Market structure and technological change* (Chur, Switzerland: Harwood); W. M. Cohn and R. C. Levin, 1989, Empirical studies of innovation and market structure, in R. Schmalensee and R. Willig (eds.), *Handbook of industrial organization* vol. 2 (Amsterdam: North-Holland), 1059–1107; F. M. Scherer and D. Ross, 1990, *Industrial market structure and economic performance*, 3rd ed. (Boston: Houghton Muffin).

34. F. M. Scherer and D. Ross, 1990, *Industrial market structure and economic performance*, 3rd ed. (Boston: Houghton Muffin), 613–660.

35. J. Schumpeter, 1942, *Capitalism, socialism, and democracy* (New York: Harper), 84–85.

36. In the Schumpeterian model, the manager disrupts the market and moves it away from equilibrium by taking action. When the action is undertaken, the formulator of the action outcompetes other firms and earns a profit. However, the realization of profit invites new actions and imitations by rivals, and profit therefore is competed away. Equilibrium returns until another action occurs. Each action is imitated or replaced by another action. Schumpeter refers to this process as "creative destruction." The gains realized from action give the firm means to pursue new actions. The forces of competition doom any firm that simply attempts to maintain its present position. See R. Jacobson, 1992, The "Austrian" school of strategy, *Academy of Management Review* 17: 782–807.

37. Lieberman and Montgomery and Kerin et al. reviewed the literature on first-mover advantages and found that most of the studies showed significant performance advantages in moving first versus later. See A. Kerin, P. R. Varadarajan, and R. A. Peterson, 1992, First-mover advantage: A synthesis, conceptual framework, and research propositions, *Journal of Marketing* 56: 33–52; M. B. Liberman and D. B. Montgomery, 1988, First-mover advantages, *Strategic Management Journal* 9: 41–58. However, Baldwin and Childs have argued that in certain instances fast seconds can outdo first movers by avoiding the uncertainty of moving first. See W L. Baldwin and G. L. Childs,1969, The fast second and rivalry in research and development, *Southern Economic Journal* 36: 18–24.

38. H. Lee, K. G. Smith, C. Grimm, and A. Schomberg, 2000, Timing, order, and durability of new product advantages with imitation, *Strategic Management Journal* 21: 23–30.

39. R. A. Bettis and D. Weeks, 1987, Financial returns and strategic interaction: The case of instant photography, *Strategic Management Journal* 8: 549–563.

40. M. J. Chen and I. MacMillan, 1992, Non-response and delayed response to competitive moves: The roles of competitor dependence and action

irreversibility, *Academy of Management Journal* 35: 539–570; M. J. Chen, K. G. Smith, and C. M. Grimm, 1992, Action characteristics as predictors of competitive responses, *Management Science* 38: 439–455; A. Schomberg, C. Grimm, and K. Smith, 1994, Avoiding new product warfare: The role of industry structure, in P. Shrivastava, A. Huff, and J. Dutton (eds.), *Advances in strategic management* (Greenwich, CT: JAI Press) 145–174; K. G. Smith, C. Grimm, M. J. Gannon, and M. J. Chen, 1991, Organizational information-processing, competitive responses and performance in the U.S. domestic airline industry, *Academy of Management Journal* 34(1): 60–85; G. Young, K. G. Smith, and C. Grimm, 1994, Engaging a rival for competitive advantage: Firm resources and the competitive environment as predictors of competitive firm activity, paper presented at the annual meeting of the Academy of Management, Dallas.

41. R. Nelson and S. Winter, 1982, *An evolutionary theory of economic change* (Cambridge, MA: Harvard University Press).

Chapter 3

1. www.finance.yahoo.com.

2. S. Pearlstein, 2003, When business plans go bust, *Washington Post*, January 5.

3. R. Grant, 2002, *Contemporary strategy analysis: Concepts, techniques, applications.* (Oxford: Blackwell); G. Hawawini, V. Subramanian, and P. Verdin, 2003, Is performance driven by industry- or firm-specific factors? A new look at the evidence, *Strategic Management Journal* 24(1): 1–16.

4. S. Pearlstein, 2003, When business plans go bust, *Washington Post*, January 5; T. Hansson, J. Ringbeck, and M. Franke, 2002, Flight for survival: A new operating model for airlines, *strategy + business enews*, December 9.

5. R. Schmalensee, 1985, Do markets differ much? *American Economic Review* 75(3): 341–351; R. P. Rumelt, 1991, How much does industry matter? *Strategic Management Journal* 17(8): 663–664; A. M. McGahan and M. E. Porter, 1997, How much does industry matter, really? *Strategic Management Journal* 18: 15–30.

6. G. Hawawini, V. Subramanian, and P. Verdin, 2003, Is performance driven by industry- or firm-specific factors? A new look at the evidence, *Strategic Management Journal* 24(1): 1–16.

7. R. Grant, 2002, *Contemporary strategy analysis: Concepts, techniques, applications.* (Oxford: Blackwell).

8. M. Porter, 1980, *Competitive strategy: Techniques for analyzing industries and competitors* (New York: Free Press), 32.

9. R. Grant, 2002, *Contemporary strategy analysis: Concepts, techniques, applications* (Oxford: Blackwell).

10. M. Porter, 1980, *Competitive strategy: Techniques for analyzing industries and competitors* (New York: Free Press).

11. Ibid.

12. Porter has acknowledged a recent advancement to entry barriers: demand-side economies of scale or proprietary network externalities in addition

to the production-side economies of scale in his original framework. See N. Argyres, and A. M. McGahan, An interview with Michael Porter, *Academy of Management Executive* 16(2): 43–52.

13. D. Michaels, 2003, Dogfight: In the secret world of airplane deals, one battle up close, *Wall Street Journal*, March 10.

14. M. Murray, 2002, In a tailspin, *National Journal*, October 12.

15. C. Woodyard, 2003. Online travel sellers court budget-conscious corporate customers, *USA Today*, July 23.

16. Many of the airlines using the hub-and-spoke route system are now moving to a "continuous" or "rolling" hub-and-spoke system, which emphasizes using aircraft, gates, and employees more efficiently in scheduling and connecting flights. See M. Arndt and W. Zellner, 2003, Commentary: How to fix the airlines, *Businessweek Online*, April 14; T. Hansson, J. Ringbeck, and M. Franke, 2002, Flight for survival: A new operating model for airlines, *strategy + business enews*, December 9.

17. S. Tully, 2001, From bad to worse, *Fortune*, October 15.

18. In addition, consistent with the firm-specific IO literature relating strategy to performance, Porter argued that selecting the proper generic strategy is also critical in achieving competitive advantage.

19. Although Porter recognizes the role of complementors and its potential as a sixth force, he says that complements do not have a monotonic relationship, as they can promote or hinder industry profits. Thus, the real value of complements is how they affect the five forces. See N. Argyres and A. M. McGahan, An interview with Michael Porter, *Academy of Management Executive* 16(2): 43–52.

20. A. Bradenburger and B. Nalebuff, 1996, *Co-opetition* (New York: Currency Doubleday).

21. R. A. Guth, 2003, Choosing sides: Videogame giant links with Sony, snubbing Microsoft, *Wall Street Journal*, May 12.

22. M. Porter, 1980, *Competitive strategy: Techniques for analyzing industries and competitors* (New York: Free Press), 129.

23. R. E. Caves and M. Porter, 1977, From entry barriers to mobility barriers: Conjectural decisions and contrived deterrence to new competition, *Quarterly Journal of Economics* 91: 241–261.

24. See, for example, D. J. Ketchen, J. G. Combs, C. J. Russel, C. Shook, M. A. Dean, J. Runge, F. T. Lohnke, S. E. Nanmann, D. E. Haptonstahl, R. Baker, B. A. Beckstein, C. Handler, H. Honig, and S. Lamonreux, 1997, Organization configurations and performance: A meta-analysis, *Academy of Management Journal* 40: 223–240, and A. Nair and S. Kotha, 2001, Does group membership matter? Evidence from the Japanese steel industry, *Strategic Management Journal* 22(3): 221–235.

25. Anonymous, 2003, Generics firms on offensive. *Chain Drug Review*, March 17.

26. S. Tully, 2003, The airlines' new deal: It's not enough, *Fortune*, April 28.

27. Anonymous, 2002, U.S. airline industry must "restructure or die," *Aviation Week & Space Technology* reports: Low-cost airlines, not September 11, have transformed industry fundamentals, *Business Wire*, November 18.

28. K. L. Alexander, 2004, Older airlines hamstrung their own longevity, *Washington Post*, Anonymous, 2003, Song's lure, *Kiplinger's Personal Finance*, June 1; M. E. Porter, 1996, What is strategy? *Harvard Business Review* 74(6): 61–78.

29. M. J. Chen, 1996, Interfirm rivalry and competitor analysis: Toward a theoretical integration, *Academy of Management Review* 21(1): 100–134.

30. K Smith, W. Ferrier, and H. Ndofor, Competitive dynamics: Critique and future directions, in M. Hitt, R. E. Freeman, and J. Harrison (eds.), *Handbook of strategic management* (London: Blackwell).

31. M. J. Chen, 1996, Interfirm rivalry and competitor analysis: Toward a theoretical integration, *Academy of Management Review* 21(1): 100–134.

32. I. C. MacMillan, A. B. van Putten, and R. G. McGrath, 2003, Global gamesmanship, *Harvard Business Review* 81(4): 62–71.

33. R. A. Bettis and M. A. Hitt, 1995, The new competitive landscape, *Strategic Management Journal* 16: 7–20.

34. M. E. Porter and J. W. Rivkin, 2000, Industry transformation, article no. 9-70-008 (Boston: Harvard Business School).

35. N. Argyres, and A. M. McGahan, An interview with Michael Porter, *Academy of Management Executive* 16(2): 43–52.

36. M. E. Porter and J. W. Rivkin, 2000, Industry transformation, article no. 9-70-008 (Boston: Harvard Business School).

Chapter 4

1. www.gillette.com/company/gilletteataglance.asp.

2. The resource-based view originated in the work of Chamberlin, Penrose and Chandler. See E. H. Chamberlin, 1933, *The theory of monopolistic competition* (Cambridge, MA: Harvard University Press); E. Penrose, 1955, Limits to the growth and size of firms, *American Economic Review* 45: 531–43; E. Penrose, 1959, *The theory of the growth of the firm* (Oxford: Blackwell); A. D. Chandler, Jr., 1961, *Strategy and structure* (Cambridge, MA: Harvard University Press). The discussion here is drawn from Wernerfelt and Mahoney and Pandian; see B. Wernerfelt, 1984, A resource-based view of the firm, *Strategic Management Journal* 5: 171–180; B. Wernerfelt, 1989, From critical resources to corporate strategy, *Journal of General Management* 14: 4–12; J. Mahoney and R. Pandian, 1992, The resource-based view within the conversation of strategic management, *Strategic Management Journal* 13: 363–380.

3. J. Barney, 1991, Firm resources and sustained competitive advantage, *Journal of Management* 17: 99–120.

4. M. Lewis, 1999, *The new new thing: A Silicon Valley story* (New York: Norton).

5. Barney's fourth dimension was substitutability, which was discussed in chapter 3.

6. M. A. Hitt, R. D. Ireland, and R. E. Hoskisson, 1995, *Strategic management: Competitiveness and globalization* (St. Paul, MN: West).

7. See I. Dierickx and K. Cool, 1989, Asset stock accumulation and sustainability of competitive advantage. *Management Science* 35: 99–120.

8. See D. Teece, G. Pisano, and A. Shuen, 1997, Dynamic capabilities and strategic management. *Strategic Management Journal* 18: 509–533.

9. Porter introduced the notion of value chain or the resource chain as a way of disaggregating the firm into its relevant resource activities. Every firm is a collection of resources that are arranged in such a way as to design, produce, deliver, and support its product or service. See M. Porter, 1985, *Competitive advantage: Techniques for analyzing industries and competitors* (New York: Free Press).

10. See M. Porter, 1985, *Competitive advantage: Creating and sustaining superior performance* (New York: Macmillan), 38.

11. Ibid., 39–45.

Chapter 5

1. P. M. Rosenzweig, 1991, Bill Gates and the management of Microsoft, case no. 9-392-019 (Boston: Harvard Business School); P. Zachary, 1994, A winning deal: Microsoft will remain dominant despite pact in antitrust dispute, *Wall Street Journal*, July 18; E. Corcoran, 1995, On-line rivals appeal to Microsoft, *Washington Post*, July 20; M. G. Rukstad and D. B. Yoffie, 2002, Microsoft in 2002, case no. 9-702-411 (Boston: Harvard Business School).

2. M. G. Rukstad and D. B. Yoffie, 2002, Microsoft in 2002, case no. 9-702-411 (Boston: Harvard Business School).

3. G. Young, 1993, *Engaging a rival: Industry and firm-specific predictors of rivalrous firm conduct in the US. software industry, 1983–1991* (Ph.D. diss., University of Maryland, College Park); W. Ferrier, 1995, *Creative destruction: An action-based study of industry leaders and challengers* (Ph.D. diss., University of Maryland, College Park).

4. P. M. Rosenzweig, 1991, Bill Gates and the management of Microsoft, case no. 9-392-019 (Boston: Harvard Business School).

5. P. Zachary, 1994, A winning deal: Microsoft will remain dominant despite pact in antitrust dispute, *Wall Street Journal*, July 18, A1.

6. E. Corcoran, 1995, On-line rivals appeal to Microsoft, *Washington Post*, July 20, D11.

7. J. A. Newburg, 2003, The narrative construction of antitrust (working paper, University of Maryland, College Park).

8. M. G. Rukstad and D. B. Yoffie, 2002, Microsoft in 2002, case no. 9-702-411 (Boston: Harvard Business School).

9. 2002 Annual Report, www.microsoft.com.

10. W. Ferrier, 1995, *Creative destruction: An action-based study of industry leaders and challengers* (Ph.D. diss., University of Maryland, College Park).

11. T. Parsons, 1937, *The social structure of action* (New York: McGraw Hill).

12. J. Thompson, 1967, *Organizations in action* (New York: McGraw Hill).

13. The focus on competitive actions is consistent with Schumpeter and the Austrian school of economics. Joseph Schumpeter argued that the market is a mechanism whereby firms experiment in taking specific actions; some firms undertake actions in a clear and explicit attempt to lead, whereas others simply

follow and imitate. See J. Schumpeter, 1950, *Capitalism, socialism and democracy*, 3rd ed. (NewYork: Harper). The roots of competitive action within the Austrian school stem from its focus on purposeful organizational behavior. Kirzner noted that any theory that does "not draw attention to the dimension of purpose gives a truncated picture of the real world." See I. M. Kirzner, 1976, On the method of Austrian economics, in E. C. Dolan (ed.), *The foundations of modern Austrian economics* (Kansas City, MO: Sheed and Ward), 40–45. The focus on competitive actions also has a parallel in Porter's model of competitive advantage, whereby firms act to position themselves relative to industry forces or act in some way to influence those forces. See M. Porter, 1980, *Competitive strategy: Techniques for analyzing industries and competitors* (New York: Free Press).

14. Mahoney and Pandian identified different types of rents generated by different type of resources. They contended that entrepreneurial rents are generated by uncertainty, Ricardian rents are generated by ownership of scarce resources, and monopoly rents are generated through market power. Our definitions of action alternatives are consistent with this viewpoint. See J. Mahoney and R. Pandian, 1992, The resource-based view within the conservation of strategic management, *Strategic Management Journal* 13: 363–380.

15. J. Schumpeter, 1938, *Capitalism, socialism, and democracy* (New York: Harper), 68.

16. S. Oster, 1999, *Modern competitive analysis* (New York: Oxford University Press).

17. C. R. Christensen, K. R. Andrews, J. L. Bower, R. G. Hamermesh, and M. E. Porter, 1982, *Business policy: Text and cases*, 5th ed. (Homewood, IL: Irwin); J. Barney, 1986, Types of competition and the theory of strategy: Toward an integrative framework, *Academy of Management Review* 11: 791–800; M. Porter, 1985, *Competitive advantage: Creating and sustaining superior performance* (New York: Free Press).

18. P. Heilbroner, 1953, *The worldly philosophers* (New York: Simon and Schuster).

19. J. Barney, 1991, Firm resources and sustained competitive advantage, *Journal of Management* 17: 99–120; E. Penrose, 1959, *The theory of the growth of the firm* (Oxford: Blackwell).

20. J. Bain, 1956, *Barriers to new competition* (Cambridge, MA: Harvard University Press); P. Sylos-Labini, 1962, *Oligopoly and technical progress*, E. Henderson (transl.) (Cambridge, MA: Harvard University Press); D. Gaskins, 1971, Dynamic limit pricing: Optimal pricing under threat of entry, *Journal of Economic Theory* 3: 306–322.

21. Of course, the response may not be in kind.

22. R. Nelson and S. G. Winter, 1982, An evolutionary theory of economic change (Cambridge, MA: Harvard University Press); S. G. Winter, 1987, Knowledge and competence as strategic assets, in D. Teece (ed.), *The competitive challenge: Strategies for industrial innovation and renewal* (Cambridge, MA: Ballinger), 159–184.

23. J. Barney, 1991, Firm resources and sustained competitive advantage, *Journal of Management* 17: 99–120; S. C. Winter, 1987, Knowledge and

competence as strategic assets, in D. Teece (ed.), *The competitive challenge: Strategies for industrial innovation and renewal* (Cambridge, MA: Ballinger), 159–184.

24. Porter referred to these factors of production as strategic variables, mobility barriers, and more recently as sources of value. See M. E. Porter, 1980, *Competitive strategy: Techniques for analyzing industries and competitors* (New York: Free Press); M. E. Porter, 1985, *Competitive advantage: Creating and sustaining superior performance* (New York: Free Press). Rumelt described these factors as potential isolating mechanisms. See R. Rumelt, 1987, Theory, strategy and entrepreneurship, in D. Teece (ed.), *The competitive challenge: Strategies for industrial innovation and renewal* (Cambridge, MA: Ballinger), 137–159.

25. S. C. Winter, 1987, Knowledge and competence as strategic assets, in D. Teece (ed.), *The competitive challenge: Strategies for industrial innovation and renewal* (Cambridge, MA: Ballinger), 173.

26. F. M. Scherer and D. Ross, 1990, *Industrial market structure and economic performance*, 3rd ed. (Boston: Houghton Mifflin).

27. W. Fellner, 1949, *Competition among the few* (New York: Knopf).

28. J. Schumpeter, 1942, *Capitalism, socialism, and democracy* (New York: Harper).

29. M. Sutherland, K. DuBois, and R. Burgelman, 2000, Charles Schwab & Co. Inc. in 1999, case no. SM-35 (Stanford University: Graduate School of Business); M. J. Cascales, A. Farhoomand, and P. Lovelock, 2000, Charles Schwab Inc.: Creating an International Marketspace, case no. HKU067 (Hong Kong: University of Hong Kong School of Business).

30. H. Lee, K. G. Smith, C. M. Grimm, and A. Schomberg, 2000, Timing, order, and durability of new product advantages with imitation, *Strategic Management Journal* 21: 23–30.

31. Miles and Snow argued that firms can choose to exploit their low-cost production capability with a low-price defender strategy or introduce new products with a prospector strategy. Firms that fail to find a fit between resources and strategy are labeled "reactors" and are doomed to lower performance. See R. Miles and C. Snow, 1978, *Organizational strategy, structure, and process* (New York: McGraw-Hill). Similarly, Porter contended that the firms with the lowest cost production capability should seek to be the lowest cost producers, which implies taking low-price actions. He also argued that firms with differentiated advantages in production quality, service, or innovation should seek to differentiate themselves with actions that emphasize quality, service, or innovation. As Miles and Snow argued, Porter implied that firms failing to achieve a fit between resources and actions would be "stuck in the middle." See M. E. Porter, 1980, *Competitive strategy: Techniques for analyzing industries and competitors* (New York: Free Press).

32. R. Rumelt, 1987, Theory, strategy and entrepreneurship, in D. Teece (ed.), *The competitive challenge: Strategies for industrial innovation and renewal* (Cambridge, MA: Ballinger), 142.

33. Kwoka showed how dominant firms like GM altered prices to deter entry. See J. Kwoka, 1984, Market power and market change in the U.S.

automobile industry, *Journal of Industrial Economics* 32: 509–522. Moreover, Schmalensee, in his study of the ready-to-eat cereal market, showed how from 1950 to 1972 the market leaders Kellogg, General Mills, General Foods, and Quaker Oats acted to introduce more than 80 new brands in an attempt to fill all market niches and deter entry. See R. Schmalensee, 1978, Entry deterrence in the ready-to-eat breakfast cereal industry, *Bell Journal of Economics* 9: 305–328. Similarly, Gilbert and Newberry developed models to show that a monopoly firm has incentive to maintain its power by patenting new technologies before potential competitors, even if such patents are never used or licensed to others. See R. Gilbert and D. Newberry, 1982, Preemptive patenting and the persistence of monopoly, *American Economic Review* 72: 514–526.

34. A Brandenburger, A. Costella, and J. Kou, 1995, Bitter competition: The Holland Sweetener Company versus NutraSweet, case no. 9-793-098 and case no. 9-794-081 (Boston: Harvard Business School).

35. Antitrust implications of such actions are discussed in detail in chapter 9.

36. R. Reed and R. J. DeFillippi, 1990, Causal ambiguity: Barriers to imitation, and sustainable competitive advantage, *Academy of Management Review* 15: 88–102.

37. A. Chandler, 1961, *Strategy and structure* (Cambridge, MA: MIT Press); L. Griener, 1972, Evolution and revolution as organizations grow, *Harvard Business Review* 50: 37–46; B. Scott, 1968, *Stages of corporate development, Parts 1 & 2* (Cambridge, MA: Harvard Graduate School of Business).

Chapter 6

1. J. Dee, 2003, This grass is always greener, *New York Times*, April 20; C. Turner, 2002, Turf war: How a small Montreal company battles AstroTurf, *National Post*, April 1.

2. K. G. Smith, 1980, *Enterprise Manufacturing Co.* (College Park, MD: University of Maryland Cases).

3. S. P. Bradley and S. Foley, 1994, Wal-Mart Stores, Inc., case no. 9-724-024 (Boston: Harvard Business School).

4. I. Kirzner, 1973, *Competition and entrepreneurship* (Chicago: University of Chicago Press).

5. Our own view on this subject is that there are powerful forces for equilibrium but that equilibrium is never achieved because of the competitive process.

6. I. Kirzner, 1992, *The meaning of market process* (London: Routledge).

7. Ibid.

8. Ibid., 161.

9. J. Schumpeter, 1939, *Business cycles* (Philadelphia: Porcupine Press), 103.

10. I. Kirzner, 1992, *The meaning of market process* (London, Routledge), 105.

11. T. Laseter, B. Berg, and M. Turner, 2003, What FreshDirect learned from Dell, *strategy + business*, spring.

12. I. Kirzner, 1992, *The meaning of market process* (London: Routledge), 221.

13. J. Schumpeter, 1934, *The theory of economic development* (Cambridge, MA: Harvard University Press), 85.

14. J. Timmons, 1985, *New venture creation* (Homewood, IL: Richard D. Irwin), 26.

15. Ibid.

16. K. I. Vesper, 1990, *New venture strategies* (Englewood Cliffs, NJ: Prentice Hall).

17. J. Timmons, 1985, *New venture creation* (Homewood, IL: Richard D. Irwin), 78.

18. Ibid.

19. Hambrick, 1989, *Reinventing the CEO: Twenty-first century report* (New York: Columbia University Graduate School of Business).

20. C. Hammel and C. K. Prahalad, 1994, Competing for the future, *Harvard Business Review* 72(4): 122–130.

21. R. H. Koller, 1988. On the source of entrepreneurial ideas, in B. H. Kirchhoff, W. A. Long, W. E. McMillan, K. H. Vesper, and W. E. Wetzel, Jr. (eds.), *Frontiers of entrepreneurship research* (Wellesley, MA: Babson Centre for Entrepreneurial Studies), 200.

22. A. C. Cooper et al., 1990, *New business in America* (Washington, DC: National Federation of Independent Business Foundation).

23. J. Timmons, 1985, *New venture creation* (Homewood, IL: Richard D. Irwin), 78.

24. M. J. Chen and D. Hambrick, 1995, Speed, stealth, and selective attack: How small firms differ from large firms in competitive behavior, *Academy of Management Journal* 38(2): 453–482.

25. M. J. Chen, 1996, Competitor analysis and inter-firm rivalry: Toward a theoretical integration, *Academy of Management Review* 21(1): 100–134.

26. Chen's argument is derived from the mutual forbearance literature, which suggests that competitors interacting in multiple markets would be less motivated to compete aggressively in a market because of their awareness of possible retaliation. See D. D. Edwards, 1955, Conglomerate bigness as a source of power, in *Business concentration and price policy: A conference of the Universities National Committee for economic research* (Princeton, NJ: Princeton University Press), 331–352.

27. G. Young, K. G. Smith, and C. Grimm, 1996, "Austrian" and industrial organization perspectives on firm-level competitive activity and performance, *Organization Science* 7: 243–254.

28. K. Eisenhardt and J. Bourgeois, 1989, Politics of strategic decision making in high-velocity environments: Toward a midrange theory, *Academy of Management Journal* 31: 737–770; S. Wally and J. Baum, 1994, Personal and structural determinants of the pace of strategic decision making, *Academy of Management Journal* 37: 932–956.

29. C. Stalk and T. M. Hout, 1990, *Competing against time* (New York: Free Press).

30. J. L. Bower and T. M. Hout, 1988, Fast-cycle capability for competitive power, *Harvard Business Review* 67(6): 113.

31. Ibid.

32. C. Stalk and T. M. Hout, 1990, *Competing against time* (New York: Free Press).

33. M. J. Chen and D. Hambrick, 1995, Speed, stealth, and selective attack: How small firms differ from large firms in competitive behavior, *Academy of Management Journal* 38: 453–482.

34. R. A. Melcher, 1993, How Goliaths can act like Davids, *Business Week,* special issue, October 22, 193.

35. S. Oster, 1999, *Modern competitive analysis* (NewYork: Oxford University Press).

36. K. H. Vesper, 1990, *New venture strategies* (Englewood Cliffs, NJ: Prentice Hall).

37. J. Case, 1989, The origins of entrepreneurship, *Inc.,* June, 53.

38. H. Lee, K. C. Smith, C. Grimm, and A. Schomburg, 2000, Timing, order, and durability of new product advantages with imitations, *Strategic Management Journal* 21: 23–30.

39. C. Williams, 1981, *Lead, follow, or get out of the way* (New York: Times Books); J. Kao, 1991, *The entrepreneur* (Englewood Cliffs, NJ: Prentice Hall), 62.

40. K. Vesper, 1990. *New venture strategies* (Englewood Cliffs, NJ: Prentice Hall).

41. B. Lloyd, 2003, Armour and the man: Under Armour's Kevin Plank rules the compression performance market with a 67 percent share, *Daily News Record,* April 14; E. Shannon, 2003, They're what everyone's wearing this season, *Time,* January 13.

42. Ibid.

43. P. Ghemawat, 1986, Wal-Mart Stores' discount operations, case no. 9-387-018 (Boston: Harvard Business School).

44. Ibid.

45. Ibid.

46. K. Vesper, 1900, *New venture strategies* (Englewood Cliffs, NJ: Prentice Hall); J. Timmons, 1985, *New Venture creation* (Homewood, IL: Richard D. Irwin), 78.

47. C. K. Prahalad and R. A. Bettis, 1986, The dominant logic: A new linkage between diversity and performance, *Strategic Management Journal* 7(6): 485–501.

48. M. E. Porter, 1980, *Competitive strategy: Techniques for analyzing competitors* (NewYork: Free Press), 59.

49. Alternatively, one could model this aspect of the game with an initial period where the rival either responds or does nothing, and a subsequent period in which the late response occurs.

50. P. Ghemawat and B. Baird, 1998, Leadership online: Barnes & Noble vs. Amazon.com, case no. 9-789-063 (Boston: Harvard Business School).

51. This example is drawn from A. Brandenburger, 1993, Signal jamming, case no. 9-793-126 (Boston: Harvard Business School); and from D. Fudenberg and J. Tirole, 1986, A "signal-jamming" theory of predation, *Rand Journal of Economics* 17: 366–376.

52. M. E. Porter and R. Wayland, 1991, Coca-Cola versus Pepsi-Cola and the soft drink industry, case no. 9-391-179 (Boston: Harvard Business School).

53. From authors' interviews with PETSTUFF managers, Silver Spring, MD.

54. S. Zahra and S. Chaples, 1993, Blind spots in competitive analysis, *Academy of Management Executive* 7: 7–28.

55. U. S. Rangan and C. A. Bartlett, 1985, Caterpillar Tractor Co., case no. 9-385-276 (Boston: Harvard Business School); C. A. Bartlett and U. S. Rangan, 1985, Komatsu Limited, case no. 9-385-277 (Boston: Harvard Business School); C. A. Bartlett, 1986, Caterpillar-Komatsu in 1986, case no. 9-387-095 (Boston: Harvard Business School).

56. J. Porac and H. Thomas, 1990, Taxonomic mental models in competitor definition, *Academy of Management Review* 15(2): 224–240.

57. S. Zahra and S. Chaples, 1993, Blind spots in competitive analysis, *Academy of Management Executive* 7: 7–28.

58. Ibid.

59. H. Sutton, 1988, *Competitive intelligence* report no. 913 (New York: Conference Board).

60. P. Ghemawat and H. J. Stander, 1992, Nucor at a crossroads, case no. 9-793-039 (Boston: Harvard Business School).

Chapter 7

1. K. A. Porter and S. P. Bradley, 2001, eBay, Inc., case no. 9-700-007 (Boston: Harvard Business School.

2. Ibid.

3. N. Wingfield, 2001, Ebay watch: Corporate sellers put the online auctioneer on even faster track, *Wall Street Journal*, June 1.

4. M. Warner, 2003, eBay's worst nightmare, *Fortune*, May 26; M. A. Ostrom, 2003, eBay revenue surpasses $1 billion for first time, *San Jose Mercury News*, January 17.

5. M. E. Porter and R. Wayland, 1991 , Coca-Cola versus Pepsi-Cola and the soft drink industry, case no. 9-391-179 (Boston: Harvard Business School).

6. P. Ghemawat, 1986, Wal-Mart Stores' discount operations, case no. 9-387-018 (Boston: Harvard Business School).

7. M. Pressler, 1995, Former rival named to lead recovery drive at Kmart, *Washington Post*, June 6.

8. R. Kerber, 1995, Discount chains in the Northeast get squeezed, *Wall Street Journal*, October 9.

9. For a review, see M. A. Hitt, D. Ireland, and R. E. Hoskisson, 1995, *Strategic management: Competitiveness and globalization* (St. Paul, MN: West).

10. J. Barney, 1991, Firm resources and sustained competitive advantage, *Journal of Management* 17: 99–120; E. Penrose, 1959, *The theory of the growth of the firm* (Oxford: Blackwell); M. E. Porter, 1985, *Competitive advantage: Creating and sustaining superior performance* (New York: Free Press).

11. L. Heilbroner, 1953, *The worldly philosophers* (New York: Simon and Schuster).

12. John Bates Clark placed Ricardian ideas in the traditional equilibrium model by contending that in equilibrium the price per unit of each productive resource is the measure of the market value of that resource. For Clark, it was axiomatic that each resource owner received the market value of what his or her resource produced. Moreover, in a competitive world in which production is always a function of resources, what a resource has produced is to be measured by the marginal product of the resource. See J. B. Clark, 1988, *The distribution of wealth* (New York: Macmillan).

13. M. E. Porter, 1980, *Competitive strategy: Techniques for analyzing industries and competitors* (New York: Free Press), 36.

14. Ibid., 75.

15. D. E. Hastings, 1999, Lincoln Electric's harsh lessons from international expansion, *Harvard Business Review* 77(3): 162–173.

16. W. J. Abernathy and K. Wayne, 1974, The limits of the learning curve, *Harvard Business Review* 52(5): 109–119.

17. This is in some respects similar to the limit price strategy discussed in chapter 8.

18. G. Hamel and C. K. Prahalad, 1985, Do you really have a global strategy? *Harvard Business Review* 63(4): 139–149.

19. R. E. Govory, 1989, From the ladder of science to the product development cycle, *Harvard Business Review* 67(6): 103.

20. S. Carey and S. McCartney, 2003, Reeling under losses, airlines turn to workers for big savings, *Wall Street Journal*, February 18.

21. J. Barney, 1988, Returns to bidding firms in mergers and acquisitions: Reconsidering the relatedness hypothesis, *Strategic Management Journal*, special issue, 9: 71–78.

22. I. Magaziner and M. Patinkin, 1989, Fast heat: How Korea won the microwave war, *Harvard Business Review* 67(1): 88.

23. Ibid., 92.

24. M. E. Porter, 1980, *Competitive strategy: Techniques for analyzing industries and competitors* (New York: Free Press).

25. Ibid., 120.

26. R. Foster, 1986, *Innovation: The attacker's advantage* (New York: Simon and Schuster), 121–129.

27. The competitive landscape of the instant camera industry has clearly changed with the advancements in digital technology and growth of digital cameras. Polaroid filed for bankruptcy in 2001 and emerged shortly thereafter as a privately held firm. It still sells instant cameras, such as the popular iZone, as well as digital cameras and photo-printing kiosks. Kodak still retains its leadership position in film sales and a strong presence in digital camera and photo-quality inkjet paper markets. See J. Krasner, 2003, A developing story: Polaroid aims to make name for itself by licensing brand to others, *Boston Globe*, May 10; B. Upbin, 2000, Kodak's digital moment, *Forbes*, August 21.

28. S. Winter, 1987, Knowledge and competence as strategic assets, in D. Teece (ed.), *The competitive challenge: Strategies of industrial innovation and renewal* (Cambridge, MA: Ballinger), 159–184.

29. S. Oster, 1994, *Modern competitive analysis* (New York: Oxford University Press).

30. U.S. Patent and Trademark Office, 1988, General information concerning trademarks (Washington, DC: U.S. Department of Commerce), 1–3.

31. R. Grant, 2002, *Contemporary strategy analysis: Concepts, techniques, applications* (Cambridge, MA: Blackwell).

32. O. E. Williamson, 1979, Transaction cost economics: The governance of contractual relations, *Journal of Law and Economics* 19: 233–261.

33. C. Brown and M. Reich, 1989, When does union-management cooperation work? A look at NUMMI and GM-Van Nuys, *California Management Review* 31(4): 26–44.

34. Anonymous, 1994, Moving the merchandise, *New York Times*, July 31.

35. K. Brooker, 2004, Just one word: Plastic, *Fortune*, February 23.

36. E. Mansfield, 1986, Patents and innovation: An empirical study, *Management Science* 32: 175.

37. R. C. Levin, A. K. Klevorick, R. R. Nelson, and S. G. Winter, 1987, Appropriating the returns from industrial research and development, *Brookings Papers on Economic Activity* 3: 794.

38. E. Mansfield, M. Schwartz, and S. Wagner, 1981, Imitation costs and patents: An empirical study, *Economic Journal* 91: 907–918.

39. R. C. Levin, A. K. Klevorick, R. ft. Nelson, and S. G. Winter, 1987, Appropriating the returns from industrial research and development, *Brookings Papers on Economic Activity* 3: 794.

40. N. Wingfield, 2002, The other eBay: Amazon is winning over small vendors, *Wall Street Journal*, July 22.

41. G. Young, K. G. Smith, and C. Grimm, 1996, "Austrian" and industrial organization perspectives on firm-level competitive activity and performance, *Organization Science* 7: 243–254.

Chapter 8

1. A. Backover, 2003, Verizon tops Sprint in long-distance, *USA Today*, January 8.

2. J. Quinn, 1988, General Motors Corporation: The downsizing decision, in J. Quinn, H. Mintzberg, and R. James (eds.), *The strategy process: Concepts contexts and cases* (Englewood Cliffs, NJ: Prentice Hall), 131.

3. S. Freeman, 2003, U.S. auto sales are mixed, *Wall Street Journal*, June 4.

4. J. Barney, 1991, Firm resources and sustained competitive advantage, *Journal of Management* 17: 99–120; E. Penrose, 1959, *The theory of the growth of the firm* (Oxford: Blackwell).

5. See, for example, W. Shepherd, 1972, The elements of market structure, *Review of Economics and Statistics* 54: 25–37; R. Buzzell. B. Gale, and C. Sultan, 1975, Market share: A key to profitability, *Harvard Business Review* 53(1): 97–106; H. K. Christensen and C. A. Montgomery, 1981, Corporate economic performance: Diversification strategy and market structure, *Strategic Management Journal* 2(4): 327–344; C. Woo, 1981, Market share leadership: Does it

always pay off? *Proceedings of the Academy of Management*, 7–11; K. Cool, I. Diericks, and D. Jemsion, 1989, Business strategy, market structure, and risk-return relationships: A structural approach, *Strategic Management Journal* 10: 507–522.

6. G. Edmondson, C. Palmeri, B. Grow, and C. Tierney, 2003, BMW like clockwork, *Business Week*, June 9.

7. M. Kempner, 2002, Rise of Fox puts CNN in strange no. 2 role, *Atlanta Journal Constitution*, April 7.

8. W. Ferrier, *Creative destruction: An action-based study of industry leaders and challengers* (Ph.D. diss., University of Maryland, College Park).

9. R. Schmalensee, 1978, Entry deterrence in the ready-to-eat breakfast cereal industry, *Bell Journal of Economics* 9: 305–328; R. Smiley, 1988, Empirical evidence on strategic entry deterrence, *International Journal of Industrial Organization* 6: 167–180.

10. M. B. Lieberman and D. B. Montgomery, 1988, First-mover advantages, *Strategic Management Journal* 9: 41–58; R. A. Kerin, P. R. Varadarajan, and R. A. Peterson, 1992, First-mover advantage: A synthesis, conceptual framework, and research propositions, *Journal of Marketing* 56: 33–52.

11. P. Milgrom and J. Roberts, 1982, Predation, reputation, and entry deterrence, *Journal of Economic Theory* 27: 280–312.

12. K. G. Smith, C. M. Grimm, and M. J. Gannon, 1992, *Dynamics of competitive strategy* (Newbury Park, CA; Sage), ch. 3.

13. C. Fombrun and M. Shanley, 1990, What's in a name? Reputation building and corporate strategy, *Academy of Management Journal* 33: 233–258.

14. N. A. Berg and C. W. Merry, 1976, Polaroid-Kodak, case no. 9-376-266 (Boston: Harvard Business School).

15. J. Teresko, 2000, New image, *Industry Week*, July 17; B. Upbin, 2000, Kodak's digital moment, *Forbes*, August 21.

16. In addition to the role of actions in maintaining dominance, economists have explored structural determinants of monopoly persistence. One of the earliest studies was by Gort (1963), who examined the stability and change of market shares of leading firms, using a 1947–54 sample across 205 manufacturing industries. See M. Gort, 1963, Analysis of stability and change in market shares, *Journal of Political Economy* 71: 51–61. His model focused on structural factors in the industries in question. Factors such as market growth, technological change, the number of firms in the industry, barriers to entry, and scale economies were found to be important. Stability is fostered by an absence of disequilibrating forces such as high rates of growth or technological change. Growth attracts entry; technological change enables a smaller firm to leapfrog a dominant rival. Barriers to entry reduce the chance that a challenger will enter and overtake the dominant firm. They can stem from many sources, such as scale economies, brand identification, distribution channels, and patents. Interestingly, Gort also found that if there are other strong firms in the industry, dominance can be more precarious. Size of the leading firm did not prove to be an important factor in explaining stability. The hypothesis that stability occurs more often when products are highly differentiated was supported. This can he

related to increased entry barriers. Caves and Porter (1978) studied the stability of oligopoly market shares, examining how much the share of the top four firms changed from year to year. Independent variables were change in demand, growth, entry, exit, imports, R & D, capital intensity, age, product life cycle, development time, and advertising. Those structural factors were also found to play an important role in the persistence of a dominant firm or set of firms. See R. E. Caves and M. E. Porter, 1978, Market structure, oligopoly, and stability of market share, *Journal of Industrial Economics* 26: 289–313.

17. J. Bain, 1956, *Barriers to new competition* (Cambridge, MA: Harvard University Press); P Sylos-Labini, 1962, *Oligopoly and technical progress*, trans. Elizabeth Henderson (Cambridge, MA: Harvard University Press); D. Gaskins, 1971, Dynamic limit pricing: Optimal pricing under threat of entry, *Journal of Economic Theory* 3: 306–322. Over time the limit-pricing literature has advanced, with more formal mathematical models and empirical testing, as well as case studies of actual limit pricing.

18. J. Quinn, 1988, General Motors Corporation: The downsizing decision, in J. Quinn, H. Mintzberg, and R. James (eds.), *The strategy process: Concepts, contexts and cases* (Englewood Cliffs, NJ: Prentice Hall), 131.

19. See, in particular, J. Kwoka, 1984, Market power and market change in the US automobile industry, *Journal of Industrial Economics* 32: 509–522.

20. For a readable discussion of this oft-researched topic, see T. J. DiLorenzo, 1993, The myth of predatory pricing, *USA Today* 121(2572): 38.

21. Anonymous, 1993, Wal-Mart loses a case on pricing, *Wall Street Journal*, October 13.

22. E. McDowell, 1992, Suit on air fare cuts raises doubts, *New York Times*, June 11.

23. T. J. DiLorenzo, 1993, The myth of predatory pricing, *USA Today* 121(2572): 38.

24. Ibid.

25. W. Comanor and T. Wilson, 1967, Advertising, market structure, and performance, *Review of Economics and Statistics* 49: 423–440.

26. M. Spence, 1977, Entry, capacity, investment, amid oligopolistic pricing, *Bell Journal of Economics* 8: 534–544.

27. R. Schmalensee, 1978, Entry deterrence in the ready-to-eat breakfast cereal industry, *Bell Journal of Economics* 9: 305–328. Schmalensee developed a model to analyze how a firm can occupy the best "locations" on the grocery shelf, drawing from Hotelling's (1929) work on location theory See H. Hotelling, 1929, Stability in competition, *Economic Journal* 39: 41–57.

28. These actions are analyzed in Harvard Business School case. See A. Brandenburger and V. Krishna, 1990, Product proliferation and preemption, case no. 9-190-117 (Boston: Harvard Business School).

29. R. Gilbert and D. Newberry, 1982, Preemptive patenting and the persistence of monopoly *American Economic Review* 72: 514–526.

30. Bureau of National Affairs, 1982, SCM urges high court to rehear Xerox case amid reject new economics, *Antitrust & Trade Regulation Report* 42(1061): 827.

31. Anonymous, 2001, Ironically, more rigorous patent legislation could stifle innovation, *Economist*, June 23.

32. G. J. Stmgler, 1968, *The organization of industry* (Homewood, IL: Richard D. Irwin).

33. W Shepherd, 1993, Long-distance telephone service: Dominance in decline? in L. Duetsch (ed.), *Industry studies* (Englewood Cliffs, NJ: Prentice Hall), 346–352.

34. Ibid., 353–354.

35. D. Gallagher, 1992, Was A T & T guilty? *Telecommunications Policy* 16(3): 317–326.

36. The breakup of A T & T resulted in the creation of seven independent providers of local telephone service, the "Baby Bells," that were granted regulated monopolies in their own regions. These local telephone service providers were limited in the products and services they could offer. The Telecommunications Act of 1996 allows the Baby Bells to enter the long-distance market after they sufficiently open their local telephone markets to competition.

37. L. Weiss, 1980, *Case studies in American industry*, 3rd ed. (NewYork: Wiley), 170.

38. R. Smiley, 1988, Empirical evidence on strategic entry deterrence, *International Journal of Industrial Organization* 6: 167–180.

39. N. K. Kubasek, B. A. Brennan, and M. Neil Browne, 1996, *The legal environment of business: A critical-thinking approach* (Upper Saddle River, NJ: Prentice Hall), 680–682, 704–705.

40. A. Jacquermin, 1987, *The new industrial organization* (Cambridge, MA: MIT Press).

41. A. Brandenburger, 1995, Bitter competition: The Holland Sweetener Company versus NutraSweet, case no. 9-793-098 and case no. 9-794-081 (Boston: Harvard Business School).

42. A. Gallun, 2001, NutraSweet facing some bitter realities, *Crain's Chicago Business*, February 26.

43. This is discussed in more detail in Australia Bureau of Transport and Communication Economics, 1991, Deregulation of domestic aviation, report 73.

44. W. Ferrier, 1995, *Creative destruction: An action-based study of leaders and challengers* (Ph.D. diss., University of Maryland, College Park).

45. An overview of the antitrust laws and recent enforcement patterns is provided in a Harvard Business School case. See, J. Kou and A. McGahan, 1995, Antitrust and competitive strategy in the 1990s, case no. 9-795-039 (Boston: Harvard Business School).

46. A Harvard Business School case involving FTC charges of monopolization is: P. Ghemawat, 1985, Du Pont in titanium dioxide (B-6), case no. 9-386-074 (Boston: Harvard Business School).

47. *Standard Oil Co. of New Jersey v. United States*, 221 U.S. 1 (1911), 58.

48. Ibid., 76.

49. *United States v. Aluminum Co. of America*, 148 F.2d 416 (2d Cir. 1945), 427.

50. R. Noll and B. Owen, 1982, The anticompetitive uses of regulation: *United States v. AT&T* (1982), in J. Kwoka and L. White (eds.), *The antitrust revolution* (New York: HarperCollins), 328–375.

51. P. Zacharv, 1994, A winning deal: Microsoft will remain dominant despite pact in antitrust dispute, *Will Street Journal*, July 18.

52. Ibid.

53. J. Newberg, 2003, The narrative construction of antitrust, working paper (University of Maryland, Smith School of Business); J. Krim, 2002; Judge accepts settlement in Microsoft case, *Washington Post*, November 2.

54. E. I. Klayman, J. W. Bagby, and N. S. Ellis, 1994, *Irwin's business law: Concepts, analysis, perspectives* (Burr Ridge, IL: Richard D. Irwin), 998.

55. Anonymous, 1998, FTC upholds charges that Toys "R" Us induced toy makers to stop selling to warehouse clubs, *M2 Presswire*, October 15.

56. B. Drummond and G. Stohr, 1997, Anheuser-Busch joins those bitten by antitrust bug, *Journal Record*, October 3.

57. R. S. Greenberger, 2003, Justices to decide postal service antitrust case, *Wall Street Journal*, May 28.

58. Of course, the railroads' aggressive actions to prevent entry targeting their key commodity, coal, may well have been profit-maximizing actions, despite this antitrust judgment against them, if successful entry would have occurred in the absence of those aggressive tactics.

59. J. Shenefield and I. Stelzer, 1993, *The antitrust laws: A primer* (Washington, DC: AU Press), 36.

60. *United States v. Grinnell Corp.*, 384 U.S. 563 (1966). The Grinnell Corporation had a dominant position (more than 80 percent market share) in central station fire and burglary protection services.

61. J. Shenefield and I. Stelzer, 1993, *The antitrust laws: A primer* (Washington, DC: AEI Press).

Chapter 9

1. G. Subramanian and M. Kalka, 2002, Price-fixing vignettes, case no. 9-902-068 (Boston: Harvard Business School).

2. J. Forster, 2002, General malaise at General Mills, *Business Week*, July 1.

3. K. S. Corts, 1996, The ready-to-eat breakfast cereal industry in 1994, case no. 5-796-133 (Boston: Harvard Business School).

4. G. Hay, 1994, Practices that facilitate cooperation: The ethyl case (1984), in J. Kwoka and L. White (eds.), *The antitrust revolution*, 2nd ed. (New York: HarperCollins).

5. K. C. Smith, C. M. Grimm, and M. Gannon, 1992, *The dynamics of competitive strategy* (Newbury Park, CA: Sage).

6. M. E. Porter, 1980, *Competitive strategy: Techniques for analyzing industries and competitors* (New York: Free Press).

7. Indeed, D'Aveni makes a similar contention. See R. D'Aveni, 1994, *Hypercompetition: Managing the dynamics of strategic maneuvering* (New York: Free Press).

8. Antitrust Division, U.S. Department of Justice, www.usdoj.gov/atr/public/10108.pdf.

9. R. Gibson, 1996, Kellogg cutting prices on some cereals in hid to check loss of market share, *Wall Street Journal*, June 10; R. Gibson and E. S. Browning, 1996, Investors have to wait to milk cereal stocks, *Wall Street Journal*, June 11; J. P. Miller, 1996, Cereal makers fight bagels with price cuts, *Wall Street Journal*, June 20.

10. S. Morrison, 2003, Clash of the PC titans, *Financial Times*, May 28; P. Thibodeau, 2003, Sun undercuts Intel server competition, *Computerworld*, May 26; B. Brewin, 2002, Dell takes a swipe at IBM, HP with new blade servers, *Computerworld*, December 2.

11. O. E. Williamson, 1965, A dynamic theory of interfirm behavior, *Quarterly Journal of Economics* 79: 579–607.

12. The increasing difficulty of coordinating as the number of firms increases is analyzed more formally by D. K. Osborne, 1976, Cartel problems, *American Economic Review* 66: 835–844.

13. A. Schomburg, C. Grimm, and K. G. Smith, 1994, Avoiding new product warfare: The role of industry structure, in P. Shrivastava, A. Huff, and J. Dutton (eds.), *Advances in strategic management* (Greenwich, CT: JAI Press), 145–174.

14. M. Dollinger, 1990, The evolution of collective strategies in fragmented industries, *Academy of Management Review* 15: 266–285.

15. D. F. Wood and J. C. Johnson, 1989, *Contemporary transportation* (New York: Macmillan).

16. K. G. Smith, C. Grimm, and M. Gannon, 1992, *The dynamics of competitive strategy* (Newbury Park, CA: Sage).

17. P. Dempsey, 1993, Must the airline industry collapse? address before the Transportation Research Forum, New York, October 14.

18. P. Asch and J. Seneca, 1975, Characteristics of collusive firms, *Journal of Industrial Economics* 23: 223–236.

19. R. E. Caves and M. E. Porter, 1977, From entry barriers to mobility barriers: Conjectural decisions and contrived deterrence to new competition, *Quarterly Journal of Economics* 91: 241–262.

20. G. Young, 1993, *Engaging a rival: Industry- and firm-specific predictors of rivalrous firm conduct in the U.S. software industry* (Ph.D. diss., University of Maryland, College Park).

21. See, for example, the verified statement of W. Robert Majure, Department of Justice, filed with the Surface Transportation Board on April 12, 1996 (finance docket no. 32760). For a general discussion of multimarket contact, see F. M. Scherer and D. Ross, 1990, *Industrial market structure and economic performance* (Boston: Houghton Mifflin).

22. Table 7.1 indicates that the outcome of cooperative actions is "unstable." By that we mean one cannot predict with certainty the intensity of rivalry in a given situation, and the intensity of rivalry in a given industry may well oscillate over time.

23. M. E. Porter, 1980, *Competitive strategy: Techniques for analyzing industries and competitors* (New York: Free Press); L. Miller, S. Schnaars, and

V. Vaccaro, 1993, The provocative practice of price signaling: Collusion versus cooperation, *Business Horizons* 36: 59–65; O. Heil and T. Robertson, 1991, Toward a theory of competitive market signaling: A research agenda, *Strategic Management Journal* 12: 403–418.

24. M. E. Porter, 1980, *Competitive strategy: Techniques for analyzing industries and competitors* (New York: Free Press), 75.

25. I. Stelzer, 1976, *Selected antitrust cases* (Homewood, IL: Richard D. Irwin).

26. For a more comprehensive discussion of similar trade association actions, including relevant antitrust issues, see T. W. Dunfee, J. R. Bellace, and D. B. Cohen, 1983, *Business and its legal environment* (Englewood Cliffs, NJ: Prentice Hall).

27. Ibid., 89.

28. R. A. Bettis and D. Weeks, 1987, Financial returns and strategic interaction: The case of instant photography, *Strategic Management Journal* 8: 549–563.

29. M. Arndt and W. Zellner, 2003, How to fix the airlines, *Business Week Online*, April 14.

30. P. Dempsey, 1993, Must the airline industry collapse? address before the Transportation Research Forum, New York, October 14. This has also been known as destructive or excessive competition: Dempsey has argued that such competition is a rationale for restricting competition through regulation.

31. A. Wells, 1989, *Air transportation* (Belmont, CA: Wadsworth). As discussed by Scherer and Ross, destructive competition can be illustrated with diagrams of cost and demand curves. See F. M. Scherer and D. Ross, 1990, *Industrial market structure and economic performance* (Boston: Houghton Muffin). Firms with high fixed costs (FC) that have a sharp decline in demand face a sharp reduction in the profit-maximizing price. For high FC firms, in contrast to those with lower FC, prices cut sharply result in severely eroded profit. With more firms competing, initial losses may subject a firm to financial crisis. The decision-making horizon shortens; a firm may try to undercut others to increase output and reduce losses. It takes just one firm in such straits ("one fool who cuts") to force the rest to follow. This process can continue until prices fall to marginal costs (MC). In industries with high FC and relatively low MC, losses can be substantial.

32. S. Morrison and C. Winston, 1995, *The evolution of the airline industry* (Washington, DC: Brookings Institute).

33. W. J. Ferrier, C. Mac Fhionnlaoich, K. G. Smith, and C. M. Grimm, 2002, The impact of performance distress on aggressive competitive behavior: A reconciliation of conflicting views, *Managerial & Decision Economics* 23: 301–316.

34. G. Hay, 1994, Practices that facilitate cooperation: The ethyl case (1984), in J. Kwoka and L. White (eds.), *The antitrust revolution*, 2nd ed. (New York: HarperCollins).

35. As discussed later in this chapter, firms must be sure not to violate antitrust laws when pursuing such actions.

36. See, for example, A. Q. Nomani, 1990, Airlines may be using a price-data network to lessen competition, *Wall Street Journal*, June 28.

37. Information about price moves is immediately and totally available to competitors through computer reservation systems, in contrast to situations in which prices are secret. This readily available price information can facilitate collusion but can also exacerbate price wars. Firms cannot undercut each other without detection, so retaliation is sure and rapid once a war begins. Hence, if these conditions do not deter war, they can indeed exacerbate destructive competition.

38. L. A. Sullivan, 1977, *Handbook of the law of antitrust* (St. Paul, MN: West).

39. Antitrust Division, U.S. Department of Justice, www.usdoj.gov/atr/public/10108.pdf.

40. David N. Danforth, 1995, The case that wouldn't fly: Using antitrust to attack fare wars, in C. E. Bagley (ed.), *Managers and the legal environment: Strategies for the twenty-first century*, 2nd ed. (St. Paul, MN: West), 595–597.

41. This source provides several additional examples of price fixing. See R. N. Corley, O. L. Reed, P. J. Shedd, and J. W. Morehead, 1993, *The legal and regulatory environment of business* (New York: McGraw-Hill), 612.

42. *Wall Street Journal*, 1993, Firms are alleged to have fixed baby food prices, January 18.

43. Anonymous, 1993, $126.8 million baby-formula settlement includes payments to Peter J. Schmitt Co., *Buffalo News*, May 26.

44. G. Subramanian and M. Kalka, 2002, Price-fixing vignettes, case no. 9-902-068 (Boston: Harvard Business School).

45. C. Quintanilla and A. D. Wilde, 1995, You dirty rat, say Decatur, Ill., of mole at Archer Daniels, *Wall Street Journal*, July 13.

46. N. Tait and E. Szewczyk, 1999, Three given jail sentences over ADM price-fixing, *Financial Times*, July 10.

47. F. M. Scherer and D. Ross, 1990, *Industrial market structure and economic performance* (Boston: Houghton Mifflin).

48. L. Miller, S. Schnaars, and V. Vaccaro, 1993, The provocative practice of price signaling: Collusion versus cooperation, *Business Horizons* 36: 59–65.

49. Ibid., 60.

50. A. Q. Nomani, 1991, NWA, TWA agree to alter pricing actions, *Wall Street Journal*, June 21.

51. Ibid.

52. I. Van Bael and J. Bellis, 1987, *Competition law of the EEC* (Bicester, UK: CCH Editions).

53. Ibid., 231.

54. Ibid., 231.

55. C. E. Bagley, 1995, *Managers and the legal environment: Strategies for the twenty-first century*, 2nd ed. (St. Paul, MN: West), 593–594.

56. R. N. Corley, O. L. Reed, P. J. Shedd, and J. W. Morehead, 1993, *The legal and regulatory environment of business* (New York: McGraw-Hill), 387–389.

Chapter 10

1. Hotel and Motel Management, Duluth, 1998, October 5. Marty Whitford.

2. www.hoover.com, Starbucks Company file.

3. M. J. Chen, 1996, Competitor analysis and interfirm rivalry: Toward a theoretical integration, *Academy of Management Review* 21: 100–134.

4. Cendant Corporation, Annual Report, 2002.

5. Six Continents PLC, Annual Report, 2002.

6. *Holiday Inn Worldwide Newsletter*, 1994, November 13.

7. Six Continents PLC, Annual Report, 2002.

8. www.ifis.com/ifis/news/hosp.html.

9. Starbucks, Annual Report, 2001.

10. Second Cup Ltd., Annual Report, 2001.

11. Starbucks, Annual Report, 2001.

12. G. Hamel and C. K. Prahalad, 1993, Strategy as stretch and leverage, *Harvard Business Review* 71(2): 75–85.

13. J. Gaibraith and R. Kazanjian, 1986, *Implementing strategy: Structure, systems and process* (Minneapolis: West).

14. G. Hamel and C. K. Prahalad, 1989, Strategic intent, *Harvard Business Review* 67(3): 63–76.

15. M. Porter, 1980, *Competitive strategy: Techniques for analyzing industries and competitors* (New York: Free Press).

16. Porter introduced the notion of value chain or the resource chain as a way of disaggregating the firm into its relevant resource activities. Every firm is a collection of resources that are arranged in such a way as to design, produce, deliver, and support its product or service. See M. Porter, 1985, *Competitive advantage: Techniques for analyzing industries and competitors* (New York: Free Press).

17. *Holiday Inn Worldwide Newsletter*, 1995, October 15.

18. E. Pizzinato and J. Lewis, 1995, Second Cup Coffee Co. asserts its market leadership position, *Canada News Wire*, August 2.

19. Second Cup Ltd., Annual Report, 2001.

20. Second Cup Ltd., Annual Report, 2001.

Chapter 11

1. We would argue that such actions are still within a Schumpterian perspective, as we interpret it, in that the emphasis is on firm actions.

2. R. R. Nelson and S. G. Winter, 1982, *An evolutionary theory of economic change* (Cambridge, MA: Belknap Press), 99.

3. Ibid.

4. L. A. Schlesinger, 1983, People Express, case no. 9-483-103 (Boston: Harvard Business School).

5. This literature is discussed in more detail by Ferrier, 1995. Weiss and Pascoe, 1983, found that the dominant firms identified in 1950 were the same as those in 1975 for only 39 percent of the industry segments in their study. Mueller found market leadership stability in only 44 percent of the industries studied. Collins and Preston found that only 36 percent of the largest 100 U.S.

corporations remained in the top 100 after a 50-year period. See W. Ferrier, 1995, *Creative destruction: An action-based study of industry leaders and challengers* (Ph.D. diss., University of Maryland, College Park); L. Weiss and G. Pascoe, 1983, The extent and performance of market dominarice, paper presented at E.A.R.I.E. meeting, August; N. Collins and L. Preston, 1961, The size structure of the largest industrial firms, *American Economic Review* 51: 986–1011; D. Mueller, 1986, *Profits in the long run* (Cambridge: Cambridge University Press).

6. F M. Scherer and D. Ross, 1990, *Industrial market structure and economic performance* (Boston: Houghton Mifflin).

7. W. Ferrier, 1995, *Creative destruction: An action-based study of industry leaders and challengers* (Ph.D. diss., University of Maryland, College Park).

8. C. K. Prahalad and G. Hamel, 1990, The core competence of the corporation, *Harvard Business Review* 68(3): 7–14.

9. R. H. Hayes and W. J. Abernathy, 1980, Managing our way to economic decline, *Harvard Business Review* 58(4): 67–77; R. Reich, 1983, *The next American frontier* (New York: Times Books).

10. Anonymous, 1991, 60,000 and counting, *Economist*, November 30.

11. S. Thomke and A. Nimgade, 2002, Innovation at 3M (A), case no. 9-699-012 (Boston: Harvard Business School).

12. E. von Hippel, S. Thome, and M. Sonnack, Creating breakthroughs at 3M, *Harvard Business Review* 77(5): 47–55.

13. Anonymous, 1991, 60,000 and counting, *Economist*, November 30.

14. Anonymous, 1999, How to merge: After the deal, *Economist*, January 9.

15. R. Sidel, 2002, Year-end review of markets and finance 2001, *Wall Street Journal*, January 2.

16. N. Kulish, 2002, Pfizer, Pharmacia combination raises little antitrust concern, *Wall Street Journal*, July 16.

17. P. Tam and S. Thurm, 2002, Married at last: H-P, Compaq face real test, *Wall Street Journal*, May 8.

18. Antitrust enforcement with respect to mergers, like other areas of antitrust law discussed in preceding chapters, has varied over time. For example, the merger policy of the Reagan administration was more permissive than that of the Clinton administration.

19. I. Van Bael and J. F. Bellis, 1987, *Competition law of the EEC* (Bicester, UK: CCH Editions).

20. R. Watson, 1995, Kansas City Southern: Merger hits shippers, *Journal of Commerce*, September 21; R. Watson, 1995, Southern Pacific shareholders embrace $25-a-share offer, *Journal of Commerce*, September 8; R. Watson, 1995, BN, Santa Fe tap top executives to lead company into the future, *Journal of Commerce*, September 7.

21. M. Porter, 1990, *The competitive advantages of nations* (New York: Free Press); F. Contractor and P. Lorange, 1992, Competition vs. cooperation: A benefit/cost framework for choosing between fully-owned investments and cooperative relationships, in F. Root and K. Visudtibhan (eds.), *International strategic management: Challenges and opportunities* (Washington, DC: Taylor and

Francis); S. Flicop, 1995, *The effects of international airline alliances on demand and price* (Ph.D. diss. proposal, University of Maryland, College Park).

22. D. B. Yoffie, 1994, Swissair's alliances, case no. 9-794-152 (Boston: Harvard Business School).

23. L. Fedor, 2003, NWA, Delta marketing deal begins, *Star-Tribune,* June 24.

24. J. Ott, 2003, Change, or else! *Aviation Week and Space Technology,* July 21.

25. T. W. Ferguson, 1993, Intel's success hasn't taken its mind off Washington, *Wall Street Journal,* January 19.

26. Anonymous, 1993, Sematech claims major advance by halving size of chip circuits, *Wall Street Journal,* January 22.

27. E. Ramstad, 1998, Foreign chip firms to boost funding of Sematech Group, *Wall Street Journal,* February 4.

28. B. Davis and D. Wessel, 1993, Clinton's good cop–bad cop stance on trade mirrors divisions within his administration, *Wall Street Journal,* March 1.

29. K. Done, 2003, Airbus beats Boeing but warns of tough 2003, *Financial Times,* January 14.

30. Anonymous, 2000, Reorganization of Airbus renews concern over aircraft deflation, *Aircraft Value News,* July 3.

31. R. Givens, 1993, *Antitrust: An economic approach* (New York: Law Journal Seminars Press).

32. In recent years, innovation has been encouraged by the relaxation of antitrust enforcement in other areas as well. Mergers, tying, vertical linkages, and the like have been allowed more often when the activity promotes innovation arid efficiency.

33. S. Balakrishnan, S. Feinberg, S. Lenway, and B. McEvily, 1995, Antitrust policy and cooperative R & D: "Much ado about nothing?" Carlson School of Management working paper, University of Minnesota.

34. T. M. Jorde and D. J. Teece, 1992, *Antitrust, innovation, and competitiveness* (New York: Oxford University Press).

35. D. Stockdale, 1993, Antitrust and international competitiveness: Is encouraging production joint ventures worth the cost? *High Technology Law Journal* 7(2): 269–314.

36. Ibid., 280

37. Ibid., 284. In addition, Clarke found that pooling of information facilitates collusion, and Mead found that bidding joint ventures resulted in restrained bidding in subsequent competition. See R. Clarke, 1973, Collusion and the incentive for information sharing, *Bell Journal of Economics* 14: 383–384; W. Mead, 1967, The competitive significance of joint ventures, *Antitrust Bulletin* 12: 819–821.

38. D. Stockdale, 1993, Antitrust and international competitiveness: Is encouraging production joint ventures worth the cost? *High Technology Law Journal* 7(2): 285.

39. M. E. Porter, 1990, *The competitive advantage of nations* (New York: Free Press).

INDEX

Note: Information presented in tables and figures is indicated by t or f respectively.

Ackerman, Jason, 107
action-based model, 86–100, 86f, 97–100, 97t, 98f, 99f, 202–219
advertising
  in coffee industry, 207
  as deterrent action, 167
  restrictions on, 16
  and Ricardian actions, 147
Airbus, 54, 234
Airline Deregulation Act, 18t
airline industry, 9, 10, 226–228
  and 9/11, 48, 194
  antitrust violations in, 199–200
  in Australia, 169
  buyer power in, 54–55
  and co-optive action, 194–196, 233
  and deregulation, 16, 18t
  deterrent actions in, 169
  entrants in, 55
  in five forces model, 53–56, 53f
  intraindustry advantage in, 50f, 59–61
  performance of, 48–49, 49f, 50t
  predatory pricing in, 163
  price fixing in, 198
  prices in, 11
  Ricardian actions in, 56

  rivalry in, 56, 186
  substitutes in, 55–56
  supplier power in, 53–54, 53f
AirTran, 60
Alcoa, 173
Amazon.com, 117–118, 129, 152
AMD, 58
America Online, 85, 232
American Airlines, 55, 163, 196, 198
American Express, 149–150
American Viscose, 143
Ames Department Stores, 130
Amtrak, 55–56
Ando, Kunitake, 12
Anheuser-Busch, 176
Ansett Airlines, 169
antiknock compounds, 181, 188, 191, 192–193
antitrust laws, 171–179. See also monopoly; Sherman Act
Apple (computers), 83–84, 122, 139–140
Archer Daniels Midland, 199
Arkansas Unfair Trade Practices Act, 163
Asia, wireless market in, 6
assets, specialized, 147–148

AstroTurf, 101
AT&T, 5–6, 12
   and deregulation, 17, 18*t*
   and deterrent actions, 156
   and information manipulation,
      165–166
auction industry, 129–130, 180
Australia, 16, 169
automobile industry, 10–11
   asset development in, 148
   and capacity, 139
   deterrent actions in, 156
   history of, 137, 138
   imports in, 15*f*
   limit pricing in, 162–163
   and performance measures, 50*t*

baby food, 198
Bain, Joe, 35
banking industry, 16, 18*t*
Barnes & Noble, 117–118
Barney, Jay, 70
Barr Laboratories, 59
beer industry, 9, 122, 176
beliefs, competitor, 208–210
Bell & Howell, 160
Benco Pet Foods, 7
Bertrand model, 34
Bettis, Richard, 45
BMW, 11, 159
Boeing, 54
Bolivia, 16
book retailing industry, 117–118
Bradlee's Inc., 130
brand loyalty, 147
Braniff International, 198
Bumlet, Richard, 94
Burlington Northern-Santa Fe,
      232–233
Burr, Donald, 226, 227
buyer power, 52, 54–55

Cable Communications Policy Act,
      18*t*
Caldor Corporation, 130
Canada
   antitrust laws in, 200
   deregulation in, 16
Canon, 71, 123
capacity, 138–139

Capitalism, Socialism, and Democracy
      (Schumpeter), 43
cars. *See* automobile industry
Carter Wallace, 59
Caterpillar, 122–123
Celanese, 143
cell phones, 5–6, 58. *See also*
      telecommunications industry
Cendant Corporation, 202–205,
      205*f*, 206*f*, 212–214, 215–216
cereal industry, 164, 180–181
The Chamber (Grisham), 145
Chamberlin, Edward, 32–33
chemical industry, 50*t*, 151
Chile, 16
China, 6
Christensen, Clayton, 8
Christie's International, 180
Clark, J. P., 19
Clark, Jim, 70
Clayton Act, 176, 232
The Client (Grisham), 145
CNN, 17, 112–113, 159
co-optive actions, 89, 180–201,
      231–237
   and antitrust considerations,
      197–201
   applicability of, 183–184
   definition of, 183
   and demand, 187–188
   and game theory, 190–191,
      193–196, 195*f*
   and homogeneity, 188–189
   and IO economics, 182–183
   legality of, 184
   and number of competitors,
      185–187
   types of, 189–193
   vs. deterrent actions, 182*t*
   vs. entrepreneurial actions, 182*t*
   vs. Ricardian actions, 182*t*
coal, 176–177
Coca-Cola
   brand awareness of, 70
   and new product introduction,
      112
   and pricing, 11, 198
   and Ricardian actions, 130
   and rivalry, 118–119
coffee industry, 202–208

Cold War, 38–40
collusion, 197, 200. *See also* co-optive actions; monopoly
Compass Airlines, 169
Competitive Strategy (Porter), 154
competitor-specific knowledge, 109–110
complementors, 56–58, 57*f*
Compuserve, 85
Computer Age, 121
Computer Associates, 85
computer industry, 9, 10. *See also* software industry
computer server industry, 12
consumer inertia, 159
Continental Airlines, 61, 163
cooperation. *See* co-optive actions
Coors, 122
copyrights, 145
cost actions, 134–135
Costco, 176
Cournot model, 34
Crandall, Robert, 198
Cray Computers, 71
credit card industry, 149–150
CSI (competing-under-strategic-interdependence) framework, 62

Darwin, Charles, 46
D'Aveni, Richard, 21
DEC, 159
defensive innovation, 164–165
Dell, 12
Deloitte & Touche, 7
Delta Airlines, 61
demand, 187–188
deregulation, 7, 16–17
  and industry dynamics, 63
  of telephone industry, 17, 18*t*, 156
design, of product, 139–140
deterrent actions, 88–89, 95–96, 156–179, 158*f*
  advertising as, 167
  combining, with others, 228–231, 229*f*
  definition of, 157–158, 161
  and game theory, 167–168, 168*f*, 170–171
  of General Motors, 162–163
  and incumbency, 159
  information manipulation as, 165–166
  and innovation, 164–165
  legality of, 158
  and market position, 158–171
  pricing as, 162–164
  product proliferation as, 164
  and reputation, 159–160
  types of, 161–167
  vs. co-optive actions, 182*t*
  vs. entrepreneurial actions, 157*t*, 182*t*
  vs. Ricardian actions, 157*t*, 182*t*
discovery, 106–108
disequilibrium, 104–112
Disney, 129
Domino's Pizza, 123–124
DOS (disk operating system), 83
Dr. Pepper, 148
"dumping," 163–164
Dun & Bradstreet, 201
DuPont, 143, 160, 181
dynamics, industry, 63–66

Eastman Kodak, 13
  Justice Department decree on, 160
  market position of, 160–161
  Ricardian actions of, 140, 143–145
  rivalries of, 123
eBay, 129–130, 152
economics, 31–47
  equilibrium theory in, 104–112
  evolutionary, 46–47
  industrial organization type of (*See* IO economics)
  neoclassical type of, 32–34
electricity, 17, 18*t*, 197–198
Electronic Arts, 57
electronics industry, 11
  effect of imports in, 15*f*
  Ricardian actions in, 142, 151*t*
England, deregulation in, 16
Enterprise Manufacturing, 77–78, 78*f*, 101–102
entrepreneurship, 88, 101–128, 104*f*
  action/reaction in, 115–128
  benefits of, 103

entrepreneurship (*continued*)
definition of, 106
discovery process in, 106–108
of FieldTurf Inc., 101
and game theory, 116–119, 117*f*
and market position, 103
and Ricardian actions, 225–228
and rivalry, 93–94
Schumpeterian view of, 44–45,
112
and timing, 123–124, 124*f*
types of, 112–115
vs. co-optive actions, 182*t*
vs. deterrent actions, 157*t*, 182*t*
vs. Ricardian actions, 135, 136*t*,
157*t*, 182*t*
and world view, 122–123
entry barriers, 52
entry determent, 164
equilibrium, 104–112
espionage, 7–8
Ethyl, 181
ETSI, 178
EU (European Union), 14
Europe, antitrust laws in, 200
evolutionary economics. *See under*
economics
*An Evolutionary Theory of Economic
Change* (Nelson and Winter), 46
Expedia, 55
eye surgery, laser, 12

farming, 132–134
fast-acting firms, 110–111
FCC (Federal Communications
Commission), 6, 166
Fedel, Joseph, 107
Federal Trade Commission (FTC).
See FTC
FieldTurf Inc., 101
Filene's Basement Corporation, 130
financial resources, 72*t*. *See also*
resources
Firestone, 143
The Firm (Grisham), 145
Five Forces model. *See* Porter Five
Forces model
Flamingo Industries, 176
Flemmings, M. C., 19
Ford, Henry, 137, 138

Ford Motor Company, 137, 138,
156
Fox (television network), 17, 159
Franklin, Ben, 114
FreshDirect, 107–108
Frito Lay, 12, 176
Frontier Airlines, 227
FTC (Federal Trade Commission), 36

Gaines Pet Foods, 6–7
game theory, 38–43
and co-optive actions, 190–191,
193–196, 195*f*
and deterrent actions, 167–168,
168*f*, 170–171
and entrepreneurship, 116–119,
117*f*
extensive form, 42–43, 42*f*
normal, 40–42
and Ricardian actions, 141–143,
141*f*, 148–149
games, video. *See* video games
Gary, Judge, 166
gas, natural, 17, 18*t*
gasoline, 181, 195
Gates, Bill, 83–85, 91. *See also*
Microsoft
General Electric, 142
General Mills, 180–181, 185
General Motors, 11, 148, 156,
162–163
Gerber Products, 198
Gillette, 68, 144
globalization, 14–16, 14*f*
Goodyear, 143
Great Depression, 16
Grinnell Corporation, U. S. *vs.*,
177–178
Grisham, John, 145
grocery delivery, 107–108
Grove, Andy, 154

Healtheon, 70
Heinz, 198
Hewlett Packard, 12, 146
Hill, Barry, 149
Holiday Inn, 202–205, 205*f*, 206*f*,
212–214, 216
Holland Sweetener Company, 70,
95–96, 168–169

hotel industry, 202–205
human resources, 71, 73t. *See also*
    resources

IBM
    and Microsoft, 83
    and monopoly, 173
    and product design, 139
    and rivalry, 122, 123
implementation knowledge,
    110–112
imports, foreign, 14–15, 15f
incumbency, 159
industry
    advantage in, 51–58
    analysis checklist, 67
    definition of, 50–51
    dynamics, 63–66
    life cycle, 64, 64f, 65t, 66
inertia, consumer, 159
information gathering, 218–219
information manipulation, 165–166
information technology, 19,
    149–150
innovation, 44–46, 143–146
innovation, defensive, 164–165
inputs, low-cost, 140–141
Intel, 58, 154
intellectual property, 84
Intelsat, 18t
intent, competitor, 210–211
Intercontinental Corporation. *See*
    Holiday Inn
interdependence, competitor,
    152–153
International Harvester, 122
internet
    and airline industry, 55
    auctions, 129–130
    bookselling on, 117–118
    grocery delivery on, 107
    stock trading on, 93
Interstate Commerce Commission
    Termination Act, 18t
intraindustry advantage, 58–61, 60f
introduction, product, 112–113
IO economics, 34–38, 44–46,
    182–183
Ireland, privatization in, 16
Iverson, Ken, 127

Jamesway Corporation, 130
Japan
    deregulation in, 16
    and "dumping," 163–164
J.C. Penney, 142
JetBlue, 60
Jobs, Steve, 146
John Deere, 122

Kaiser Aluminum, 173
Kelleher, Herb, 111–112
Kellogg (cereal company), 180–181,
    185
Kevlar, 143
Kmart, 76–77, 102, 118, 130, 152
Kodak. *See* Eastman Kodak
Komatsu, 122–123
Kraft, 12
Kroc, Ray, 115

Landauer, Greg, 214
laser eye surgery, 12
LaserSight, 12
layoffs, airline industry, 54
Levitt, Ted, 108
life cycle
    industry, 64, 64f, 65t, 66
    product, 20
Lim Kunstoff Technology, 143
limit pricing, 162–163.
    See also price
Lincoln Electric, 71, 137–138
logic, dominant, 116
long-distance industry, 12. *See also*
    telecommunications industry
    and deregulation, 17
    and deterrent actions, 156
    and information manipulation,
        165–166
    monopoly in, 173
loyalty, brand, 147
luxury products, 11

machinery, 15f
management
    and antitrust laws, 175–179,
        200–201
    and co-optive actions, 197–201
    knowledge for, 108–112
Marion Laboratories, 59

market
  disequilibrium in, 104–112
  Schumpeterian view of, 44
  signaling, 147, 190–191,
    199–200
market position, 48–66, 204
  and defensive innovation,
    164–165
  definition of, 159
  and deterrent actions, 158–161,
    161–171
  and five forces model, 51–56
  and industry complementors,
    56–58
  and industry dynamics, 63–66
  and intraindustry advantage,
    58–61
  and pair-wise advantage, 61–63
  and rivalry, 91–92
Mason, Edward, 35
Mastercard, 149–150
Matthews, Francis P., 39
McDonald's, 115
McEwen, Alton, 214
MCI, 12, 156, 165
  merger, 232–233
Micro Systems, 121
Microsoft
  competitive advantage of, 83–86
  and entrepreneurship, 94
  monopoly of, 174–175
  and product design, 139–140
  reputation of, 161
  spying on, by Oracle, 7
  in video game industry, 12
  and Windows 95 launch, 43–44
microwave oven, 142
Ming-jer Chen, 110
Minolta, 123
monopoly, 32–34, 85, 171–179
  of Alcoa, 173
  of AT&T, 173–174
  in auction industry, 180
  avoiding legal action over, 177
  and co-optive actions, 197–201
  in coal industry, 176–177
  definition of, 178–179
  disadvantages of, 176
  of IBM, 173
  legality of, 177–178

  and management, 175–179
  of Microsoft, 174–175
  in railroad industry, 178
  of Standard Oil, 172–173
Motor Carrier Act, 18t, 187
MS-DOS, 83
mutual forbearance, 184

NAFTA (North American Free Trade
  Agreement), 14
Nalco, 181
National Cooperative Research Act,
  234–235
National Energy Policy Act, 18t
natural gas. See gas, natural
Natural Gas Policy Act, 18t
natural selection, 46
Nelson, Richard, 46, 47
Netherlands, deregulation in, 16
Netscape, 70
new product introductions, 10–11,
  11f
New Zealand, 16
Nigeria, 16
Nike, 159
Nintendo, 12, 74–75, 127–128, 154
Nissan, 139
Northwest Airlines, 200
Nucor, 71, 127, 139, 154
Nutrasweet, 70, 95–96, 140,
  168–169
nylon, 143

office machinery, 15f
oil industry, 163, 172–173
oligopoly, 34
Oracle Corporation, 7
Organizations in Action (Thompson),
  87

pair-wise advantage, 61–63, 63f
Panke, Helmut, 12
Parsons, Talcott, 86
Parson's theory of action. See
  action-based model
patents, 10, 10f
  and defensive innovation, 165
  effectiveness of, 151
  laws on, 145
  and monopoly, 33

People Express, 226–228
Pepsi, 115, 118–119, 121
  and Nutrasweet, 140
  and price fixing, 198
  Ricardian actions of, 130, 131, 134
Pepsi Challenge, 88, 121, 130
performance measures, 48–49, 50t
pet food, 6–7
PETSTUFF, 122
Pfizer, 232
pharmaceutical industry
  intraindustry advantage in,
    59–61, 60f
  patents in, 151
  and performance measures, 50t
  performance of, 1998–2002,
    48–49, 49f
Pharmacia, 232
Philippines, privatization in, 16
photography industry, 140,
    143–144, 160–161. See also
    Eastman Kodak
Pilot (newspaper), 39
pizza industry, 123–124
Plank, Kevin, 113–114
Polaroid, 45, 143, 143–144,
    144–145
polyerts, 143
population, and Ricardian action,
    133
Porter Five Forces model, 31, 37–38
  and industry advantage, 51–56,
    52f, 53f
  and intraindustry advantage,
    58–61, 60f
  and life cycle, 66
  vs. resource-based view, 69–70
Post (cereals), 185
Postal Service, 176
Poundstone, William, 39
PPG, 181
predatory pricing, 163–164, 178.
    See also price
prediction, 208–212
price(ing)
  in action-based model, 96–97
  in airline industry, 169, 198
  base point, 192–193
  and co-optive actions, 189–193
  in competition, 11–12

as deterrent action, 162–164
in equilibrium theory, 105–106
fixing, 180, 198, 198–199
leadership, 166–167
limit, 162–163
and marketing, 147
predatory, 163–164, 178
and Ricardian actions, 138
and rivalry, 184–185
Schumpeterian view of, 45
Prisoner's Dilemma (Poundstone),
    39
privatization, 16–17
Procter & Gamble, 7, 12
Prodigy, 85
product
  design, 139–140
  improvements, 113–114
  introduction, 112–113
  proliferation, 33, 164
production joint ventures,
    235–236
profit
  in airline industry, 60–61
  and buyer power, 52
  Schumpeterian view of, 44
proliferation, product, 33, 164
property, intellectual, 84
property rights, 145, 146
Public Utilities Regulatory Act, 18t
Purina. See Ralston Purina
Putnam, Howard, 198

Quaker Oats, 6–7, 161

radicality, of action, 121–122
radio, 6
railroads
  and deregulation, 18t
  mergers in, 232–233
  and monopoly, 176–177
Ralston Purina, 6–7, 161, 198
Ravenscraft, David, 36
rayon, 143
razors, 68, 144
Reagan administration, 173, 174
rent, as Ricardian action, 132–134
reputation, 147, 159–160
reputational resources, 71, 72t.
    See also resources

resource-based view, 69–71,
72t–73t
resource position, 68–79, 90–92
resources
    adjustment of, 126
    advantage creation with,
        124–128
    definition of, 90–91
    differentiation, advantages,
        143–150
    examples of, 69
    imbalance of, 150–151
    intangible, 91
    internal, 91, 204
    low-cost, advantages, 135–143
    market position as, 158–161
    and Ricardian actions, 134–150,
        136f, 136t, 141f
    tangible, 71
    types of, 71, 72t–73t
revenge, 130
Reynolds (aluminum), 173
Ricardian actions, 88, 94–95,
        129–155. See also rivalry
    of American Express, 149–150
    definition of, 133–134
    and demand, 133
    and differentiation resource
        advantage exploitation,
        148–150
    disadvantages of, 153
    of eBay, 130, 131
    and economies of learning,
        137–138
    and economies of scale, 136–137
    and entrepreneurial actions,
        225–228
    and game theory, 141–143, 141f,
        148–149
    and innovation, 143–146
    and interdependence, 152–153
    and low-cost inputs, 140–141
    and low-cost resource advantages,
        141–143, 141f
    and marketing, 146–147
    of Pepsi, 130, 131, 134
    and population, 133
    and prediction of reaction,
        150–154
    and price, 138

rents as, 132–134
and resources, 134–150, 136f,
    136t, 141f
response times to, 150–151, 151t,
    153
and specialized assets, 147–148
and threat, degree of, 151–152
and trade secrets, 146
and utilization of capacity,
    138–139
and value chain, 153–154
vs. co-optive actions, 182t
vs. deterrent actions, 157t, 182t
vs. entrepreneurial actions, 135,
    136t, 157t, 182t
of Wal-Mart, 130, 131, 134
Ricardo, David, 88
rivalry. See also monopoly;
    Ricardian actions
    in airline industry, 56
    avoiding, 96–97
    blindness to, 118–119
    definition of, 38
    in five forces model, 53
    intensity of, 184–189
    and interdependence, 152–153
    and signal jamming, 119–120
    and world view, 122–123
Rockefeller, John D., 163, 172
Russell, Bertrand, 39
Russo, Patricia, 13

S-C-P (structure-conduct-
    performance) framework, 31,
    35, 35–36, 171–172
Samsung, 11, 142
satellite radio, 6
satellite television, 6
satellites, 18t
Schick, 68, 144
Schumpeter, Joseph, 8, 43
Schumpeterianism, 43–46
Schwab, 93
scientific instruments, 15f
SCM Corporation, 165
scope, of action, 121
Scully, John, 121
Sears, 102, 118
Second Cup, 202–208, 214–215,
    216–218

secrets, trade, 146
Sega, 57
Sematech, 233–234
semiconductor industry, 233–234.
    See also software industry
    complementarity in, 57–58
    memory chips in, 154
    monopoly in, 173, 174–175
    response time to Ricardian actions
        in, 151*t*, 153
    scope in, 121
    and Windows 95 launch, 43–44
September 11, 2001, 48, 54, 194
servers, computer. *See* computer
    server industry
7-Up, 148
shaving products, 68
Sherman Act, 171, 172–175, 184,
    197. *See also* monopoly
signal jamming, 119–120
signaling, 147, 190–191, 199–200
Silicon Graphics, 70
soft drinks, 11, 50*t*, 93. *See also*
    specific types
software industry, 10. *See also*
    computer industry
    complementarity in, 57–58
    and design, 139–140
    and Microsoft, 83–86
    monopoly in, 174–175
    and performance measures, 50*t*
Sony, 12
Sotheby's Holdings, 180
South America, privatization in,
    16
Southern Pacific, 232–233
Southwest Airlines, 58, 60, 61,
    111–112
Southwest Recreational Industries,
    101
sportswear, 113–114
Sprint, 12
spying. *See* espionage
Stackleberg model, 34
Staggers Act, 18*t*
Standard Oil Company, 163,
    172–173
standardization, 20
Starbucks, 202–208, 214–215,
    216–218

steel industry, 192–193
    and capacity, 139
    deterrent actions in, 166–167
    and performance measures, 50*t*
    and resources, 127
Steele, Alfred, 115, 118–119
Stigler, George, 34–35
stock trading, online, 93
structure-conduct-performance
    framework (S-C-P). *See* S-C-P
    framework
substitutes, 52–53
    in airline industry, 55–56
Summit Technology, 12
suppliers, 53–54, 53*f*
supply shortages, 115
sustainability, in Schumpeterian
    view, 46
sweetener industry, 70, 95–96,
    168–169

Target (retail store), 76–77, 102,
    118
technological resources, 71, 72*t*.
    See also resources
technology, 17–20
Telecommunications Act of 1996,
    17, 18*t*
telecommunications industry, 9, 11.
    See also cell phones;
    long-distance industry
    complementarity in, 58
    deregulation in, 17
    history of regulations on, 16–17
    and performance measures, 50*t*
telephone industry. *See* long-distance
    industry
television, 6, 17, 18*t*, 64, 112–113,
    122, 159
terrorism. *See* September 11, 2001
Teva Pharmaceutical, 59
textiles, 15*f*
    and performance measures, 50*t*
theory of action. *See* action-based
    model
The Theory of Monopolistic Competition
    (Chamberlin), 32–33
Thomas Register (magazine), 102
Thompson, Jane, 87
threat, of action, 121, 151–152

3M, 71, 144, 230–231
Time Warner, 232
timing, 123–124, 124f
tire industry, 143
tobacco industry, and performance
    measures, 50t
tool manufacture, 77–78, 78f
Toyota, 11, 156
Toys "R" Us, 176
trade secrets, 146
trademarks, 146
train travel, 55–56
transportation industry
  changes in, 20
  regulations on, 16–17
TransWorld Airlines, 200
Travelocity, 55
trucking industry, and deregulation,
    18t
Turner, Ted, 112–113

U. S. Postal Service, 176
U. S. Steel, 166–167
U. S. vs. Grinnell Corporation,
    177–178
Under Armour, 113–114
underwear, 113–114
Unilever, 7
Union Pacific, 232–233
United Airlines, 48, 61, 140, 149, 196
United States, deregulation in, 16
US Airways, 48, 61

value, 74–78, 76f, 77f, 78f
  definition of, 74
  production of, 75, 75f

vaporware, 85, 96, 174, 175
Vesper, Carl, 112
video games, 12, 57, 127–128
Visa, 149–150
Visx, 12
Von Neumann, John, 39

Wal-Mart
  and economies of scale, 137
  entrepreneurship of, 94, 102,
      114, 118
  logistics of, 74
  and predatory pricing, 163
  in resource-based view, 70
  resources of, 76–77, 77f
  Ricardian actions of, 130, 131,
      134, 152
  trucking fleet of, 137
Walton, Sam, 102, 114, 118.
    See also Wal-Mart
war metaphor, 181–182
Washington Post, 121
Weeks, David, 45
Windows (software), 43–44, 84, 85.
    See also Microsoft
Winter, Sidney, 46, 47, 144
wireless, 5–6, 10. See also
    telecommunications industry
World Trade Organization (WTO).
    See WTO
World War II, 16
Wozniak, Steve, 146
WTO (World Trade Organization),
    14

Xerox, 123, 129, 165